Diversity, Inequality & Canadian Justice

Douglas E. King &
John A. Winterdyk

de Sitter Publications

Diversity, Inequality and Canadian Justice

by Douglas E. King and John A. Winterdyk

ISBN 978-1-897160-32-9

Library and Archives Canada Cataloguing
in Publication data

A catalogue record for this book is available from the Library and Archives Canada.

Cover image: Escalator crowd © Pavel Losevsky
Cover and book design by de Sitter Publications

de Sitter Publications
111 Bell Dr
Whitby, ON, L1N 2T1
CANADA

289-987-0656
www.desitterpublications.com
sales@desitterpublications.com

▌Acknowledgement

The development of this volume was supported, in part, by funding provided by Mount Royal University's Academic Development Centre and E-Campus Alberta.

▌About the Authors

Douglas E. King

Doug King is the Chair of the Department of Justice Studies at Mount Royal University in Calgary, Alberta. Doug brings a combination of extensive academic credentials and practical experience in the justice system to his teaching practice at Mount Royal. He began his studies with an undergraduate degree in economics and earned a Master of Arts in Sociology before attending the doctoral program in sociology at Columbia University in New York City.

For seven years, Doug worked as a research and planning analyst with the Calgary Police Service. There he developed a keen interest in different models of policing, police recruitment and police performance. In 1993, he began his full-time, post-secondary teaching career as a professor in the Department of Criminology at the University of the Fraser Valley. In 1997, he accepted a full-time teaching position in the Department of Justice Studies at Mount Royal. Doug is a past recipient of the University's Distinguished Faculty award. He was a key player in the development of both the Police Studies Certificate and the Human Justice Certificate offered through the University's Faculty of Continuing Education. Doug has chaired the Department of Justice Studies for seven years and guided it in the development of the Bachelor of Arts – Criminal Justice degree. His primary academic areas of concentration are policing trends and issues, human rights/civil liberties and quantitative research methods.

John A. Winterdyk

Dr. John Winterdyk is the Director of the Center for Criminology and Justice Research at Mount Royal University in Calgary, Alberta. John's primary areas of interest include young offenders, criminological theory, research methodology, bio-social explanations of crime and comparative criminology/criminal justice. John has published extensively in the areas of criminological theory, youth at risk, corrections and criminal justice related issues as well as on a host of comparative themes.

Dr. Winterdyk recently co-edited the texts: *Qualitative and Quantitative Research Methods Reader: a Canadian Orientation* (Pearson, 2006); *Racist Victimization: International Reflections and Perspectives* (Ashgate, 2008) – with G. Antonopolous; *A Guided Reader for Comparative Criminology/Criminal Justice* (Universitatsverlag, 2009) – with P. Reichel & H. Dammer; and is working on several new international projects including the most recent book titled *Border Security in the Post 9/11 era* with K. Sundberg (CRC Press, 2010) and a forthcoming text on human trafficking which involves international contribution. In addition, he recently served as guest editor for a Special Issue on genocide for the *International Criminal Justice* review journal (2009: 19(2)) as well as co-guest editor (with Philip Reichel) for a Special Issue on human trafficking for the *European Journal of Criminology*.

In 2008, John received the "Effective Team Award" for leading an interdisciplinary research team to completing a major study of the evaluation of the effects of different strategies to help students deal with the stresses of balancing academic and personal life. In 2009, he became the first recipient of the "Distinguished Faculty Scholarship Award" for his scholarly endeavors.

Table of Contents

PART ONE

 Theories of Diversity and Justice

▌ Introduction

The influence of diversity is all around us. We often hear about the growing number of elderly Canadians and the impact this trends is having on healthcare, housing and finances. The issue of homelessness and poverty are pressing ones in all Canadian cities. Colleges and universities have to turn away many applications from younger Canadians because of a lack of funded spaces. Public concern about youth crime remains high. The political debate about the most appropriate level of immigration into Canada continues. Gender remains one of the more important factors in the work-place. Sexual preference has shaped some of the more important legal decisions in this country.

Issues of justice are also commonplace in Canadian society. Canada's political parties use justice issues to appeal to voters. Our news media is filled with stories of crimes that take place locally, nationally and internationally. The public's fascination with policing, crime forensics and criminal court proceedings has translated into numerous television series, motion pictures and books of fiction.

How are issues of diversity and of justice interrelated?

Because diversity is one of the defining aspects of Canadian society, it should come as no surprise that its consequences are also found in Canada's criminal justice system. Consider the following facts:

■　　While persons of aboriginal ancestry make up less than 5% of Canada's population but 19% of provincial/territorial inmates and 17% of federal inmates (Goff, 2004:271).

■　　Approximately 5% of all self-reported crime victimization incidents in Canada are believed to be victims of "hate crime" (Statistics Canada, 2004:1).

■　　In more than three-quarters of all spousal homicides recorded in Canada since 1974, women are the victims (Statistics Canada, 2002:1).

■　　Individuals between the ages of 15 and 24 are 1.5 to 1.9 times more likely to be a victim of violence than older individuals (Statistics Canada, 2005:7).

■　　In 1999, around 7% of elderly respondents to a Canadian survey reported being a victim of some form of elder abuse (Sacco and Kennedy, 2002:229).

Why consider theories of diversity and theories of justice?

The social sciences use theories to "make sense" of human behaviour. For example, there is no "laws" of diversity in the social sciences but several theories of diversity. Occasionally, there is some consensus within the social sciences that a particular theory is the better explanation than other theories. However, it is more common that a handful of theories offer alternative explanations for the same behaviour. For example, there is no single theory that is recognized as the "best" explanation why a small number of people commit crime in our society while the majority do not. Instead, we have several different theories that are credible.

Understanding the more commonly recognized theories of diversity and theories of justice will help you recognize how the social sciences explain these important concepts. This knowledge will provide you with an academic foundation to analyse the links between justice and diversity in Canada.

Learning Outcomes

What are the learning outcomes for this section?

The information this section is designed around an explicit set of outcomes. These outcomes represent the types of learning that you will be able to satisfactorily demonstrate upon completion of this section. You will be able to:

- explain the role of theories in the social sciences,
- articulate the core ideas in the major theories of diversity,
- articulate the core ideas in the major theories of justice,
- compare and contrast the major theories of diversity, and
- compare and contrast the major theories of diversity.

Learning Activities

A series of learning activities have been embedded in each chapter of this unit. These include such activities as entries in a course journal, online research, reflection on key points, case studies, summarization and discussion points. Learning activities are designed to enhance the readers understanding of the material presented in each chapter of this unit.

References

Goff, C. (2004). *Criminal justice in Canada.* 3rd ed. Toronto, ON: Nelson.

Sacco, V., and Kennedy, L. (2002). *The criminal event: An introduction to criminology in Canada.* Toronto, ON: Nelson.

Statistics Canada. (2002). *National trends in intimate partner homicides, 1974-2000.* Catalogue no. 85-002-XIE, vol. 22, no. 5. Retrieved May 12, 2007, from http://www.statcan.ca/english/ freepub/85-002-XIE/0050285-002-XIE.pdf.

Statistics Canada. (2004). *Hate crime in Canada.* Catalogue no. 85-002-XPE, vol. 24, no. 4. Retrieved April 23, 2007, from http://dsp-psd.tpsgc.gc.ca/Collection-R/Statcan/85-551-XIE/0009985-551-XIE.pdf.

Statistics Canada. (2005). *Criminal Victimization in Canada, 2004.* Catalogue no. 85-002-XPE, vol. 25, no. 7. Retrieved April 10, 2007, from http://www.statcan.ca/bsolc/english/bsolc? catno=85-002-X20050078803.

Statistics Canada. (2006). *Crime statistics in Canada.* Catalogue no. 85-002-XIE, vol. 26, no. 4. Retrieved April 12, 2007, from http://www.statcan.ca/Daily/English/040601/d040601a.htm.

PART ONE

Chapter 1
Defining Diversity and Inequality

Learning Activity 1 - Fun Quiz

Defining diversity is a challenging task as it has many different dimensions. Take this fun quiz before you read the chapter. Answer "True" or "False":

1. Diversity is always a positive feature.

2. Diversity is a term that has many different shades or degrees.

3. In common language, homogeneity means "differences".

4. Heterogeneity is the opposite of homogeneity.

5. Characteristics such as age, gender and ethnicity are forms of achieved status.

6. A meritocracy has no social stratification.

7. Social mobility based on ascribed status leads to social inequality.

8. Karl Marx believed that economics was the core of social inequality.

9. Prejudice and discrimination are the same things.

10. Minority groups are always smaller in number compared to the dominant group.

    ANSWERS: 1F, 2T, 3F, 4T, 5F, 6F, 7T, 8T, 9F, 10F

In this chapter, we investigate some of the more well-known theories of diversity and stratification. The term "diversity" is often used but rarely defined. This unit provides an overview of the different "levels" of diversity. It concludes with a model of diversity that can be used to measure different degrees of diversity.

Defining Diversity

What is "diversity"?

It is surprising how little effort has taken place within the social sciences to develop a formal definition of the term "diversity." Most authors who use the term elect not to define the concept and may even use such common terms as "minorities" interchangeably to refer to such things as people with intellectual disabilities, the elderly, ethnic minorities, and people of whose sexual preference is not the norm (e.g., gays and lesbians)(see below for further discussion). As a result, the concept of diversity in the social sciences has taken on an implied value statement—diversity is a positive attribute. For example, Abella (1991) suggests that formal laws, rules and practices that encourage diversity within a group, community or society contribute to the social good. Further, some proponents of diversity equate the absence of the active promotion of diversity as passive form of discrimination and prejudice (Canadian Human Rights Foundation, 1987). As discussed by Roberts and Clifton (1990), the discussion about diversity seems to have moved past an exploration of its value and has become centered on a debate regarding the best means to protect and enhance social, cultural, and demographic diversity.

In no way should the above concerns about the informal understanding of diversity as a social science concept be interpreted as a rejection of diversity. Instead, it is intended to draw attention to the limitations associated with its current lack of precise definition. For example, most advocates of diversity implicitly place some limitations of its value. Only the most ardent civil libertarian would find positive value in an organization that tolerates a fully diverse range of attitudes and actions. Consider how most advocates of diversity would respond to the idea that neo-Nazi proponents be allowed to expose and practice their beliefs at meetings of the Canadian Human Rights Commission. Indeed, the Canadian Criminal Code (CCC) places limitations on one of the more extreme expressions of diversity—"hate propaganda" (see sections 318 & 319 in the CCC).

In the absence of a commonly accepted social science definition and drawing on a review of some of the existing literature, let's develop our own definition of diversity:

> *Diversity is the degree of socially meaningful differences among and between individuals, groups, communities, cultures and societies. As an empirical measure, diversity is neither a positive or negative attribute.*

Our definition has several key points.

1.   Diversity is not a "black or white" quality; instead, it is a matter of degree. This way, we will be able to measure "how much" or "how little" diversity there is.
2.   Diversity relates to "socially meaningful differences"—that is, diversity is a social prescribed concept. There are many qualities of individuals that have no significant social meaning or consequence. For example, the thickness of your fingernails, the colour of your car or your shoe size are not socially meaningful in our society. However, your gender, age and personal wealth are socially meaningful.
3.   Diversity is a quality or characteristic of individuals and the different levels of groups

to which they belong.

4.   Diversity is something that can be operationalised and measured.
5.   Diversity is a social fact. By itself, it is not necessarily "good" or "bad." It only takes on these value judgements when it is used as part of a political or ideological agenda.

Our social science understanding of diversity can be enriched by linking it to sociological concepts of heterogeneity, social stratification, social inequality and minority group status (Winterdyk and King, 1999:4-10).

Learning Activity 2 - Reflect and Research

The topic of diversity in the workplace can lead some people to express very strong opinions (positively or negatively). Linking back to our discussion in Unit 1, these are opinions rather than theories.

1.   What is your opinion about diversity in the classroom? Why do you hold these opinions? How do they relate to your own personal biography and experiences?

2.   Ask a few friends and/or family members what are their opinions about diversity? Try and assess if these opinions are based on their own biography and experience.

Diversity as Heterogeneity

What does heterogeneity mean?

The sociological concept of **heterogeneity** is the first building block of diversity. In his book entitled: "Heterogeneity and social inequality: A primitive theory of social structure" (1977), Peter Blau offers this definition: "Heterogeneity or horizontal differentiation refers to the distribution of a population among groups in terms of a nominal parameter" (Blau as cited in Winterdyk and King, 1999:4).

The following diagram illustrates Blau's concept of heterogeneity.

Heterogeneity

In the above figure, the blue horizontal line represents all of the members (what Blau calls "the distribution of a population") within a group. In a heterogeneous group, it is possible to divide the group into different subgroups (what Blau calls "heterogeneity or horizontal differentiation"). To have value, these subgroups need to be socially meaningful (what Blau calls a "nominal parameter"). For example, in the group (or "population") of students taking this class, it would be possible to assign everyone into one of two gender groups. Gender is a socially meaningful "nominal parameter." Assuming that there are both females and males taking this class, we can say there is gender heterogeneity.

What is the opposite of heterogeneity?

Homogeneity is the polar opposite of heterogeneity. When a group or population cannot be subdivided along a socially meaningful characteristic, the group is homogenous in that characteristic.

Homogeneity

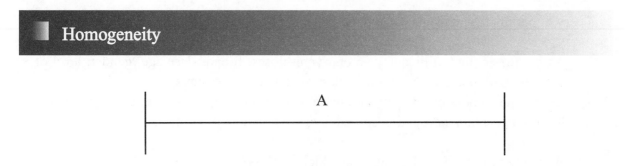

For example, assume that there are no males taking this class. This means that the group students (represented in the above illustration) is homogeneous in terms of gender.

Learning Activity 3 - Discuss

Most of us work in teams in our employment or at school. With several of your friends, discuss your thoughts on the value of "homogeneity" within the team. Next, discuss the importance of heterogeneity within the team.

Heterogeneity as an Empirical Starting Point

Can we measure heterogeneity?

As a dimension of diversity, heterogeneity gives us an empirical and quantitative starting point (Winterdyk and King, 1999:5). Within a group, we can assess the degree of heterogeneity in a straight-forward manner. Again, let's use the students taking this class as an example. Suppose everyone taking a course at a college or university had a different ethnic background. That would be a very heterogeneous and diverse class. What if **everyone but one** student had the same ethnic background? This class would have virtually no diversity along this quality and would be very homogeneous.

Heterogeneity can be used as an empirical and quantitative measure *between groups* as well. Let's take a real situation this time. We know that less than 5% of all Canadians are of First-Nations ancestry. Yet, First-Nation inmates make up approximately 22% of those in provincial/territorial custody and 17% of federal inmates (Statistics Canada, 2006:15). The different rate of heterogeneity for First-Nations people (as found in the general population and in federal prisons) provides the social sciences with an important question to be addressed—why?

Learning Activity 4 - Research

It is very important that students understand the concept of heterogeneity. Try this exercise.

1.   Assess the amount of diversity among your closest friends. Use age, gender, level of education, occupation and ethnic background as your measures.
2.   Assess the amount of diversity among your work colleagues. Again, use age, gender, level of education, occupation and ethnic background as your measures.

Which group has more diversity and which has less? Why?

Diversity as Social Stratification

How is social stratification different from heterogeneity?

All groups and societies value some social characteristics or qualities more than others. This "rank ordering" of social characteristics results a hierarchical ranking of social status. For example, education is a meaningful social characteristic (or nominal parameter) in our society. However, it goes beyond heterogeneity because our society (or groups or organizations) place greater social value on higher levels of educational achievement. This valuing results in a hierarchical ranking. This explains why most people with higher education earn more income and have better employment benefits.

Ascribed and Achieved Status

Does a person control her/his social status?

Ascribed Status

Some social characteristics are beyond the control of any individual. For example, a person has no control over her/his age, ethnicity, race and sex. These types of social qualities are called "**ascribed status**" characteristics. Ascribed status means that individuals are socially valued (or ranked) within society on characteristics that they cannot control. For example, in earlier times, much of North America negatively valued non-Caucasians. In the United States, "Jim Crow" laws enforced segregation between the races starting in the 1860s. In Canada, the Indian Act of 1876 established aboriginal reserves to segregate the races.

Achieved Status

Individuals also possess "**achieved status**" characteristics. These are socially valued qualities that an individual has some control over. A person has considerable control over the amount of education they earn or the occupation they choose.

Social Roles

A person's social status (ascribed + achieved) can be described as his/her social identity. This social status is reinforced through the social roles that the person has within the group or society. A social role is best described as the expected behaviour that is associated with the numerous positions within society. For example, being a

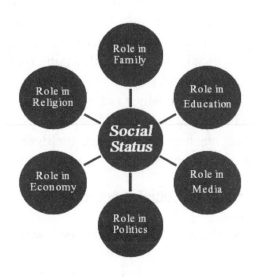

student is a social role. In that position, there is a range of behaviour that is expected from those individuals occupying the role. The expected behaviour of a student includes studying, completing assignments and required reading and so forth.

Individuals have many social roles. They emerge from your involvement in society's institutions. As part of the family, you may have one or more role that can include parent, sibling, spouse, child and so forth. You can begin to appreciate the many social roles that one person can have when you consider the other social institutions such as education, government, religion and the media.

Learning Activity 5 - Reflect

In your mind, what are the socially meaningful characteristics of individuals in Canadian society (e.g., age? income? employment?)? What social rewards to people get because of these characteristics?

How many different social roles do you perform? List them. Which are based primarily on achieved status and which are based primarily on ascribed status?

Structural Functionalist Theory of Social Stratification

Is social stratification inevitable in any group or society?

Some social scientists labelled "structural functionalist" theorise that our society is more closely organized around achieved status and an open stratification system (Waters, 1994:336-339). They observe that some form of social stratification is present in all societies so it must be a necessary part, or function, of society. In complex societies like ours, there are many crucial social roles that have to be filled in order for society to maintain itself. These include such roles as doctors, judges and business leaders. In order to attract capable individuals to aspire to fill these demanding roles, we have developed a system of social rewards to compensate them. These social rewards can include income and social prestige. Social ranking (or status) is achieved through a combination of talent, intelligence and effort.

The degree to which our society's social ranking is based on achieved status is debatable. As we shall see when we next look at the social inequality dimension of diversity, some theorists contend that much more than talent, intelligence and effort is at play in our society's social ranking. Some groups have more social power than others.

Diversity as Social Inequality

How is social inequality different from social stratification?

Social stratification becomes social inequality through the exercise of social power. As pointed out by Winterdyk and King (1999:6):

> If an individual or group can restrict the claim that another individual or group has on social rewards, then social stratification moves towards social inequality. The inclusion of social inequality into the definition of social diversity introduces the possibility that some expressions of diversity are not positive.

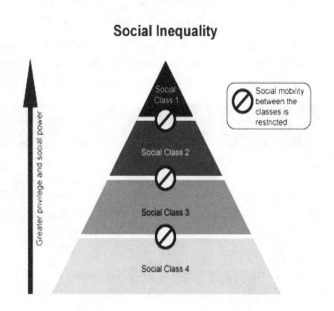

The degree to which social inequality exists is seen in the amount of social mobility within a group or society. In a meritocracy, the capacity of an individual to increase her/his social status depends on that individual's talent, intelligence and personal effort. Individuals move up and down the social status hierarchy based on achieved status. Social mobility is a reality (Butler, 2007:231-232).

Learning Activity 6 - Journal Entry

In your course journal or notes, discuss the following questions:

1.   All societies have some degree of social inequality. Are some groups in Canada afforded special advantage because of who they are? If so, who are they and what is their source of social power?
2.   Are there some groups in Canada that are disadvantaged for reasons of than merit? If so, what is the source of their social disadvantage?
3.   If you have concluded that social inequality exists in Canadian society, what does this mean for the Canadian Criminal Justice System?

However, when an individual's place on the social hierarchy is influenced by ascribed status characteristics, social mobility is restricted and social inequality is increased. Racial policies originating as far back as Canada's Indian Act (1867) and the "Jim Crow" laws in the southern United States (1876) prevented the social mobility of aboriginals in Canada and blacks in the United States because of their racial background (Hicks, 1998; Friederes and Gadacz, 2004; Henry, Taylor, Mattis and Rees, 2000).

The sociological concepts of "class" and "class structure are keys to an understanding of social inequality. Theories of social inequality contend that our society is not a meritocracy. Instead, we can uncover broad social groupings or "classes." Each class can be described in terms of the similar lifestyles and life-opportunities for those within the class. Social inequality theorists maintain that social mobility between the classes is restricted. The more privileged the social class, the greater its social power within society.

Theories of Social Inequality

Why do we have social inequality in our society?

Within the social sciences, there is no single theory explaining the source of social inequality. Instead, there are several competing theories. Here is a brief summary of a few.

Karl Marx (1818-1883) is credited with the introduction of the concept of social inequality. His ideas are generally associated with the functionalist school which focuses on what how societies maintain continuity and stability. The classic Marxist theory asserts that economic relations are the foundation of a society's class structure (Waters, 1994:299-301). In a capitalist society, the capitalist class, or **bourgeoisie**, control the economic and non-economic institutions (e.g., government, religion, and media). The working class, or the **proletariat**, have no real social power within society. Members of proletariat have no option but to sell their labour to the capitalist class for wages. Through their control over all society's institutions, the bourgeoisie are able to keep wages down and exploit the labour of the working class. According to Marx, class refers to the relationship that social groups have to the production of goods and services in society. There is no genuine social mobility as the bourgeoisie prevent the proletariat from gaining any real foothold in the economic structure of society.

Max Weber (1864-1920) agreed with Marx that economic class played an important role in social inequality. However, he contended that hierarchies of prestige and political power influence social inequality (Wallace and Wolf, 1995:183-188). Weber believed that the goal(s) and the means are rationally chosen based on ones understanding (i.e., "verstehen") of the situation in question. Instead of using Marx's idea of economic classes, Weber said that social inequality in society is a product of "social class." He suggested that there were four (4) social classes—the **working class**, the **small entrepreneur**, the **professional class** (technicians and "white-collar" employees) and the **owning class**. Mobility between the social classes is greatly restricted through the exercise of social power but not necessarily impossible.

Feminist theories contain many branches (e.g., liberal, Marxist, radical, socialist, postmodernist, and more recently eco-feminist) but they generally share a common premise and focus. That is, feminist theories are based on the social inequality between females and males or "gender ratio" issues (Siegel, 2004). The basic structure of society is patriarchal, or male-dominated. While there are several different varieties of feminism, all maintain that the patriarchal foundation of our society places males in positions of control in both the public sphere (e.g., economy, law, and politics) and the private sphere (e.g., family and interpersonal relations) (Water, 1994:250-288). Social power is the privilege of men in our society.

Learning Activity 7 - Summarize

In your own words, summarize the difference between Marx's theory and Weber's theory. As well, what aspects of Marx's and Weber's theories are found in Feminist theories? What makes a feminist explanation unique?

Diversity as Minority Group

What is a minority group?

American sociologist Louis Wirth (1897-1952) and member of the Chicago School of Sociology, is credited with one of the earliest discussions of minority groups in his 1945 article entitled: "The Problem of Minority Groups." For his work, he drew heavily from his own first-hand experience as an immigrant Jews in the United States. In his article, Wirth (1945: 347) defined a minority group as:

(a) group of people who, because of their physical or cultural characteristics, are singled out from the others in society in which they live for differential and unequal treatment, and who therefore regard themselves as objects of collective discrimination.

Wirth's definition adds another dimension to our understanding of diversity. It is the idea that a **possible outcome** of social inequality is the realization by some individuals that personal merit is not the deciding factor in their lives. These individuals begin to recognize that the outcome of their lives is shaped by prejudice, discrimination, disenfranchisement, and/or social inequality. According to Wirth's definition, the degree to which this awareness is shared among members of the same group is the degree to which it can be classified as a "minority group." In other words, a minority group does not represent a politically dominate plurality of the general population and may have their civil rights and collective rights compromised on some manner.

The everyday understanding of the term "minority group" is often limited to ethnic or racial groups who make up less than 50 percent of the population. However, the technical use of the concept is broader and more developed.

- The "physical and cultural characteristics" that establish group membership can include such things as gender, sexual preference, age, social class; as well as ethnicity and race.

- The definition of "minority group" is not based a group's numbers. It is based on their disadvantaged access to social power. For example, in South Africa's former racial system of apartheid, the majority of the population were black. However, their access to social power was severely restricted because of the apartheid's elaborate system of racial segregation and discrimination.

- The existence of social inequality and minority groups logically means the existence of "dominant groups." Members of a dominant group are socially advantaged by the inequality within a group or society. They benefit from a system of discrimination. Members of a dominant group may not recognize the reasons for their positions of advantage as the system of discrimination may be rooted in history, customs and traditions.

How do minority groups develop?

It is rare that all individuals in a minority group respond in the same way to their minority group status. As first observed by Wirth in his 1945 article, it is often the case that "subgroups" (e.g., outlaw motorcycle gangs, rave groups, urban street gangs, Hippies from the 1970s, etc.) emerge within a minority group. Some may work to make changes within the group or society to address the social inequality (e.g., The Squamish Five during the 1980s—also known as the Vancouver Five or Direct Action). Others many resign themselves to their positions of social disadvantage. In some instances, members of the minority group may have the goal to segregate themselves from the dominant group completely and form their own group or society (e.g., handicapped citizen groups, linguistic minority groups, and cultural minority groups such as Polish folk dancers).

The Civil Rights movement in the United States during the 1960s and 1970s is an example of social change that emerged out of minority group concerns. In Canada, the enhanced activism of First Nations peoples in the 1970s and early 1980s significantly influenced the inclusion of some Aboriginal group rights in the Canadian Charter of Rights and Freedoms. The women's movement of the 1970s and 1980s is another social movement that produced social change. Some argue awareness among gays and lesbians of their minority group status over the past decade is becoming more public. As a result, some notable action has been taken to address social discrimination on the basis of same sex preferences. (Most of these themes will be covered in various chapters throughout the text.)

Prejudice, Stereotyping and Discrimination

How is social inequality maintained?

Many theories of social inequality indirectly see prejudice, stereotyping, discrimination as primary ways that social inequality is maintained. Let's consider what these terms mean.

- *Prejudice* is "the prejudging of people because of characteristics assumed to be shared by all members of their social category" (Teevan, 1989:376). It is an attitude or opinion that can be either negative or positive. For example, one might believe that all persons with PhDs are arrogant and absent-minded (negative attitude or opinion). Someone else might believe that all persons with PhDs are the most intelligent people in our society (positive attitude or opinion).

- *Stereotypes* are mental images that exaggerate the traits (real or assumed) of all members of a social group (Teevan, 1989:379). For example, Canada's racist practice of residential schools in the early to mid-twentieth century was based on a stereotype that all Aboriginals were primitive, savage and god-less.

- *Discrimination* is the "acting out of prejudice" and stereotyping to favour or disfavour someone on the basis of their group members. *De jure discrimination* is built into laws and policies of a society or group. For example, many police departments once had policies that prohibited females from applying to become police officers (Seagraves, 1997). *De facto discrimination* is built into the customs, traditions and practices of a society or group. Using IQ tests as to determine someone's "intelligence" is now a disputed practice because these tests are often biased against non-white, middle-class individuals.

Towards An Integrated Theory of Social Diversity

Drawing on our earlier definition of diversity, we can use the four dimensions of diversity (heterogeneity, social stratification, and social inequality) to construct an integrated theory of social diversity.

Learning Activity 8 - Case Study

The Death of Neil Stonechild

Read the following case study.

In late November of 1990, the body of 17-year old Neil Stonechild was found in a remote field in Saskatoon. An autopsy revealed that he had frozen to death in the sub-zero temperatures that had settled into the region for several days. Stonechild's body showed minor signs of trauma. What made the discovery of Stonechild's body more alarming was the fact that he was not the first such discovery. Several men (mostly Aboriginal) had been found frozen to death in remote parts of Saskatoon. The police explained the discovery of these men as the unfortunate result of alcohol and cold weather.

In February of 2000, another Aboriginal man, Darrell Night, came forward and accused two police officers of leaving him in a remote field in the frigid temperature. After an RCMP investigation, two Saskatoon police officers were found guilty of unlawful confinement and sentenced to 8 months in prison.

Rumours and accusations spread quickly that the Saskatoon Police regularly engaged in what are now referred to as "starlight tours." Regardless of the temperature, some police officers would transport "problem drunks" they encountered to remote areas of the city and let them out of the patrol car, regardless of the person's physical state.

The Government of Saskatchewan ordered a public inquiry into Neil Stonechild's death in 2003. The inquiry confirmed that some Saskatoon police officers participated in the "starlight tours" which were an illegal form of detention.

Further, evidence was collected that incriminated two police officers in the death of Neil Stonechild. Despite the two police officers denials, police records show that the two responded to a call-for-service that involved an inebriated Neil Stonechild late in the evening before his body was discovered. As well, several eye witnesses reported seeing Stonechild being transported somewhere by the two police officers after they responded to the call-for-service.

The public inquiry concluded that Neil Stonechild death was not an accident but the product of the negligence of the two police officers and the inappropriate nature of the "starlight tours."

How do the circumstances surrounding Neil Stonechild's death relate to the concepts of prejudice, discrimination and stereotyping? Generally, do you thing First Nations peoples in Canada are treated differently by the justice system? Why or why not?

If you want more information on the results of the public inquiry, follow this URL link:
http://www.stonechildinquiry.ca/finalreport/default.shtml

How are the four dimensions of diversity interrelated?

1.   **Heterogeneity** is the foundation of diversity. If there is no social differentiation within a group or society, there is no socially meaningful basis for diversity.

2.   **Social stratification** is a necessary feature of social diversity. It exists when a hierarchy of social status is linked to the heterogeneity in the group or society. If the status is based on heterogeneous characteristics that an individual has no control over, it is ascribed status. If the individual has some control over the characteristic, it is achieved status.

3.   It is not logically necessary that **social inequality** results from conditions of social stratification. In a meritocracy (a system/process by which those with talent/skills are moved ahead on the basis of their achievement(s)), everyone has an equal opportunity to succeed or fail. Nonetheless, social inequality is often the outcome of social stratification. When groups are able to protect their status position through the exercise of social power, social inequality exists.

4.   Socially disadvantaged group may acquire **minority group status** if there is widespread recognition within the group that their life chances are negatively impacted by societal discrimination. A variety of responses can follow from this recognition (e.g., challenging the source of the inequality, passive acceptance of the disadvantage, and separating entirely from the group or society).

In the next Chapter we will examine some of the main theories as they relate to the different dimensions that underpin the concept of justice. Specifically, natural justice, procedural justice, retributive justice, restorative justice and human justice will be discussed.

Integrated Theory of Social Diversity

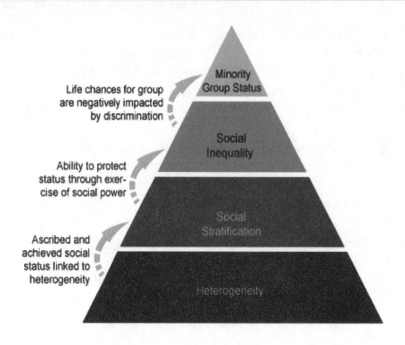

Learning Activity 9 - Summarise and List

In your own words, summarise the key aspects of the four different dimensions of diversity (i.e., heterogeneity, social stratification, social inequality and minority group status). Based on what you currently know, what dimensions of diversity (heterogeneity, social stratification, social inequality and minority group) do the following groups in Canada society exhibit?

- Aboriginals
- Women
- Gays and lesbians
- Post-secondary students
- Police officers
- Elderly
- Physically disabled
- Mentally disabled

References

Abella, R. (1991). "Equality and human rights in Canada: Coping with the new isms." *University Affairs* June/July (21-22).

Blau, P. (1977). *Inequality and heterogeneity: A primitive theory of social structure.* New York: The Free Press.

Butler, L. (2007). "Diversity and conformity: The role of gender." In P. Angelini (ed.), *Our society: Human diversity in Canada.* 3rd ed. Toronto, ON: Thomson Nelson.

Canadian Human Rights Foundation. (1987). *Multiculturalism and the charter.* Toronto, ON: Carswell.

Frideries, J. and Gadacz, R. (2004). *Aboriginal peoples in Canada.* 7th ed. Toronto, ON: Pearson Education Canada.

Henry, F., Tator, C., Mattis, W. and Rees, T. (2000). *The colour of democracy: Racism in Canadian society,* 2nd ed. Toronto, ON: Harcourt Brace Canada.

Hicks, S. (1998). Indian Act, 1876. Retrieved April 12, 2007, from http://www.socialpolicy.ca/cush/m8/m8-t7.stm.

Seagraves, J. (1997). *Introduction to policing in Canada.* Scarborough, ON: Prentice Hall Canada.

Siegel, L. (2004). *Criminology: Theories, Patterns, & Typologies.* 8th ed. Belmont, CA: Wadsworth/Thomson Learning.

Statistics Canada. (2006). *Adult correctional services in Canada, 2004/2005.* Catalogue no. 85-002-XIE, Vol. 26, no. Retrieved April 10, 2007, from http://www.statcan.ca/english/freepub/85-002-XIE/85-002-XIE2006005.pdf.

Teevan, J. (1989). "Glossary." In J. Teevan (ed.), *Basic sociology: A Canadian introduction.* 3rd ed. Scarborough, ON: Prentice Hall Canada.

Wallace, R. and Wolf, A. (1995). *Contemporary sociological theory: Continuing the classical traditions.* 4th ed. Englewood Cliffs, NJ: Prentice Hall.

Waters, M. (1994). *Modern sociological theory.* London, England: Sage Publications.

Winterdyk, J. and King D. (1999). "Introduction." In J. Winterdyk and D. King (eds.), *Diversity and justice in Canada.* Toronto, ON: Canadian Scholars' Press.

Wirth, L. (1945). "The problem of minority groups." In R. Linton (ed.), *The science of man in the world crisis.* New York, NY: Columbia University Press.

Chapter 2

Theories of Justice

Learning Activity 1 - Fun Quiz

Take this fun quiz before you read the chapter. Answer "True" or "False":

1. Our understanding of justice is all about punishing criminals.

2. Natural justice is the earliest from of justice.

3. Retributive justice is also called the theory of punishment.

4. The phrase "punishment must fit the crime" means that all crime should be punishe severely.

5. Distributive justice argues that society should ensure that some individuals get more justice than others.

6. Most of our legal rights in Canada are based in procedural justice.

7. The statement that "it is better that 100 guilty men go free than 1 innocent man suffer" is an example of retributive justice.

8. Restorative justice is the same as retributive justice.

9. Having an offender met his/her victim face-to-face is a bad idea.

10. Social justice is a combination of other forms of justice.

ANSWERS: 1F, 2T, 3T, 4F, 5T, 6T, 7F, 8F, 9F, 10T

There are many different theories related to the concept of justice. Some look at justice as an "end" in itself. Other theories link the concept to models of social equality and argue that justice is not equality distributed within our society. In this chapter, we investigate some of the more well-known theories of justice.

Common Perceptions about Justice

What is "justice"?

Here are some ways that people commonly use the term "justice:

- Justice is often seen as law, or fairness, or punishment, or revenge, or restitution.

- Some people look to the criminal justice system as the source of justice in our society while others see justice as a product of all aspects of our lives.

- Still others contend that justice is a process or the "means to an end"; whereas others see it as an outcome or an "end" itself.

- Finally, some view justice as a standard that has to be imposed "by society" on its members and others maintain that justice is a product of social consensus.

Academic debates about justice are as numerous as those found within everyday life. Philosophers before the time of Socrates have debated the essential components of justice. It is a question pursued in the disciplines of sociology, economics, criminology and legal studies. Justice is a concept that informs religious beliefs and religious lives.

For our purposes, let's consider some of the mainstream definitions of justice in the social sciences. These include "natural justice", "retributive justice", "distributive justice", "procedural justice" and "restorative justice."

Natural Justice

What is natural justice?

To appreciate what is meant by "natural justice," we have to start by understanding the concept of natural law. Natural law is the theory that some guidelines separate human beings from other forms of life. These guidelines or norms make us human but are not created by us. Natural law is not subject to continuous change or true in some cultures and not in others.

There are several explanations about the source of natural law (Natural law, n.d.). The ancient Greek philosophers called the Stoics (around 300 BC), developed the first known theory of natural law. They believed that we could discover the universal norms of human conduct through **human reasoning**. Human-made laws (also called positive laws) were just only if they conform to the higher natural law. The Greek philosopher Aristotle believed that societies should be ruled by "philosopher

Learning Activity 2 - Case Study

The Murder of Tracy Latimer*

The death of 12-year old Tracy Latimer on a farm just outside of Wilkie Saskatchewan on October 24, 1993, received national and international attention. Tracy had a form of cerebral palsy that left severely mentally challenged and physically disabled. In her short lifetime, she had undergone several major surgical procedures to help minimize the bending of her long bones and spine due to continual muscle tension. Despite the surgeries, little could be done to alleviate Tracy's constant pain. As well, she had chronic problems with her respiratory and digestive systems. She was unable to walk or talk. Tracy could not swallow food without having her throat massaged. She frequently vomited and spent most of her time in bed. Tracy's condition was degenerative which meant that her health was getting worse and would ultimately lead to her early death.

Tracy was found in her bed by her mother who had returned from Sunday church services. When the RCMP arrived at the family farm, they were immediately suspicious about the cause of Tracy's death. The condition of her body pointed to carbon monoxide poisoning. The result of the subsequent autopsy confirmed this as the official cause of death.

Eleven days after Tracy's death, her father Robert Latimer confessed that he had planned and carried out her death. While the rest of the family was at church, Robert put Tracy into the family's pickup truck and hooked a hose to its exhaust pipe. He started the vehicle and feed the other end of the hose through a small crack in the front window. After Tracy had died, Robert placed her body in bed and waited for his wife to discover her.

The Crown charged Robert Latimer with first-degree murder based on his confession and the premeditated nature of his actions. At his trial, Latimer's defence team argued the defence of necessity – an accepted legal defence for those situations when a person is compelled to commit a criminal act because of "imminent danger". The jury acquitted Latimer of first-degree murder but found him guilty of second-degree murder. He was sentenced to life in prison with parole eligibility after 10 years. Latimer remained free on bail as his lawyers appealed the decision to the Saskatchewan Court of Appeals. That court subsequently denied his appeal.

Latimer's defence team launched another appeal when it learned that the Crown prosecutor in his original trial had the RCMP screen potential jurors regarding their views of "mercy killing". This time, the Supreme Court of Canada ordered a new trial for Latimer because of the misconduct of the Crown prosecutor. At the second trial, the Crown decided to pursue a conviction on second-degree murder charges. On November 5, 1997, Latimer was again convicted of second-degree murder.

...continued on next page

However, the jury recommended that he not be sentenced to the legally mandatory minimum sentence of 10 years before being eligible for parole. Instead, the jury wanted to see Latimer eligible for parole in one year. His defence team also argued that Latimer should be given a "constitutional exemption" to the required 10 year minimum sentence because such a sentence would be "cruel and unusual punishment" in the Latimer case. The judge agreed that a 10 year minimum sentence was inappropriate and sentenced Latimer to 2 years less one day, with ½ of the sentence to be served under house arrest.

The Crown appealed the court's decision to the Saskatchewan Court of Appeal. The higher court upheld the Crown's appeal and reinstated the minimum 10 year sentence. The Supreme Court of Canada was asked to reconsider the 10 year minimum sentence. In January 2001, the Supreme Court ruled that the 10 year minimum sentence was not "cruel and unusual punishment" and thereby Latimer began his 10 year sentence for the second-degree murder of his daughter. A public opinion poll just after the final ruling found that 73% of Canadians felt Latimer's sentence was too harsh. Forty-one percent expressed support to legalise euthanasia (i.e., "mercy killing").

The Government of Canada has the power to grant a "royal prerogative of mercy" (i.e., a pardon) to any criminal. Latimer and his supporters have not been successful in securing his release from federal prison.

* Source: Goff (2004:1-3).

Consider the following questions:

- Did Robert Latimer receive justice?
- Did Tracy Latimer receive justice?
- Did the Canadian public receive justice?
- Did Canadian society receive justice?

kings" because they could better comprehend natural law due to their skill at human reasoning.

In his consideration of the source of natural law, Christian philosopher St. Thomas Aquinas (1225 – 1274 AD) linked the concept to religion. He maintained that natural law was common to all peoples – Christian and non-Christians. However, Christians were better able to comprehend natural law as God had chosen them over all other forms of religion (Natural law, n.d.). For Aquinas, the Bible was God's way of leading Christians to a better understanding of natural law.

More contemporary expressions link natural law to universal ethical standards and human rights. This focus is seen in the development of international law that followed World War II. In particular, the horrors of the Nazi holocaust accelerated the concern for some universal ethical/moral code for nations.

There are two primary rules in natural justice (Natural law, n.d.):

1. *"Audi alteram partem"* which is Latin for "hear the other side." Natural justice cannot occur until all individuals who have been wronged, or accused of doing wrong, have the opportunity to speak.

2. *"Nemo debet esse judes in propria sua causa"* which means "no one shall be judged in his own case." This means that the administration of natural law and justice must be objective and without personal bias.

Are there any other ways natural justice theory is found in today's society?

A second example of natural law and justice in today's society is the United Nations' Universal Declaration of Human Rights. Adopted in December of 1948, the Universal Declaration of Human Rights was established in response to the Nazi Holocaust in World War II. By articulating the universal rights of all humans, members of the United Nations agreed to uphold the rights of their own citizens and intervene internationally when countries failed to do so.

■ Learning Activity 3 - Online Research

Many natural law principles have been incorporated into the United Nation's Universal Declaration of Human Rights. Follow this URL link to the United Nation's electronic posting of the Universal Declaration. Read it closely looking for those rights that relate specifically to justice.

http://www.un.org/Overview/rights.html

■ Retributive Justice

Doesn't retribution mean revenge?

The theory of retributive justice is also known as the "theory of punishment" (Griffiths and Cunningham, 2003:67). It is based on the reasoning that society in general is harmed when someone's actions violate the society's customs, traditions, ethics, morals or laws.

Society has to take some form of action against the violator in order to bring balance back into the social order. If society takes no action, the imbalance will grow as more violations will take place. Society's inaction will encourage individuals who have been harmed to take matters into their own hands; thereby creating a "war of all against all" or anarchy.

The theory of retributive justice is based in the *"just deserts" model* (Schmalleger, MacAlister and McKenna, 2004:284). Punishment in this model should be proportional to the harm caused by the individual's violation. Echoed in the biblical quotation of "an eye for an eye and a tooth for a tooth", the more contemporary expression of proportional punishment is the statement that the "punishment must fit the crime."

What is the "right" punishment?

Jeremy Bentham (1748 - 1832) is credited with making the statement that "the punishment must fit the crime." (Schmalleger, MacAlister and McKenna, 2004:286). His theory provides much of the foundation for our contemporary sentencing practices. Bentham contended that human beings are motivated by rewards and deterred by punishments. Each one of us makes a "cost-benefit" assessment before taking any action. If the benefits outweigh the costs, we will take action. Crime is like any form of human action in that people make a "cost – benefit" assessment. If people believe that the potential benefits of the crime are greater than the potential costs, we all will engage in the criminal action. Punishment, therefore, is a potential cost.

Punishment must be proportional to the potential social harm of the crime. If punishment is too lenient, the potential cost of the crime may not act as a sufficient deterrent. However, if a punishment is too severe for the crime, it will call into question people's overall support of the system of justice. For example, if police officers were directed to kill anyone who was caught speeding, the amount of speeding would drop. However, the authority of the police would no doubt be challenged; thereby eroding the entire justice system.

Learning Activity 4 - Discussion

What are your thoughts on the following questions?

1.   Does punishment deter crime?
2.   What evidence should we look for to answer this question?
3.   Is sending criminals to prison the best way to punish people?

Distributive Justice

What is distributive justice?

Equality and fairness are the core principles of distributive justice (Cook and Hegtvedt, 1983). As developed by philosopher John Rawls (1921 to 2002), distributive justice is closely linked to the ideal of a *meritocracy*. As we discussed in Unit Two, a society is a meritocracy when a person's social status is determined by her/his own merit (talent, intelligence and effort). Instead of being judged on ascribed characteristics (such as age, gender or ethnicity), a person is evaluated on the basis of achievement.

Equality of opportunity is a necessary component of a meritocracy and a system of achieved status. This form of equality is based on the assumption that all persons are "born equal" and that each succeeds according to personal merit. Differences in personal achievement result in differences between people in terms of social rewards.

In a meritocracy, equality of opportunity also applies to the distribution of justice. Everyone is "born equal" in terms of the justice system. It is through a person's own actions that they "get the justice" they deserve, regardless of their level of achievement in other aspects of their lives. This results in fairness.

Is a meritocracy realistic?

As we discussed in Unit Two, a meritocracy is more of an ideal than a reality. Most agree that social rewards and penalties are not distributed in a completely fair manner. There is a concern that social inequality is also evident in our justice system. For example, many people believe that "money buys justice" or racial discrimination is a factor.

Rawl's theory of distributive justice advocates for positive social action to alleviate social inequality. In conditions of inequality, social remedies based on **equality of condition** are necessary (Rubinstein, 1998). Simply put, socially disadvantaged groups should be afforded "more justice" to make up for their position of disadvantage.

The notion of equality of condition is commonplace in many aspects of our society. For example, our public school system, health system and income subsidy system are designed to "level the playing field."

In our system of justice, the availability of legal aid is one example of distributive justice based on equality of condition. As well, alternative sentences such as conditional release, probation and intermediate sentences (electronic monitoring, and "house arrest") are forms of distributive justice. Treatment programs in prisons also fall within this category.

Learning Activity 5 - Online Exploration

Legal Aid services are examples of distributive justice in Canadian society. They are based on the assumption that the financial inability of some persons should not prevent them from accessing qualified legal support.

Have a look at the types of services that Legal Aid typically offers. Follow these URL links to Legal Aid services in Alberta, Ontario and British Columbia:

http://www.legalaid.ab.ca/   http://www.lss.bc.ca/   http://www.legalaid.on.ca/

Procedural Justice

What is procedural justice?

Procedural justice is the foundation of the *"due process model"* in our system of justice (Goff, 2004:19). It also uses fairness and equality as basic principles but in a somewhat different way. Procedural justice maintains that justice is best served when society ensures that the rules and procedures in the justice system are fair. If the rules and procedures are fair, the outcome of justice (e.g., the determination of guilt or innocence) will also be fair.

The rights of individuals in the face of the legal powers of agents of the justice system (e.g., police, prosecutors, judges) are essential to procedural justice. As a person becomes a legitimate target of concern to the justice system, the onus is placed on the justice system to follow proper procedures. The rights of individuals and the proper procedures that representatives of the justice system can legally use are found in natural law and in our system of common law. The rights of individuals under procedural justice include

- the presumption of innocence,
- the right to silence,
- the right to legal counsel,
- the right to be informed of the reasons for an arrest, detention or criminal charge,
- the right of "habeus corpus" (being brought before a judge to ensure that an arrest or detention valid),
- the right to speedy trial,
- the right to disclosure (you have a right to know what evidence is going to be used against you at trial), and
- the right to be free from "cruel and unusual punishment."

What does it mean that "it is better that 100 guilty men go free than 1 innocent man suffer?"

The sentiment that "it is better that 100 guilty men go free than 1 innocent man suffer" is rooted in both procedural justice and natural justice. There is no greater injustice from these perspectives than a system that unfairly convicts an innocent person. It violates the basic rights of all human beings and is evidence of the unjust application of law.

Learning Activity 6 - Online Research and List

The Canadian Charter of Rights and Freedoms enshrines many of our procedural rights. Prepare a list of the procedural legal rights that are mentioned in the Charter.

Follow this URL link to Canada's Department of Justice Charter webpage:

http://laws.justice.gc.ca/en/charter/index.html

Restorative Justice

What is restorative justice?

Restorative justice is seen as an ***alternative to retributive justice*** (or the "punishment model"). Restorative justice is an approach to problem-solving that involves the victim, the offender, their social networks, justice agencies and the community. The fundamental principle informing restorative justice is that criminal behaviour injures not only victims but also communities and the offend-

Table 2.1 - Differences between Retributive Justice and Restorative Justice

Retributive Justice	Restorative Justice
Crime is an act against the state, a violation of a law, an abstract idea.	Crime is an act against another person or the community.
The criminal justice system controls crime.	Crime control lies primarily with the community.
Offender accountability is defined as taking punishment.	Accountability is defined as assuming responsibility and taking action to repair harm.
Crime is an individual act with individual responsibility.	Crime has both individual and social dimensions of responsibility.
Victims are peripheral to the process.	Victims are central to the process of resolving a crime.
The offender is defined by deficits.	The offender is defined by the capacity to make reparation.
Emphasis is on adversarial relationships.	Emphasis is on dialogue and negotiation.
Pain is imposed to punish and deter/prevent.	Restitution is a means of restoring both parties; goal of reconciliation/restoration.
Community is on the sidelines, represented by the prosecutor and the judge.	Community is facilitator in restorative process.
Response is focused on offender's past behaviour.	Response is focused on harmful consequences of offender's behaviour; emphasis on the future and on reparation.
Dependence is upon proxy professionals.	There is direct involvement by both the offender and the victim.

Source: Schmalleger, F., MacAlister, D. and McKenna P. (2004:299).

ers themselves. To completely resolve all the issues involved in crime, it is important that all parties have a say. A widely used definition of restorative justice states that "restorative justice is a process whereby parties with a stake in a specific offence collectively resolve how to deal with the aftermath of the offence and its implications for the future" (Marshall quoted in Griffiths and Cunningham, 2003:31).

Table 2.1 compares the basic features of restorative justice with those of retributive justice.

Restorative justice has become a viable option in our system of justice. Initiatives such as Victim Offender Reconciliation Programs (VORPS), youth justice committees and community service sentences are frequently used for adult and youth first-time offenders. As well, the role of crime victims in criminal proceedings has been greatly enhanced through changes such as Victim Impact Statements and Victim Assistance Programs.

Learning Activity 7 - Reflect

Is restorative justice better suited for certain types of criminals and victims?

If yes, what types of criminals and victims? Be sure to outline the reasons for your answer.

If no, give some explanation for your answer.

Towards An Integrated Theory of Justice

Can we tie all the theories of justice together?

Canada's approach to justice has evolved as a synthesis of the various forms of justice discussed in this unit. At different points in our history, some forms of justice have greater influence than others. However, it is not correct to say that one form of justice is "better" than another. As we have seen, each has contributed to the evolution of our system of justice.

We can use the term "human justice" to describe the justice system in Canada. As represented in the figure below, social justice is the end product of a system of justice that synthesises the various forms of justice into a coherent societal response to crime and wrong-doing.

In the following reading entitled "Perspectives of Racial Profiling in Canada" authors Frances Henry and Carol Tator highlight the intersection of diversity concerns and the perceptions and actions of some who work within the Canadian justice system. Often thought to be an American phenomenon, racial profiling can occur in Canada.

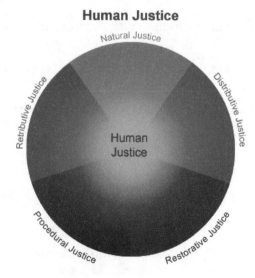

Human Justice

Learning Activity 8 - Summarize

In your own words and using your own examples, summarize the 5 different theories of justice. Give examples of each of the 5 different theories.

How do the five different theories of justice combine to become "human justice?" Compose your own definition of human justice.

References

Cook, K. and Hegtvedt, K. (1983). "Distributive justice, equity, and equality." *Annual Review of Sociology* 9:217-241. Retrieved November 12, 2006 from JSTOR database.

Goff, C. (2004). *Criminal justice in Canada, third edition.* Toronto, ON: Nelson.

Griffiths, C. and Cunningham, A. (2003). *Canadian criminal justice: A primer.* Scarborough, ON: Thomson Nelson.

Natural law. *The internet encyclopaedia of philosophy.* Retrieved on November 14, 2006, from http://www.iep.utm.edu/n/natlaw.htm.

Rubinstein, D. (1998). "The concept of justice in sociology." *Theory and society* 17(4):527-550. Retrieved November 12, 2006 from JSTOR database.

Schmalleger, F., MacAlister, D., and McKenna, P. (2004). *Canadian criminal justice today.* Toronto, ON: Pearson Education Canada.

Yerbury, C. and Griffith, C. (1999). "Minorities, crime, and the law." In J. Winterdyk and D. King (eds.), *Diversity and justice in Canada.* Toronto, ON: Canadian Scholars' Press.

PART ONE

Chapter 3

Perspectives on Racial Profiling in Canada

Frances Henry and Carol Tator

Learning Activity 1 - Fun Quiz

Take this fun quiz before you read the chapter. Answer "True" or "False":

1. Racial profiling in criminal justice agencies is found only in the United States.

2. Racial profiling is a from of discrimination.

3. In Canada, members of visible minority groups report being stopped and questioned by the police at a greater rate than non-visible minorities.

4. Terrorism acts in the United States on September 11, 2001 are one of the reasons racial profiling in Canada has increased.

5. The Supreme Court of Canada has ruled that minority groups in Canada are over policed and that this practice can be a violation of the Canadian Charter of Rights and Freedoms.

6. The concept of "white gaze" means that a person of colour are stereotyped by non-visible minorities primarily by the colour of their skin.

7. "Whiteness Studies" prove that persons of colour are equally prejudicial to individuals in non-visible minority groups.

8. Racial profiling focus on what a person looks like rather than what a person does.

9. In North America, too many people associate "blackness" of skin colour with danger and criminality.

10. In Canada, Aboriginal persons are at greater risk of being the target of racial profiling.

ANSWERS: 1F, 2T, 3T, 4T, 5T, 6T, 7F, 8T, 9T, 10T

Introduction

The term "racial profiling" has been much in the news in recent years and, it has, in fact increasingly become part of the public agenda. Originally an American term, it is now used almost routinely to refer to the form of racism practiced primarily, but not exclusively, by policing organizations. The scholarly literature on the subject is not as extensive in Canada as it is in the U.S. (Kennedy, 1997; Jernigan, 2000; Harris, 2002). There are many definitions of racial profiling, but a fairly comprehensive one is offered by Tanovich:

> Racial profiling occurs when law enforcement or security officials, consciously or unconsciously, subject individuals at any location to heightened scrutiny based solely or in part on race, ethnicity, Aboriginality, place of origin, ancestry, or religion or on stereotypes associated with any of these factors rather than on objectively reasonable grounds to suspect that the individual is implicated in criminal activity Racial profiling operates as a system of surveillance and control. (2006:20)

It is important to note that the term racial profiling is most closely associated with law enforcement and security systems.[1] Of particular significance is that racial profiling is identified as a means of maintaining social control and it is based on surveillance. The question immediately arises as to what is being controlled and who is being surveilled and why. Racial profiling can be differentiated from the traditional and routine use of criminal profiling because it is most frequently based on ethno-racial characteristics.[2]

This chapter will present some of the compelling evidence of racial profiling in Canada by reviewing studies of Indigenous and various racialized communities. It will review the case law that has been developed by the justice system to show how racial profiling is increasingly being put forward as a defense in courts of law. We will also briefly discuss the evidence of racial profiling at the border since the points of entry into the country have come under increasing surveillance. Finally, the chapter concludes by reviewing the various theoretical perspectives designed to explain the existence and prevalence of racial profiling.

---

[1]   Some scholars, notably Tator and Henry (2006), understand racial profiling as just another label for "racism" and identify it in many institutions such as policing, systems of governance, media, and other authorities, in their efforts to rationalize and justify racialized behaviours and practices.

[2]   Although racial profiling is a relatively new term, "profiling" is a well known and established technique used by policing organization around the world. Certain individuals are profiled by police based on what they look like and the observations of their behaviour. Thus, for example, if a poor looking person is seen in an affluent neighborhood, police are likely to suspect criminal intent. Many police organizations engage specialists who are "profilers," often trained in psychology, whose job is to provide a picture of the background and behavioural characteristics of a potential criminal.

The Evidence for Racial Profiling in Canada

There are several research strategies that can identify the evidence of racial profiling. For example, empirical studies include those undertaken by the *Toronto Star* (2002) which was based on data secured from the Toronto Police Service and obtained under the Freedom of Information Act. This study based on a substantial corpus of empirical data present clear cut evidence of the use of racial profiling by police. In the 2002 study, Blacks were charged more frequently, treated more harshly and more likely to be denied bail and held in custody for a bail hearing. These differences are maintained even when relevant legal factors such as previous records, and the like were controlled. Another example is the work done by Wortley and Marshall (2005), who were commissioned by the Kingston police to determine if racial profiling exists within their police practices. They found that Blacks were four times more likely to be stopped by police than White drivers and Aboriginals were also more likely to be stopped. The study also found that younger Black males were far more likely to be stopped than young White drivers and Black drivers were more likely than Whites to be arrested and charged.

In another empirical study by the *Toronto Star* on "Race Matters" (2010), the newspaper obtained police data (again through the Freedom of Information Act) on the actual contact cards that police fill out after each stop or incident. This recent study reveals a number of pricipal findings:

- "Between 2003 and 2008 Blacks remain much more likely to be ticketed for "out-of-sight" driving offences than Whites...Blacks are still more likely to be held for bail than whites when facing a simple drug possession charge.
- As in 2003, the present study found that when compared to their baseline population, blacks are charged for criminal and drug offences and ticketed for certain HTA offences at an overall rate of three times their baseline population in census data. They are also more likely to have been arrested or ticketed more than once. Blacks are disproportionately arrested for violent crimes. Jamaican-born Black men continue to be over represented in this category.
- Toronto police filled out 1.7 million cards between 2003 and 2008, most resulting from non-criminal encounters with citizens. Police attempted to control for those with multiple contacts, but the matching was not 100 percent. However, according to the data, about 1.3 million people were documented over those six years.
- The number of contact cards filled out where skin colour was black is three times higher than the proportion of blacks in Toronto. The rate for "Brown" is slightly higher. While, the document card rate for white people is proportionate to the white population.

An important tool in the study of racial profiling is to ask racialized groups about their experiences with, and perceptions of, the police and the justice system, and whether they felt they were being treated fairly by the police, judges, crown attorneys, and other authorities. Wortley and Tanner's (2003) study of the racial profiling of high school students shows that Black students who were not involved in any activity likely to attract the notice of police were nevertheless 4 times more likely to have been stopped and 6 times more likely to have been searched than White students.

Solomon and Palmer's (2004) study of incarcerated Black youth found that the policies of zero tolerance safe school and the ongoing practice of racial profiling appear to converge in moving Black students through the "school-prison pipeline." They argue that the police are incrreasingly making their way into schools to reinforce school authority structures.

An important study on racial profiling of male residents living in Toronto conducted by the Commission on Systemic Racism in the Ontario Criminal Justice System (1995) reported that 43 percent of Blacks, 25 percent of Whites and 19 percent of Chinese reported being stopped by police in the previous two years. It also noted that both racialized people and those who are White believed that judges made decisions based on race (p.178).

In recent studies, racialized people have been asked to describe their experiences of racial profiling by the police and in other institutional settings. For example, in a proactive move the Ontario Human Rights Commission launched an inquiry on racial profiling and received more than 800 responses. In the final report, *Paying the Price: The Human Cost of Racial Profiling* (2003), the Commission stated that there was no longer any doubt that racial profiling was a deeply serious problem for many racialized and Indigenous communities in Ontario. Evidence came from many of the new communities including immigrants from Asia, Africa, the Caribbean, as well as Canadian born racialized people from a variety of ethnic backgrounds. The Commission report also documented how Aboriginal peoples in Ontario experience racial profiling. The narratives revealed the everyday experiences of fear, humiliation, and differential treatment that Aboriginal peoples suffer at the hands of the police, and more specifically the abuse suffered by Aboriginal youth. The respondents commented about the fuitility of complaining to police or other organizations. Some spoke about feeling humiliated when they complained to storekeepers, security guards, transit employees, and the police. Other reports indicate frustration with health care and government agencies. A painful story was shared by an Aboriginal nurse who was immediately terminated following allegations that she had injured a patient. She commented that she would not have been accused if she was not Aboriginal.

Learning Activity 2 - Journal Entry

In your course journal or notes, discuss the following questions:

1.   How is the practice of racial profiling linked to the concepts of prejudice and discrimination?

2.   What are the dangers when a police officer engages in racial profiling while performing her/his duty?

3.   What are the dangers of racial profiling by jury members?

Racial Profiling and Aboriginality: A Case Study

The practice of racial profiling directed at Aboriginal men by law enforcement agencies is particularly insidious. In November 1990 the body of an Aboriginal teenager named Neil Stonechild (see also Learning Activity 8 in Chapter 1, p.15) was found frozen in a field outside the city four days after his death. On that night the temperature had reached -28C and Stonechild was only partially clothed, wearing one shoe and a light jacket. The Stonechild case was largely ignored for a decade until two more Indigenous men were found frozen to death during the course of a week in 2000. In 2003, the Saskatchewan minister of Justice established a judicial commission to inquire into the death of Stonechild and the investigations carried out by the Saskatoon Police Service and the RCMP. The injuries and marks on Stonechild's body were probably caused by handcuffs. A friend reported that he last saw Stonechild bleeding in the back of a police car, screaming that the police were going to kill him. In the course of the inquiry Justice David Wright determined that Mr. Stonechild was in the custody of two officers before he died, and that they had tried to conceal this fact while testifying at the inquiry. Justice Wright concluded that the police had prematurely closed their investigation into the Stonechild's death, probably because the detective leading it was aware that members of the police force could have been involved. In the Report of the Commission of Inquiry into Matters Related to the Death of Neil Stonechild (October 26, 2004) Justice David Wright wrote:

> As I reviewed the evidence in this inquiry, I was reminded again and again of the chasm that separates Aboriginal people and non-Aboriginal people in this city and province…The deficiencies in the investigation are beyond incompetence and neglect. They are inexcusable.

Racial Profiling of Muslim and Arab Communities: The War on Terror

Since 9/11, surveillance of Muslims and Arabs has become the most overt measure of racial profiling in Canada and other countries as the "War on Terrorism" is largely directed against them. While there are no direct laws that encourage racial profiling in this "War," the various institutions involved in social control have policies and directives that facilitate profiling. Bahdi (2003:300) has identified three major categories that impact on racial profiling. These are measures aimed at "Arab or Muslim communities in general; measures aimed at specific members of the Arab or Muslim communities; and neutral measures aimed at the Canadian public" as a whole but which differentially impact these communities.

With respect to the first category, airline personnel as well as security staff can subject individuals who look like Arab or Muslim men and women to higher levels of scrutiny than other passengers. Bahdi provides examples of individuals who have been removed from aircraft both here and in the U.S. Fausal Joseph, for example, a lawyer to the Canadian Islamic Congress on his way to Ottawa to meet with the Minister of Justice was pulled aside and ultimately missed his connection. Numerous examples of racial profiling are cited by Gova and Kurd (2008) including a Muslim respondent who said:

> At the border … from Canada to the US, as soon as the immigration saw me…I mean literally my name and that I was born in Saudi Arabia I was immediately asked to get out of the

car, park it, and they went and searched the heck out of the car…Another person noted that whenever he is sent back to automatic check in at a ticket counter at the airport, he "jokes about it but tells the counter agent that he will not go because I'm going to randomly get selected for the special checking, and then I have to come back to you because it won't give me a boarding pass…"

Measures aimed at specific Muslim and Arab communities, include the main law in effect to deal with terrorism – Bill C-36, the Anti Terrorism Act. One of its provisions allows banks to freeze the financial assets of persons on the terrorist list. This encourages the use of racial profiling because the agency responsible for this advises financial institutions to suspect even people whose names resemble those actually on the list. Bank managers are therefore strongly encouraged to view Arabs and Muslims with suspicion. Thus, race and religion, through the use of names becomes a proxy for risk. Because of the similarity of many Muslim names, and many people have the same name, it sometimes becomes difficult for them to prove that they are not the person named on the list. However, the measures in place to clear their names are cumbersome, overly bureaucratic, time consuming and sometimes involve costs.

Other measures that do not specifically target Arabs and Muslims but nevertheless has a strong impact on them include the recent amendments to the Aeronautics Act in which an airline carrier can give information about any of its passengers "if requested to do so by a government of a foreign state." This makes all Canadians vulnerable especially Arabs and Muslims or people who could be taken as members of these groups. Arabs and Muslims allege that they have been subjected to more surveillance especially in the United States even when they are travelling on Canadian passports.

A case in point was the controversy surrounding the case of alleged "terrorist" Maher Arar who was detained and deported to his native Syria by American officials as he made a stopover in New York on his way home to Montreal from a vacation in Tunisia. Arar is a Canadian citizen and was travelling on a Canadian passport. Agents from U.S. Immigration and Naturalization alleged that Arar had links to al-Qaeda. He was first deported to Jordan and then to Syria, where he was imprisoned and tortured for a year before being released in October, 2003. The issues raised by this case involve questions about the rights, freedoms and civil liberties of Canadian citizens who have been born in other countries are identified in some way as a threat to Canada or the United States. Smith (2007:162) observed:

In the Arar case the notions of democratic freedoms and the role of the state in protecting its citizens are suspended as the state responds to a threat, real or perceived, to its very existence and in doing so treats the authors, real or perceived, of the threat in ways that are considered aberrant to the rule of law…

The increased surveillance of Muslims and Arabs is especially evident since 9/11. Unlike the more definite racial profiling of police and other agents of social control, the border presents a far more ambiguous location. Border officials, like many police, rigorously deny the existence of racial profiling largely because there are no official regulations or laws which dictate it. Thus, is racial profiling only the result of official directives or "does profiling refer only to the use of explicit and official directives to target specific racial groups, or does it also encompass less official patterns and organizational mechanisms of racialized decision making that include 'race' but that extend also to often eclectic blends of ethnicity, culture and religion?" (Pratt and Thompson, 2008:621).

Although higher levels of government unconditionally distinguish race and nationality, the difference becomes "muddled" at the border. Pratt and Thompson, who interviewed 61 border officers, maintain that this very ambiguity is "enabling" because it not only allows for protection from scrutiny it also "facilitates the play of racialized risk knowledges" at the border and enhances the discretionary powers of border decision makers. They contend that viewing the border as a space in need of surveillance against "risky foreigners" (increased since the relationship between crime and security has become heightened) makes the border a good place for the interaction of "racialized knowledges." Indeed, there is no distinction to be made between criminal and racial profiling. Race is one of many social variables that might produce risk. Other rish factors include make of car, travel route and behavioural characteristics. All of these factors fall under the discretionary power of border agents. Racialized risk information is transmitted by means of special alerts, office postings, newsletter items as well as the expert knowledge of CSIS and Immigration intelligence on terrorist threats. Photographs are transmitted to border officers, but as one officer said, "they all look the same." Rather than consider this a racist remark, Pratt and Thompson note that it may be one of the ways that officers make decisions. While most alerts and postings were about young Black men who were pulled over for drugs, weapons or gang association, today Muslims driving (especially trucks) is another significant indicator of risk. Officers receive information though briefings on new trends, for example, hearing that several Vietnamese have been seized entering the country "so be aware of that." Although they are never told to watch for specific groups, details about each ethnic seizure is provided so "officers draw their own conclusions."

Border officials receive cultural sensitivity training, but a major message communicated in these sessions is that cultural differences will help officers deal with potential threats, especially to their own personal safety. Pratt and Thompson feel that rather than encouraging anti-racist values and inclusivity, the training focus is more on "a know your enemy" approach. The authors' main conclusion is that the concept of race is too general and that there are many variables that play a role in the discretionary decisions of border officers. Nationality is key because African Americans are not just "Black," they are also American. Similarly, Jamaican men are not merely "Black" but also Jamaican nationals. Muslims come from a variety of countries suspected as security threats. However, it is the very ambiguity of identities that allow decisions based on race or racial profiling to continue.

Another area of entry to the country is the airports where racial profiling has also been alleged to happen, especially towards South Asians and/or Muslim appearing persons. In the wake of the last major security threat in the United States in December 2009, for example, new security measures based on behavioural observations similar to Israel's highly successful system is being put in place at North American airports. Based on behavioural observations such as excessive sweating, general nervousness, rapid eye movements and any other observable "suspicious" behaviours are flagged by security officers. This system is being implemented at Pearson International airport in Toronto, the *Toronto Star* (March 11, 2010) quoted an official as saying this system will be helpful because "the ability to fall into racial profiling is so easy."

Learning Activity 3 - Reflect

Imagine you are a Aboriginal individual in Canada and you have been stopped and questioned by police officers on numerous occasions for no apparent reason. What emotions would you feel when this happens?

As a target of racial profiling, how would this influence your perceptions about police officers and the Canadian criminal justice system?

Racial Profiling of Black Communities

Generations of Black communities, especially those in urban centres, have been well aware of police racial profiling. Scholars have also come to recognize the importance of this form of profiling. Racial profiling has been described as a point of entry for analyzing how Blackness becomes equated with deviance and for measuring the social cost of linking Black skin with criminal activity (Russell, 2004).

James (2002:137) links the racial profiling and fatal shootings of Blacks to the "racial schema" used by police, which interweaves Blackness with "assumed citizenship, immigrant status and nationality (often Jamaican)...to inform their perceptions and actions...." He also suggests that the stigmatizing of Black people as a criminal group likely "to threaten the social order, safety and security of citizens turns them into racialized subject[s] that are always under suspicion."

This racialization and criminalization of the Black male, specifically Black youth, is thus structured within a social, ideological, and discursive context. In the dominant discourse of White authorities, both gangs and Jamaicans become coded language for the dangerous "other."

Individuals from the Black communities in the Greater Toronto Area have affirmed the reality of racial profiling as a persistent and systemic problem in their lives. With near unanimity, they validated the *Toronto Star*'s findings of 2002. The series was based on a two-year probe of race and crime statistics gathered from a police database that documents arrests and charges laid. The police database detailed more than 480,000 incidents in which an individual was arrested or ticketed for an offence, along with nearly 800,000 criminal and other charges laid by police from 1996-2002. The data revealed significant disparities in how Blacks and Whites are treated in law enforcement practices. The *Toronto Star*'s series on race generated hundreds of news stories, opinion pieces, editorials and letters to the editor. The series provoked an immediate and sustained hostile reaction from the police chief, the Toronto Police Services Board, the Toronto Police Association, and the president of the Toronto Police Union. Many politicians and journalists from other papers adopted a common discursive position: the categorical denial that racial profiling exists.

To address the misrepresentations of racial profiling of Blacks, key community organizations, Black leaders, and members of the African Canadian community formed the African Canadian Community Coalition on Racial Profiling (ACCCRP). The ACCCRP commissioned a study across the Greater Toronto Area to assess the nature, extent, and impact of racial profiling.

Maureen Brown (2004) interviewed youth, adults, city dwellers, GTA residents, wealthy suburban-ites, and the inner-city poor. Respondents detailed encounters with police in which they were targeted, harassed, and disrespected by police. The majority of respondents in the study firmly believed that the police use race as a factor in determining who is likely to commit or has likely committed a crime. All of the respondents spoke of their anger, pain, and loss of innocence, as well as their deep fear that as Blacks that they could not expect the same treatment or benefit of doubt as others receive in Canadian society.

The ACCCRP also commissioned a report that examined the history, current manifestations and impact of racial profiling in three countries: Canada, U.S. and U.K. The report examines the history of relations between the African Canadian community and the police in Canada and com-pares it with research findings from the other countries. The report bases its Canadian content on studies, task force reports and inquiries, public forums, community consultations, and media reports over the previous thirty years (Smith, 2004).

In October 2003, while the crisis over racial profiling was happening, the Chief of the Toronto Police Service Julian Fantino authorized a focus group of thirty-eight Black officers, led by four of the service's most senior Black officers. The group came together to discuss what it was like to be a Black officer on a force that was facing allegations of racial profiling. They also dis-cussed how racial profiling influenced their own professional and personal lives. The documents generated by this focus group demonstrated that racial profiling was consistently experienced on the force. Most of the focus group participants said they themselves had been inappropriately stopped while off duty. Three said they had been stopped more than once in a single week. They also described other forms of racism that they experienced: differential enforcement activities; derogatory comments directed at Black officers and civilians; the stereotype that Black motorists in expensive cars received extra attention was confirmed by Black officers; apathy among senior officers regarding racist behaviour; White officers who hold the stereotype that Black officers are lazy; the perception among Black officers that they are not allowed the same margin of error as White officers; a lack of change in the overall climate despite a zero tolerance taken by the Chief of Police; all the officers in the focus group had either experience or witnesses racial misconduct; and Black police officers being stopped for insufficient reason while off duty. Half a dozen said they had been stopped more than twelve times in a year. No actions were ever taken after the internal consultation and the findings were not made public until March 2005.

Case Studies of Racial Profiling in the Justice System

There have been dozens of high profile cases involving racial profiling of Blacks. Dee Dee Brown (*R. v. Brown,* April 16, 2003, Appeal Court of Ontario), was a Black Toronto Raptors basketball player who was stopped while driving a late-model, expensive car. At the trial, the judge refused to consider the defense's argument of racial profiling. The judge also clearly indicated his displeasure at this sort of argument. The appellate judges decided that there was sufficient evidence for the judge to have considered the role that racial profiling might have played in this case. Accordingly, they decided on a new trial for Brown. The landmark decision by the Ontario Court of Appeal was written by one of the longest-serving justices in the history of the Ontario Court of Appeal, Justice John Morden. He began his report with the recognition that racial profiling was a systemic issue and that the police officer need not be an overt racist. He states: "His or her conduct may be based on subconscious racial stereotyping" (Smith, 2006).

In another example of racial profiling, Kirk Johnson, one of the greatest heavy weight boxers of all time found himself constantly being stopped by Halifax police. After being stopped twenty-eight times between 1993 and 1998 he decided that he would initiate a formal complaint with the Nova Scotia Human Rights Commission in relation to an incident that occurred in 1998 when the police stopped, ticketed and towed his Texas-registered Black Ford Mustang. Johnson was a passenger with his friend in the driver's seat. In December 2003, the board concluded that Johnson was stopped, ticketed and towed because he and Fraser were Black men.

In *R. v. Ladouceur* (1990), the Supreme Court of Canada did not deal directly with racial profiling, but considered whether routine traffic stops violate the *Charter of Rights and Freedoms*, particularly sections 7, 8 and 9. While the majority in this case ruled that there was no violation of these sections, the Court expressed concern about the potential abuse of police power which caused them to comment on the need for officers to have a legal basis for requiring vehicle stops, such as checking a driver's sobriety or the condition of the vehicle. The dissent, however, specifically noted that allowing for random stops would give police officers too much discretion. The dissent noted:

> Indeed, …racial considerations may be a factor too. My colleagues states that in such circumstances, a Charter violation may be made out. If, however, no reason need be given nor is necessary, how will we ever know? The officer need only say, "I stopped the vehicle because I have the right to stop it for no reason. I am seeking unlicensed drivers." … How many innocent people will be stopped to catch one unlicensed driver? (1990:1267)

The issue of whether a vehicle stop constitutes a detention within the meaning of section 9 of the Charter was considered in *R. v. Simpson* (1993). It was determined that if a stop or detention is unrelated to road safety concerns or operation of a vehicle, a police officer has no general detention power. It noted that:

> …subjectively based assessments can too easily mask discriminatory conduct based on such irrelevant factors as the detainee's sex, colour, age, ethnic origin or sexual orientation… (1993:500-504)

R. v. Richards (1999) is the case most cited where racial profiling was clearly defined as

> criminal profiling based on race. Racial or colour profiling refers to that phenomenon whereby certain criminal activity is attributed to an identified group in society on the basis of race or colour resulting in the targeting of individual members of that group. In this context, race is illegitimately used as a proxy for the criminality or general criminal propensity of an entire racial group. (1999:295)

In *R. v. Golden* (2001) the Supreme Court suggested that "minority groups in Canada are over-policed and that *Charter* standards need to be developed to 'reduce the danger of racist stereotyping by individual police officers'" (Tanovich, 2002:52). Shortly after this case, *R. v. Peck* (2001) addressed profiling in a case where African Canadian youth were stopped and searched in an alleyway by an undercover officer who indicated race and other factors (e.g., the street location which was suspected of being a place for drug transactions) as the basis for suspicion. In finding that the race of the accused was a significant factor in the officer's decision to stop them for questioning, the Court determined that there was neither a basis for investigative detention nor reasonable grounds to suspect criminal activity. They found that race, especially that of a "young black male" either alone or in context of facts does not provide a basis for reasonable grounds for suspicion of criminal activity. In this case, the Court concluded that "[s]tereotypical assumptions linking young black men and the illegal use of narcotics do not provide a lawful basis to detain or arrest them" (2001, para.16-18).

Community Racial Profiling of Asian Canadians

The Lake Simcoe region of Ontario, a favorite spot for sport fishermen, has been the site of several serious incidents of racial profiling. In recent years, Asian anglers have been harassed, verbally and physically assaulted. The pattern is that local youth and adults from surrounding communities drive around in the middle of the night, looking for cars parked near piers, docks, and bridges. They then creep up behind the fisherman and push them into the lake. The locals call it "nippertipping." "Nip" is a derogatory word for Japanese and "tipping" refers to a rural prank known as cow tipping – sneaking up on a sleeping upright cow and pushing it over. Asian fishermen have also been confronted by men with guns, axes, and dogs. At first police dismissed the incidents as random youthful pranks. After assaults continued to increase over the last few years York Regional Police launched a hate-crime investigation. Charges were laid in four of the six incidents under investigation. The most serious of these incidents was an attack on Shayne Berwick and six of his friends. The group was fishing off a bridge at Lake Simcoe early in the morning of September 16, 2007. A group of men pushed two of the fishers off the dock and into the lake. A scuffle ensued between the members of the two groups and one local man was beaten. Berwick and his friends then got into a car and fled. But Middleton chased them down the road with his pickup truck, ramming into the car repeatedly until it crashed into a tree. Berwick was severely injured in the crash and suffered serious brain damage. Despite the finding that race played a role in the attack, the judge did not use hate crime provisions of the criminal code when he handed down his sentence of two years. The jury found Middleton guilty of four counts of aggravated assault and two counts of criminal negligence causing bodily harm. The family of the injured man questioned whether the law acts as a deterrent and is urging the Crown to appeal the sentence arguing it is not long enough.

Learning Activity 4 - Discussion

Using the course's discussion board, post your thoughts on the following questions.

1.   What actions would you take if your were Chief of Police for a large municipal police agency in Canada that has a history of racial profiling?

2.   What immediate and long-term actions would you take to make sure that racial profiling did not return?

Explanations and Perspectives on Racial Profiling

Racial profiling is essentially based on physical appearance and how that appearance is evaluated in terms of beliefs and stereotypes. But why is this phenomenon so pervasive in Westernized democratic societies? Several explanations and theoretical perspectives have been offered to explain this phenomenon in Canada. For example, the present authors have already presented their view that "racial profiling" is just another term for "racism" that has gained popularity through its usage in the United States to explain the frequency of police stops of racialized, primarily Black people (Tator and Henry, 2006). Their theory focuses on the hegemonic dominance of whiteness and the white gaze resulting in a form of racism prevalent in Westernized democratic societies where liberal values prevail, but in which elements of racism are still systemic and pervasive. They have identified this as "democratic" racism. The important work of Wortley and his associates, although largely empirical, also understands racial profiling as part of the larger dynamic of racism in Canadian society. Satzewich and Shaffir (2009), on the other hand, appear to reject these efforts and believe that it is in the nature of police work that creates a subculture in which all forms of profiling are acceptable. As race has become a variable of increasing importance in multicultural and multiracial Canada, it has been added to their long list of profiling characteristics. They contend that this leads to the frequent and vociferous denials of racism by police because they believe they are merely carrying out their professional tasks. What racial profiling does exist is a function of police subculture rather than racism or stereotyping. There are several other critical approaches to race that have been developed in the U.S. where racial profiling has a long history.

Whiteness and the White Gaze

In *Black Skins White Masks* (1967), Frantz Fanon identified the "white gaze." He describes how a young white child stares at him with its white gaze and turning to his mother says "look, a Negro (negre)." The child sees and comments only on his skin colour rather than his athletic build, the scar on his face or any other personal characteristic. Moreover, he does not refer to him as a "black" or "a man of colour" but as a "negre." Fanon's acute observation demonstrates a critical insight into the nature of racialization and the ideological construction of Blacks and other racialized groups. Whites identify racialized people and especially Blacks by their skin colour.

The importance of the White gaze – the way White people, especially White elites, perceive people of colour – is that it allows a dominant group to control the social spaces and social interactions of all other groups. Blacks, for example, can be rendered visible and invisible at the same time under the gaze of a White police officer, lawmaker, judge, journalist, educator, or filmmaker. With respect to criminality, the White gaze is central to the construction of the Black male body as the site of danger and deviance. The Black male is often perceived as a criminalized "other" who represents a serious threat that warrants surveillance, control and coercion. More recently, groups such as Arabs and Muslims have also become the targets of profiling – "brown" bodies are now also under surveillance.

Whiteness Studies

The field of "Whiteness Studies" focuses on racialization: the process of making race a relevant factor to persons or situations when it is, in fact, totally irrelevant. From the perspective of "Whiteness," however, the term is reversed to refer to the racialization of the "White" race. Whiteness scholars accept, as do all critical scholars today, that race, as a biological construct is no longer important or relevant to the understanding of human differences. Yet, social racism still places an emphasis on race as a visible trait that is used to practice racial discrimination. The nature of White identity is based on the concept that those who have traditionally held hegemonic positions of power over all other groups have done so by constructing hierarchical structures of exclusion and marginality. White-studies scholars assert that Whites must accept a race category for themselves, which does not include the assumption that they are biologically superior to other "races."

A dominant ideology in many post-modern societies is that Whiteness is hegemonic over Blackness or Brownness. This "truth" is believed not only by those who are strongly prejudiced but also by those who exercise control over the major structures and systems across all sectors of society. The beliefs, values and norms of the dominant White elite operate in the law, media, education, the criminal justice system and other systems of social control and representation. The hegemonic concept has attained its own largely unconscious reality that displays itself in terms of the meaning of "Whiteness," especially in contrast to "Blackness." Whiteness becomes another socially constructed identity, but one which has held the dominant position in perpetuating social inequity.

Whiteness studies reverse the focus on "Blackness," Muslimness, Aboriginalness and other forms of social markings, to critically examine the role of Whites in preserving and reinforcing racial bias and exclusion. Whiteness contests the often held view of colour-blindness—the notion that one does not see skin colour—as untrue and inaccurate. Whites see the "colour" in others in the same manner as they are seen as "White." Most White people do not, however, recognize themselves as a racial category and their self identification rarely includes the descriptor "White." Such people are often not even aware of being White and without that essential self recognition, find difficulty in recognizing and accepting their role as perpetrators of racial discrimination and exclusion. Many Whites often do not recognize their own identity in terms of race, as such they do not typically participate in conversations about race. The power of Whiteness is manifested by the ways in which racialized Whiteness becomes transformed into social, political and economic social and cultural capital. White culture, norms and values in all these areas becomes normative and natural. It becomes the standard against which all other cultures, groups and individuals are measured and usually found to be inferior.

Whiteness comes to mean truth, objectivity and merit. It is against this background that critical race scholars of Whiteness (Delgado, 1995; Williams, 1991; Bell, 1987) attempt to gain insight and perspective into these dynamics with the ultimate aim of exposing the power of Whiteness in order to dismantle some of its overwhelming hegemony over those who are "non-White."

Blackness Studies: Moving Towards Racial Profiling - Danger and Racialization Theory

Whiteness has become normalized, but this also means that non-Whiteness has become "abnormalized." The Black driver or the "Brown" airline passenger is quickly perceived in terms of a particular body and colour image associated almost unconsciously with either criminal or terrorist dispositions.

Proactive measures such as enhanced surveillance are developed in order to identify the abnormal by what it *looks like* rather than by what it *does.* Thus, "suspects" need not be engaged in criminal or terrorist behaviour (Fiske, 2000). The racialization, criminalization, and abnormalization of the racial "other" by means of extensive surveillance whether by video camera, in police cars, or at airports strongly relies on a process of identifying deviancy based on appearance rather than behaviour and is central to contemporary forms of racism or racial profiling.

The identification of the abnormalized racialized male has been linked to the fear of danger and threat. This is the idea that Blacks and other racialized people pose a dangerous risk in predominantly White societies. Thus, danger and racialization are brought together (Rose, 2002; Garland, 1996; Visano, 2002; Jiwani, 2002).

Blackness has long been associated with criminal danger in America (Rose, 2002). In the U.K., Garland (1996) notes that from the late 1970s, there has been "new and urgent emphasis upon the need for security, the containment of danger, and the identification and management of any kind of risk." And, in view of the massive post war migration from the former Commonwealth to the "mother" country, an important effect has been the "emergence of a criminological discourse of the 'alien other.'" This approach "represents criminals as dangerous members of distinct racial and social groups which bear little resemblance to 'us'" (pp.459-463).

Thus, racial profiling has become an adaptive or managerial approach to crime. Rose (2002) states that racial profiling "… results from the politicization of danger… it is a new way of talking about danger" (p.185). The object is not to identify a dangerous offender but to identify and manage "risky" population subgroups. This explains why the police stop and search Black drivers–not because of traffic violations but because they are "driving while Black." It also explains why border officials and airline security personnel stop and challenge Arabs and Muslims. Similarly, stopping and searching Blacks on street corners, in neighbourhoods, or in shopping malls and increasing surveillance of Arabs and Muslims is justified by suspicion of criminal activity rather than by violation of law.

The profiling of young Black men remains true "whether they are driving while Black, walking while Black, sitting while Black, bicycling while Black, or breathing while Black" (Russell-Brown, 2004:66).

Learning Activity 5 - Online Research

The Canadian Broadcasting Corporation (CBC) has an interesting webpage discussing racial profiling among police in Canada. Follow this link and review the information on the CBC website:

http://www.cbc.ca/news/background/racial_profiling/

Final Reflections

It is important to emphasize that the manifestations of racial profiling and racialized policing go far beyond law enforcement. The processes of racial profiling are deeply embedded in the interlocking systems and structures of lawmaking, immigration, criminal justice, education, the media and various vehicles of cultural production and representation. The dominant ideologies and everyday discourses of "otherness" used by the public and its authorities are marked by stereotyping, essentialization, inferiorization and the criminalization of Aboriginal peoples, Blacks, Muslims and Arabs, as well as other marginalized groups in Canadian society.

Clearly, no definition of racial profiling can capture all of the overlapping and conflicting meanings that are generally included under the term "racial profiling." Racial profiling whether it involves law enforcement specifically or the general perception of race as a dangerous "abnormality" in diverse public spaces (e.g., borders, courtrooms, schools, malls, street corners, and so on), results in particular categories being classified as requiring surveillance. Ultimately, these processes of large and small aggressions against racialized peoples reveal the huge social and psychological costs to society. Racial profiling exists in Canada. It does not keep us safe from violence. It is an act of violence.

References

Bahdi, R. (2003). "No exit: Racial profiling and Canada's war on terrorism." *Osgoode Hall Law Journal* 41(2,3):94-317.

Bell, L. (2003). "Telling tales: What stories can teach us about racism." *Race, Ethnicity and Education* 6(1):1-28.

Brown, M. (2006). "In their own voices: African Canadians in Toronto share experiences of police profiling." In C. Tator and F. Henry, *Racial profiling in Canada: Challenging the myth of 'a few bad apples.'* Toronto: University of Toronto Press.

Commission on Systemic Racism in the Ontario Criminal Justice System. (1995). Toronto. Queens Printer.

Delgado, R. (ed). (1995). *Critical race theory: The cutting edge.* Philadelphia, PA: Temple University.

Gova, A. and Kurd, R. (2008). "The impact of racial profiling." *A MARU Society / UBC Law Faculty Study* CERIS Working paper, No. 08-14 Metropolis B.C. October.

Fanon, F. (1967). *Black skins white masks.* New York: Grove Press.

Fiske, J. (2000). "White watch." In S. Cottle (ed.), *Ethnic minorities and the media.* Buckingham, UK and Philadelphia, PA: Open University Press.

Garland, D. (1996). "The limits of the sovereign state: Strategies of crime control in contemporary society." *British Journal of Criminology* 36:445-71.

Harris, D. (2002). *Profiles in justice: Why racial profiling cannot work.* New York: The New Press.

Henry, F. and Tator, C. (2009). *The colour of democracy: Racism in Canadian society.* 4th ed. Toronto: Nelson.

James, C. (2002). "Armed and dangerous!: Racializing suspects, suspecting race." In B. Schissel and C. Brook (eds.), *Marginality and condemnation; An introduction to critical criminology.* Halifax: Fernwood.

Jernigan, A. (2000). "Driving while black: Racial profiling in America." *Law and Psychology Review* 24:127-138.

Kennedy, R. (1997). *Race, crime and the law.* New York: Vintage Books.

Jiwani, Y. (2002). "The criminalization of Race/The Racialization of Crime." In W. Chan and K. Mirchandani (eds.), *Crimes of colour.* Peterborough Press: Broadview Press.

Ontario Human Rights Commission. (2003). *Paying the price: The human cost of racial profiling.* October 21. Toronto.

Pratt, A. and Thompson, S. (2008). "Chivalry, 'Race' and Discretion at the Canadian Border." *The British Journal of Criminology* 48(5):620-640.

Rose, W. (2002). "Crimes of color: Risk, profiling, and the contemporary racialization of social control." *International Journal of Politics, Culture, and Society* 16(2):179-201.

Russell-Brown, K. (2004). *Underground codes: Race, crime, and related fires.* New York and London: New York University Press.

Russell, K. (1998). *The colour of crime.* New York: New York University Press.

Satzewich, V. and Shaffir, W. (2009). "Racism versus professionalism: Claims and counter-claims about racial profiling." *Canadian Journal of Criminology and Criminal Justice* 51(2):199-223.

Smith, C. (2004). *Crisis, conflict and accountability: The impact and implications of police racial profiling.* Commissioned by The African Canadian Community Coalition on Racial Profiling. Toronto, Ontario.

Smith, C. (2007). *Conflict, crisis and accountability: Law enforcement and racial profiling in Canada.* Toronto: Centre for Policy Alternatives.

Solomon, P. and Palmer, H. (2004). "Schooling in Babylon, Babylon in school: When 'Racial Profiling' and 'Zero Tolerance' converge." *Journal of Education/Administration and Policy* 33 (September).

Tanovich, D. (2006). *The colour of justice: Policing in Canada.* Toronto: Irwin Law.

Toronto Star. (2002). "An investigation into race and crime." (October 19).

Toronto Star. (2010). Special series: "Race matters." (February 6).

Wortley, S. and Marshall, L. (2005). "Race and police stops in Kingston Ontario: Results of a pilot project." Kingston Police Services Board.

Wortley, S and Tanner, J. (2003). "Data, denials and confusion: The racial profiling debate in Toronto." *Canadian Journal of Criminology and Criminal Justice* 45:367-389.

Visano, L. (2002). "The impact of whiteness on the culture of law: From theory and practice." In C. Levine-Rasky (ed.), *Working through whiteness: International perspectives.* Albany: State University of New York Press.

PART TWO

Faces of Diversity and Justice

in Canada

Introduction

What do you mean by "faces of diversity"?

Because social diversity can be seen in most aspects of Canadian society, it is inevitable that its impact is seen within the Canadian justice system. As reflected in Part One, you can see several of the different "faces" of diversity—gender, race and age. In these next six Units, we will explore some of the realities of the different faces of diversity in Canada's justice system. In particular, we will analyze the role of gender, age, sexual orientation, race and ethnicity as they are evident in the following ways:

- Official crime rates,
- Official and self-reported rates of victimization,
- Incarceration rates, and
- Employment within the Canadian criminal justice system.

Learning Outcomes

What are the learning outcomes for these Units?

After completing Part Two, students will be able to:

- Identify and articulate the impact gender, age, sexual orientation, race and ethnicity has within the Canadian justice system,
- Critically analyze the core factors that link social diversity in Canada to its justice system, and
- Apply the alternative theories of justice and diversity covered in Part One of this course to the faces of diversity in Canada's justice system.

Unit One: Aboriginal Canadians

Chapter 4

An Overview of Justice and Canada's First Nations Peoples

Learning Activity 1 - Fun Quiz

Take this fun quiz before you read the chapter. Answer "True" or "False":

1. The term "Indian" is considered by some to be negative and possibly offensive.

2. The Supreme Court of Canada has ruled that First Nations people have a legal claim to the ownership of land in much of North America.

3. Canada's Indian Act was repealed.

4. The last Aboriginal residential school was closed in 1996.

5. The purpose of residential schools was to forcibly assimilate Aboriginals into Canadian society.

6. Using United Nations standards, Canada's Aboriginals, on average, have the standard of living found in third world countries.

7. Aboriginals make up about 4.4% of Canada's population and about 20% of those incarcerated in Canada's prisons.

8. Aboriginal people are no more likely to be a victim of crime than non-Aboriginal people.

9. Racism is the same as prejudice.

10. There is solid evidence that racism towards Aboriginal people has been a problem in Canada's criminal justice system.

ANSWERS: 1T, 2T, 3F, 4T, 5T, 6T, 7T, 8F, 9F, 10T

Perhaps the most recognized and pressing aspect of diversity within Canada's justice system is its interaction with Canada's Aboriginal or First Nations people (see, for example, Andrew, 2004; Frideres and Gadacz, 2004; Green, 1998; Patenaude, 1997). In Canada, a history of government actions such as the Indian Act, forced segregation onto reserves, residential schooling and other assimilation policies have marginalized many aboriginal people within Canadian society. As we will see, their marginalization also plays out in the justice system.

▍ Evolving Labels

Why does it matter what we call minority groups?

How we label different minority groups is often a reflection of their social standing. It is important that we recognize the sometime hidden implications in how we refer to Canadian Aboriginal peoples.

Using similar lists provided by Canada's Department of Indian Affairs and Northern Canada (2003), The Assembly of First Nations (n.d.) and Statistics Canada (2006a), here are some of the more common labels we use for Aboriginal people. These terms are legally identified in section 35(2) of the Canadian Constitution Act.

- ▍ *Aboriginal People*
  In its most general sense, "Aboriginal people" refers to the descendents of the original inhabitants of one of the seven continents. It is a term that is recognized in international law. As recognized in the Canadian Constitution, there are three distinct sub-groups of Aboriginal people: Indians, Métis and Inuit.

- ▍ *Indian*
  This term is thought to date back to the time of the explorer Christopher Columbus (1451-1506) when he mistakenly thought he had discovered the "Indies" (a medieval name for Asia). However, the term "Indian" was first legally defined in 1850 in the Statute for Lower Canada. The term Indian attempted to clearly define Indians as different from those of European heritage. Then, in 1870, additional measures under the Act to Encourage the Gradual Civilization of the Indian Tribes in the Province to Amend the Laws Representing Indians allowed for Indian men to "enfranchise" their status by surrendering their status claims in exchange for nominal financial incentives or some land. This was then followed by the Indian Act in 1869, which included provisions to allow Indian women to enfranchise by marrying outside of their own people.[3] In addition to the beginning of Metis status (see below), this is also viewed by many scholars as a covert attempt to assimilate (a process whereby a minority group adopts the culture, customs, and attitudes of the "prevailing" culture. Scholars such as Dickinson (1994) describe this process as a sort of conquest by law versus force of arms.

  Within the Canadian context, Indian peoples are the decedents of the original inhabitants of Canada, excluding the Inuit as described below. In recent years, some Aboriginal people have voiced concern that the term "Indian" is negatively tainted and potentially offensive.

- *Inuit*

  Aboriginal people of Northern Canada who live in Nunavut (meaning "our land" in their native language), Northwest Territories, Northern Quebec and Northern Labrador are referred to as "Inuit" (meaning "the people"). They share a common culture and heritage. This term replaced the slang term "Eskimo" (Algonquin loosely translated to "one who eats raw meat"), which is now considered outdated and negatively tainted.

- *Métis*

  This term refers to people of mixed Aboriginal and European ancestry. The word Metis comes from the French language meaning half-bred, mongrel and from Latin meaning "mix." Hence, it carried a negative connotation of people with no clear lineage and it is thought that the Jesuits were among the first to apply the term to the women (mostly Cree, Ojibway and Saulteaux) who married the voyageurs who travelled across the north-west for the fur trade and to establish outposts for the pioneers.

  Louis Riel (1844-1885) is perhaps the most recognized Metis who championed the plight for Metis status.[4]

- *First Nation People(s)*

  This term first appeared in the 1970s to replace "Indian" and "band Indian" that some people found offensive. While it has no legal definition in Canadian law the term refers to their heritage and ethnicity. Today, the use of First Nations People is the more contemporary and common term in Canadian Aboriginal circles.

For further information on terminology related to Indian and Aboriginal matters see www.ainc-inac.gc.ca/.

Learning Activity 2 - Reflect

From the perspective of someone who is of Aboriginal ancestry, why does it matter what "label" non-aboriginal people use? Some people argue that we are just being "politically correct" and it really doesn't matter. What do you think?

The Royal Proclamation of 1763 and the Indian Act of 1876

Why does the history of Aboriginal people in Canada matter today?

It is impossible to adequately review the impact that the past has had on contemporary Aboriginal people in Canada in the few paragraphs here. However, here are several of the more important historical incidents.

---

3   It wasn't until 1985 when Bill C-31 passed allowing women to regain their lost status if they had married outside their bands. The Bill also allowed the first born of these women to reclaim their legal status should they so choose.

4   Riel was eventually charged with treason and hung on Nov. 16, 1885 for his "insurrections."

The Royal Proclamation of 1763

The Royal Proclamation of 1763 was the first attempt by the representatives of Britain to provide a legal framework to negotiate with North American's Aboriginal peoples, the land that European settlers could occupy and which lands the Aboriginals would be protected for them. In addition, the proclamation integrated New France into the British Empire of North America and created the province of Quebec.

As the Royal Proclamation stated, its purpose was to "prevent such irregularities for the future, and to the end that the Indians may be convinced by our justice and determined resolution to remove all reasonable causes of discontent" (Royal Proclamations of 1763, n.d.).

In essence, the Royal Proclamation of 1763 negotiated the following provisions:

■   First Nations representatives agreed to turn over ownership of the land upon which the 13 British colonies were settled in exchange for the recognition that all lands west of the 13 colonies was the property of Aboriginals.

■   Any further attempts by European settlers to move into Aboriginal lands were prohibited, unless legally negotiated by the appointed representative of the King of England and First Nations peoples.

In the past 50 years, The Supreme Court of Canada and the Supreme Court of the United States have ruled that the Proclamation established legal precedent. In other words, in accordance with the proclamation, it provided the basis for subsequent treaties and related means by which to limit or restrict Aboriginal land titles even though most land in North America legally belonged to the Aboriginal people.

The Indian Act of 1876

The Indian Act of 1876 by Canadian Parliament represents one of the more controversial pieces of legislation in Canadian history. In the face of rapidly deteriorating relations between First Nations people and the Federal and Provincial governments, the Indian Act brought all Aboriginal affairs under the control of the Federal government.

What changes did the Indian Act bring?

Without consultation; as described by Hicks (1998), the Indian Act of 1876 introduced under the leadership of former Prime Minister Sir John A. MacDonald (1822-1892). The following provisions:

■   Aboriginal people became "wards" of the Federal Government. Aboriginals were told where they should reside (the reserve system), educated in non-aboriginal ways, prevented from engaging in some of their customs and denied full Canadian citizenship.

■   Instead of following the customs and traditions of their past, Aboriginal peoples were organized into bands. Each band was assigned a federal "Indian agent" who represented the band in dealings with the Federal Government.

■   Despite clear historical and cultural distinctions among Canada's First Nations, the Federal Government imposed a "white" system of classification.

- "Status Indians" were those Aboriginals who moved to government designated reserves—as specified under the Indian Act. Once registered with the government, they would be free from federal taxes, provided education and health care and allowed to fish and hunt without a license provided they continued to reside on the reserve.

- "Non-Status" Indians were those aboriginals who decided not to move to a reserve. They had none of the privileges of "Status Indians." They were essentially *persona non grata* – without status.

- "Métis" were individuals of mixed Aboriginal and European heritage. Also under the Indian Act, Metis had no special privileges.

- In accordance with Confederation in 1867, "Indians" at the time had the right to vote but only if they gave up all ties to their Aboriginal community and heritage. This situation remained in place until, then; Prime Minister John Diefenbaker's Progressive Conservative government on March 10, 1960 passed legislation granting Aboriginals and all people regardless of race or color the right to vote.

Learning Activity 3 - Journal Entry

The Supreme Court of Canada has ruled that the Royal Proclamation of 1763 established legal precedent supporting the claim of Aboriginal people that they had ownership rights to most of North America. This has become the legal foundation of the Court's ruling that First Nations Peoples are "citizens plus."

The concept of "citizens plus" asserts that First Nations Peoples enjoy all the Charter rights as non-Aboriginal citizens, as well as those rights that were agreed to by our ancestors when they negotiated treaties with First Nations peoples.

1. What are the consequences of "citizens plus" status for First Nations Peoples in Canada.

2. Given this legal status, how do you explain the social conditions that confront Canada's Aboriginal peoples?

3. Comment on the suggestion that the rhetoric of "assimilation" may have been a passive form of genocide.

Residential Schools

Are not residential schools a thing of the past?

A CBC report in 2006 noted that in 1928 "a government official predicted Canada would end its 'Indian problem' within two generations. Church-run, government-funded residential schools for native children were supposed to prepare them for life in white society. But the aims of assimilation meant devastation for those who were subjected to physical, sexual and emotional abuse." You can find out more by going to the Canadian Broadcasting Corporations Digital Archives (http://archives.cbc.ca/) and search for the video clip: *A lost heritage: Canadian residential schools* (2006).

The history of residential schools in Canada, dating back to 1874, is disturbing (see, for example: www.irsr-rqpi.gc.ca/english/index.html). Residential schools which numbered as many as 130 in all provinces except Newfoundland, New Brunswick and Prince Edward Island, were a key way that the Federal Government tried to forcibly strip Aboriginal peoples of their heritage and culture. By compelling Aboriginal children and youth to attending residential schools, the Federal Government hoped to speed the assimilation of Aboriginals into Canadian society. However, most now view the residential schools system as a primary cause of many of the challenges confronting Aboriginal people today and the Federal government has established a host of initiatives to facilitate reconciliation.

Nearly all residential schools were operated through a partnership between the Federal Government and various religious organizations (e.g., the United Church of Canada and the Roman Catholic Church). The realities of life at a residential school were stark (Indian and Northern Affairs Canada, 2004):

- Children of Status Indians as young as 7 were removed from their parents to attend year-round schooling until the age of 16.
- Parents were not allowed to visit their children.
- Trips back home were short and infrequent.
- While at the residential school, children were punished, often physically, for speaking in their cultural languages or practicing their cultural traditions.
- Children were required to practice the religious practices of those who ran the school.
- Physical punishment (in the form of caning, strapping, paddling, hitting, and kneeling on pencils or pebbles) was commonly practiced.

In essence, "extreme" measures were taken to suppress Aboriginal culture and heritage and force assimilation.

Finally, after considerable debate and even measures in 1967 to provide one half of instruction per week on some aspect of Indian culture, residential schools were closed between 1970 and 1971. By 1973, education of Native youth had been transferred to Band Councils and Indian educational committees. Some of the schools continued to operate until the final school (i.e., Gordon Residential School in Saskatchewan) was closed in 1996.[5] According to Canada's Department of Indian and Northern Affairs, 80,000 First Nations people living today attended a residential school.

What was the major impact of residential schools on Aboriginal people?

Many social scientists link Canada's history of residential schools to numerous ongoing social conditions facing Aboriginal peoples today (Frideres and Gadacz, 2005; Dickason, 1998). In particular, the schools had the impact of destroying one of the cornerstones of Aboriginal life – the family (Frideres and Gadycz, 2005). It is difficult to fully appreciate the psychological and emotional torment that children, their parents and extended family must have experienced when the children were sent off to residential school at 7 years of age.[6]

Before we move on, ask yourself these questions:

- Who provided love and affection to these children?
- What impact does this emotional vacuum have on those who attended residential schools in terms of how their own childrearing abilities?
- How long will the impact of residential schools last?

Learning Activity 4 - Watch and Listen

The Canadian Broadcasting Corporation (CBC) has developed a valuable online archive of many contemporary and historical television and radio clips covering a wide range of Canadian topics. You can visit the online archive at: http://archives.cbc.ca/index.asp?IDLan=1

The CBC's online archive has many items related to the impact of residential schools on Canada's First Nations people. Follow the link below and to watch any of the television clip:

http://archives.cbc.ca/IDC-1-70-692-4007/disasters_tragedies/residential_schools/clip5

The Reality of First Nations' Life in Canada Today

Referencing data from sources such as Health Canada, Statistics Canada and the Auditor General of Canada, Canada's Assembly of Nations (n.d.) has published a "fact sheet" documenting some of the added risks of being aboriginal in Canada.

---

5   For a more personal accounting of the school visit:
www.thecanadianencyclopedia.com/index.cfm?PgNm=TCE&Params=M1ARTM0012194 (Accessed June. 7/2010).

6   A 1907 report by the Medical Inspector for the Department of Indian Affairs reported that the death rate among "Indian" children in residential schools was nearly 50 percent.
(see: http://canadiangenocide.nativeweb.org/mort_rate_index.html (Accessed June. 7/2010).

What are some of the risks facing First Nation people today?

The following figures show the demographic shift (1991-2000) in Aboriginal population and the potential problems it may represent.

- Canadian population in 2001 was 29.6 million of which 976,305 were Aboriginal, 608,850 were North American Indian, 292,305 were Metis and 45,070 were Inuit.

- Ontario had the highest number of Aboriginals and Native American Indians while Alberta has the highest number of Metis with Nunavut the highest number of Inuit.

- Between the 1991 and 2000 census the Canadian population grew 3.9% while the Aboriginal population grew 22.2%, the Metis population grew 43.2% and Inuit grew by 12.1%.

- **Living Conditions**
  - Using the 2005 Human Development Index (HDI) created by the United Nations (UN),[7] Canada ranks fifth in the world among 174 countries. Meanwhile, the quality of life among Canada's First Nations people would rank 63rd and Aboriginal children rank 78th on the HDI. This would place Canada's First Nations among the poorest countries in the world.
  - According to Canada's Department of Indian and Northern Affairs, in 2001, 92 Aboriginal communities were among the bottom 100 of the 4,685 Canadian communities based on the "Community Well-being Index." When comparing Inuit communities with First Nation communities and "other communities", in 2001 the Inuit communities surveyed (N=51) scored marginally better (.69) than the First Nations communities (N=539), while the "other communities" (N=4,095) scored .81.[8]

- **Mortality Rates**
  - Based on 2001 census data, the First Nations infant mortality rate is 1.5 times higher than the overall Canadian infant mortality rate.
  - A First Nations man, on average, will die 7.4 years earlier than a non-Aboriginal Canadian male. For First Nation's women, they will die, on average, 5.2 years before a Non-Aboriginal woman.
  - Suicide has long been recognized as a leading cause of death for First Nations people between the ages of 10 to 24. Compared to non-Aboriginal Canadians in the same age group, the suicide rate for First Nations individuals is 6 times greater, placing it among the highest suicide rate in the world. One government report further estimates that as many as 25% of "accidental" deaths are likely the result of suicide, further exacerbating the problem. Furthermore, the suicide rate was placed at 3.3 times the national average for registered Indians and 3.9 times for Inuit (see, Suicide among Aboriginal people: Royal Commission Report, 1995).

---

[7]   For further details see: http://hdr.undp.org/reports/global/2005/pdf/HDR05_HDI.pdf (Accessed June 7, 2010) and for more specific data as it relates to First Nation peoples see: www.ainc-inac.gc.ca/pr/ra/wbp_e.pdf (Accessed June 7, 2010).

[8]   Scores range from 0 to 1 – with 1 being the highest possible score.

- First Nation peoples experience higher rates of chronic diseases than non-Aboriginal Canadians. The prevalence of diabetes among First Nation individuals is 3 times the Canadian rate and tuberculosis rates are 8 to 10 times higher. While making up about 3% of the total population of Canada, First Nations people account for over 16% of new HIV/AIDS cases. In 2002, according to a leading Canadian medical journal (CMAJ), Aboriginals living off-reserve faced in many cases even more daunting health problems.

Education

- According to 2001 census data, 48% of First Nations people have less than high-schools education compared to 31% of Non-Aboriginal students. And only 4% of the Aboriginal population has a university degree compared to 15% of Non-Aboriginal Canadians.

- While the number of non-Aboriginal post-secondary students has been increasing over the past decade, the number of post-secondary First Nations students has been declining.

Employment

- According to the rather dated information from the Assembly of First Nations website (see: www.afn.ca/article.asp?id=764#_edn16), the unemployment rate among First Nations individuals is at least double the non-Aboriginal rate.

- When employed, First Nations individuals are 3 times more likely to be employed on a part-time basis than non-Aboriginals.

- Employed First Nations individuals are paid, on average, 37% less than non-Aboriginals.

- Registered Indians have the lowest labour force participation rate of any Aboriginal group, with a rate of 54%.

Learning Activity 5 - Watch and Discuss

The CBC has developed a valuable online archive of many contemporary and historical television and radio clips covering a wide range of Canadian topics. You can visit the online archive at: http://archives.cbc.ca/index.asp?IDLan=1

Follow this link to the CBC archives and listen to a 1998 radio report on the tragically high suicide rate among aboriginal youth:

http://archives.cbc.ca/IDC-1-70-692-4008/disasters_tragedies/residential_schools/clip6

If your course includes a Blackboard or discussion board, consider posting your reaction to the social conditions facing Canada's Aboriginal People. What ongoing impact do you think residential schools have today?

Aboriginals in Canada's Justice System

How does being Aboriginal matter in relation to the justice system?

Let's start with a straightforward fact that has been well documented over the years: Canadian Aboriginal people are "over-represented" in the criminal justice system. Their disproportionate representation has been described as a clear example of institutional racism (see below). Consider the following statistics:

- According to Statistics Canada (2001), approximately 976,300 Canadians or 4.4% of all Canadians, identified themselves as Aboriginal (North American Indian, Métis or Inuit). However, adult Aboriginals represent 21% of admissions to provincial/territorial prisons and 18% of admissions to federal prisons (Statistics Canada, 2006).
- Virtually all the judges are white and less than 1% of the lawyers are First Nations Peoples (Satzewitch, 1998).

There is more evidence that the involvement of Aboriginal people in the Canadian justice system differs from non-Aboriginal people.

CRIME VICTIMIZATION

↑   Aboriginal people are nearly three times more likely to be a victim of violent crime than non-Aboriginals.

↑   About 20% of Aboriginal people report being assaulted by a current or ex-spouse in the past 5 years, compared to 7% of non-Aboriginals (Statistics Canada, 2006:7).

What about the prison system?

INCARCERATION

↑   In Saskatchewan, 80% of admissions to provincial prison are Aboriginal; in Manitoba, 68% of admissions are Aboriginal; and in Alberta, 39% of provincial prison admissions are Aboriginal (Statistics Canada, 2004:5).

↑   On average, Aboriginal offenders receive longer sentences than non-Aboriginal offenders *for the same offence* (Frideres and Gadacz, 2005:141).

RE-OFFENDING

↑   57% of Aboriginal offenders are categorized as having a high risk of re-offending compared to 44% of non-Aboriginal offenders, based on the assessment of contributing factors such as substance abuse, personal needs, employment, and family/marital needs (Statistics Canada, 2001:11).

↑   Released Aboriginal offenders are two times more likely to re-offend than non-Aboriginal offenders (Frideres and Gadacz, 2005:142).

Learning Activity 6 - Journal Entry

In your course journal or notes, address the following questions:

■   Is there a relationship between the over-representation of Aboriginal people in Canada's justice system and the information presented on the social conditions of First Nations Peoples in Canada? Consider providing concrete evidence to support your position.

■   Is the "cause" of the over-representation different, similar or the same as the high suicide rate among Aboriginals, the under-representation in terms of education and the higher rates of poverty that Aboriginals experience?

■ The Question of Racism

What is racism?

The longstanding over-representation of Aboriginal people in Canada's criminal justice has raised considerable debate regarding issues of racism. As defined by Angelini and Broderick (2007:110), "racism is the discriminatory treatment of individuals and groups on the basis of the group's race or ethnicity" and/or their culture. A core aspect of racism is to treat everyone of a particular race/ethnic or cultural group on the basis of a negative stereotype. Not only can an individual be racist but racism can be "systemic." Systemic racism exists when laws, policies, procedures, customs and traditions discriminate against individuals on the basis of race.

A perhaps more specific term that has been used to describe strong pejorative attitudes and feelings towards another group is the term "xenophobia." This term is generally reserved for those who "appear" to exhibit a fear or hatred towards another person or group as being an outsider.

Is there racism in Canada's justice system?

Have you heard the phrase: "Not liking the French? That's very English of you!"

In the 1980s and 1990s, there were a series of government studies from across Canada that concluded that pockets of racism existed within the justice system. As listed by Henry, Tator, Mattis and Rees (2002:173-174), these included Nova Scotia's *Report of the Royal Commission on the Donald Marshall Jr. Prosecution* (1989), Alberta's *Report on the Task Force on the Criminal Justice System and Its Impact on the Indian and Métis People of Alberta* (1991), *Law Reform Commission's Report on Aboriginal Peoples and Criminal Justice* (1991), Manitoba's *Report of the Aboriginal Justice Inquiry of Manitoba* (1991), Ontario's *Report of the Commission on Systemic Racism in the Ontario Criminal Justice System* (1995) and British of Inquiry *Columbia's Independent Commission into Policing* (1995).

During the 1990s, the majority of justice agencies in Canada took action to address concerns about racism. Agencies adopted community initiatives, diversity hiring and diversity training. Still, a much larger question remains open. *Is the over-representation of Aboriginal people in the justice system a symptom of the wider racism in Canadian society, or if not, why are they overrepresented?*

In September 2007 the United Nations General Assembly adopted a declaration, after some 20 years of debate, acknowledging that aboriginals around the world are entitled to all legal rights such as rights to lands, territories and resources (article 26); that governments should consult with aboriginals "in order to obtain their free, prior and informed consent" (article 19), as well as "right to self-determination." Canada was one of 4 countries among 143 nations that opposed the declaration. At the time of preparing this chapter, the decision had already raised considerable controversy over the intent of the government to rectify past actions (Caution on Native Rights, 2007).

Learning Activity 7 - Case Study

In 1971, a then young, Donald Marshall Jr. (a Mi'kmaq Aboriginal from Nova Scotia) was charged, tried and convicted of a murder he did not commit. Finally, in 1989 the Marshall Report issued by a royal commission criticized the Nova Scotia government for its handling of the case and accused the prosecution of being racist in their proceedings. The report concluded that Marshall's wrongful conviction resulted from individual and systemic racism and incompetence.

Follow this link to the CBC archives and listen to the 1990 newscast covering the release of the royal commission's findings on the Donald Marshall Jr. case:

http://archives.cbc.ca/IDC-1-70-2068-12858-11/disasters_tragedies/twt/

The CBC has developed a valuable online archive of many contemporary and historical television and radio clips covering a wide range of Canadian topics. You can visit the online archive at

http://archives.cbc.ca/index.asp?IDLan=1

Michael Harris, a former newspaper reporter with the *Globe and Mail,* wrote a book on the Marshall case titled: "Justice Denied: The law versus Donald Marshall" (1986), which was considered instrumental in helping to reopen the Marshall case.

As we have seen throughout the chapter, the plight of Canada's First Nations peoples has and continues to be fraught with controversial issues that are, to varying degrees, reflections of their historical marginalization and exclusion in Canadian society.

In the following chapter entitled "Being Aboriginal in Canada's Justice System," author John Steckley provides important historical and cultural context to the realities of being Aboriginal in Canada. He illustrates his discussion with reference to importance cases involving J.J. Harper, Neil Stonechild, Helene Osborne, and others.

References

Angelini, P. and Broderick, M. (2007). "Race and ethnicity: The obvious diversity." In P. Angelini (ed.), *Our society: Human diversity in Canada.* 3rd ed. Toronto, ON: Thomson Nelson.

Assembly of First Nations (n.d.). *Fact sheet.* Retrieved April 28, 2007, from http://www.ainc-inac.gc.ca/pr/info/tln_e.html.

Canadian Broadcast Corporation, Digital Archives Website. (2003a). *For survivors, the hurt comes back.* Retrieved May 8, 2007, from http://archives.cbc.ca/IDC-1-70-692-4007/disasters_tragedies/residential_schools/clip5.

Canadian Broadcast Corporation, Digital Archives Website. (2005a). *Abuse affects the next generation.* Retrieved May 8, 2007, from http://archives.cbc.ca/IDC-1-70-692-4008/disasters_tragedies/residential_schools/clip6

Canadian Broadcast Corporation, Digital Archives Website. (2007a). *Donald Marshall exonerated of wrongful conviction.* Retrieved May 8, 2007, from http://archives.cbc.ca/IDC-1-70-2068-12858-11/disasters_tragedies/twt/.

Caution on Native Rights. *Thestar.com.* Retrieved September 17, 2007, from www.thestar.com/printArticle/256867.

Chenier, N.M. (Feb. 1995). *Suicide among Aboriginal people: Royal Commission Report.* Retrieved September 19, 2007, from http://www.parl.gc.ca/information/library/prbpubs/mr131-e.htm#THE%20MAGNITUDE%20OF%20THE%20PROBLEM(txt).

Frideres, J. and Gadacz, R. (2004). *Aboriginal peoples in Canada.* 7th ed. Toronto, ON: Pearson Education Canada.

Henry, F., Tator, C., Mattis, W., and Rees, T. (2000). *The colour of democracy: Racism in Canadian society.* 2nd ed. Toronto, ON: Harcourt Brace Canada.

Hicks, S. (1998). Indian Act, 1876. Retrieved April 12, 2007, from www.socialpolicy.ca/cush/m8/m8-t7.stm.

Indian and Northern Affairs Canada. (2003). *Terminology.* Retrieved April 26, 2007, from www.ainc-inac.gc.ca/pr/info/tln_e.html.

Indian and Northern Affairs Canada. (2004). *Backgrounder: The residential school system.* Retrieved April 10, 2007, from www.ainc-inac.gc.ca/gs/schl_e.html.

Indian Residential Schools Resolution Canada. (n.d.). *The residential school system historical overview.* Retrieved May 1, 2007, from www.irsr-rqpi.gc.ca/english/history.html.

Royal Proclamation of 1763. (n.d.). Retrieved April 13, 2007, from www.bloorstreet.com/200block/rp1763.htm#2.

Satzewich, V. (ed). (1998). *Racism and social inequality in Canada: Concepts, controversies and strategies of resistance.* Toronto: Thompson Educational Publishing Inc.

Statistics Canada. (2001). *Aboriginal peoples in Canada.* Catalogue no. 85F0033MIE. Retrieved April 23, 2007, from www.statcan.ca/bsolc/english/bsolc?catno=85F0033M2001001.

Statistics Canada. (2004). *Adult criminal court statistics, 2003/04.* Catalogue no. 85-002-XPE, vol. 24, no. 12. Retrieved April 12, 2007, from www.statcan.ca/bsolc/english/bsolc?catno=85-002-X20040128431.

Statistics Canada. (2005). *Criminal Victimization in Canada, 2004.* Catalogue no. 85-002-XPE, vol. 25, no. 7. Retrieved April 10, 2007, from www.statcan.ca/bsolc/english/bsolc?catno=85-002-X20050078803.

Statistics Canada. (2006). *Victimization and offending among the Aboriginal population in Canada.* Catalogue no. 85-002-XIE, vol. 26, no. 3. Retrieved April 12, 2007, from www.statcan.ca/bsolc/english/bsolc?catno=85-002-X20060039199.

PART TWO

Unit One: Aboriginal Canadians

Chapter 5

Being Aboriginal in Canada's Justice System

John Steckley

Learning Activity 1 - Fun Quiz

Take this fun quiz before you read the chapter. Answer "True" or "False":

1. The largest over-representation of Aboriginal people in Canada's provincial prisons is found in Saskatchewan and Manitoba.

2. The only reason Aboriginal persons are in prison at a greater rate is that they commit more crime.

3. The Supreme Court of Canada has ruled that an Aboriginal person's exposure to systemic racism can be a factor in determining an Aboriginal offender's guilt of innocence.

4. "Gladue Courts" are based on the Supreme Court's ruling that the direct and indirect effects of racism experienced by an Aboriginal offender can be considered by a judge in determining the appropriate sentence.

5. In many Aboriginal cultures, the concept of individual guilt is a core aspect of their languages.

6. The case of J.J. Harper relates to evens that took place in Winnipeg, Manitoba.

7. One of the key outcomes of J.J. Harper's death was an public inquiry that uncovered systemic racism towards Aboriginal people by police officers in Winnipeg.

8. The name of the Aboriginal youth whose death brought to light the practice of "starlight tours" by the Saskatoon Police was Henry Beaudry.

9. The term "disposable people" refers to individuals that the law, social services and society in general treat as having little or no value.

10. Aboriginal women are at particular risk of becoming "disposable persons" in Canada's criminal justice system.

ANSWERS: 1T, 2F, 3F, 4T, 5F, 6T, 7T, 8F, 9T, 10T

In the forward to A. C. Hamilton's *A Feather Not A Gavel* (2001), Saulteaux judge, Justice Murray Sinclair wrote:

> When I was a law student, I was painfully conscious of the fact that Aboriginal people—my people—were over-represented in the justice system which I was striving to join. While the fact had been one of the reasons I went to law school—to see if I could 'do something' about it—the more I studied law, the more I felt overwhelmed by two thoughts. One was that the issue was far too large to ever do anything about. The thought pushed me toward the conclusion that becoming part of the legal system inevitably meant I would become part of the problem and not part of the solution. The second thought—resulting from the manner in which we were taught about the glorious history of the common law—was that the problem of over-incarceration must be with Aboriginal people and not with anything the justice system was doing.
>
> It wasn't until many years later, as my legal career developed, and I had an opportunity to meet with many of the elders and wisdom keepers of the Aboriginal communities within which I worked as a lawyer, that I began to see my way past the second of those two thoughts. I found that what I had observed in law school was the end result of a long process of legalized racial oppression and political deprivation. (Hamilton, 2001:5)

Introduction

Every individual experiences the criminal justice system in a different way. A major factor in this being true is the fact that the social location of each individual can strongly condition the experience he or she has with the system. By social location, I am referring to such elements as gender, age, social class, ethnicity, race and sexual orientation. Some social locations involve privilege. There are definite benefits to being rich, white, and male when experiencing the criminal justice system. Other social locations involve marginalization or a more negative experience of the system. In this chapter we will be talking largely of the experience of one such marginalized social location: being Aboriginal.

It is easy and wrong to throw all the blame on the system itself for the negative experience. Canadian society, which is by-and-large systematically discriminatory toward Aboriginal people (a systemic discrimination with a centuries old history), is the main cause. The lives of Aboriginal people are already negatively affected by this factor before individuals even face the Canadian criminal justice system. And the system itself, is, of course, profoundly influenced by that.

Let's take one small aspect to illustrate these points. A traditional and well-known feature of the prison system is the prison chaplain, a Christian minister. The chaplain is respected by the system because his (in a men's prison) position is society is well-established and respected. The work that he does in the prison is to help the individual criminal rehabilitate, guided by strong Christian principles. He can assist individuals to deal with the negative consequences of some of the actions in their lives, and can give prisoners the strength to deal with the jail term and with life after jail.

Spiritual elders in Aboriginal culture held such a position in traditional society, but after three centuries of marginalization that position would not be respected in mainstream society. All you have to do is consider the connotations of the terms "witch doctor" and "medicine man" to know the truth of that. Over the last few decades, however, the position of spiritual elder has returned to that of having a positive influence very much akin to that of minister or chaplain in most First Nations.

It took time and a lot of lobbying on the part of Aboriginal people for the spiritual elder to be able to make prison visits along similar lines to that of a chaplain. That was a flaw in the system that came from the centuries of religious prejudice in Canada. Canadian society did not respect the spiritual elder because of the European prejudice against Aboriginal religion that resulted in such actions as the banning of the potlatch of the First Nations of British Columbia, the Sun Dance of the Prairies, and a number of other ceremonies whose main role it was to strengthen society in ways similar to the major generally-recognized religions of the world (concerning the role of the potlatch see Clutesi, 1969; Goldman 1975; Nowell 1968; Spradley 1969). As tradition based Aboriginal religion gains in respect in both Aboriginal culture and in broader Canadian culture, the spiritual elder has become a positive player in the Canadian criminal justice system. Aboriginal people in prison now can experience the positive effects of a religious practitioner in ways that show respect for their culture and their identity. This had been long experienced by non-Aboriginal people prior to this time. The fight for this equality in the system is not yet completely won, as prison populations and prison staff have not been quick to see the importance of spiritual elders.

It has long been known that Aboriginal people are over-represented in the prison system and that this represents, at some level, discrimination within the justice system. Sociologist David Stymeist (1975:75) noted the latter in the following quotation from his 16 months of experience studying "Ethnics and Indians" in "Crow Lake" (aka Kenora) in northwest Ontario in 1971 and 1972:

> Most arrests in Crow Lake are for public intoxication. Ontario Provincial Police cars park outside the entrance to the Crow Lake Hotel, the town's largest central pub, for an hour or so before and after the pub closes. The waiters will ask a drunk white man, who is perhaps a relative, friend or steady customer, if he wants to call a cab. The cab will arrive at the back door of the hotel and the man in question will leave unseen. Many Indians, however, are arrested as they leave the pub, and some have been arrested for public drunkenness as they were climbing the stairs to their rooms in the hotel.

Figures of Over-Representation

The statistics consistently demonstrate that Aboriginal people are over-represented as accused and as prisoners (see Table 5.1).

In general during this period, Aboriginal adults represented 21% of admissions to provincial/territorial sentenced custody, and 18.5% of admissions to federal institutions, with an Aboriginal population generally of about 2.6% (Statistics Canada, 2006). It should be noted that the highest over-representation is in the Prairie Provinces, particularly Saskatchewan and Manitoba, as well as in Yukon and the NWT.

It is also important to note that between 1996 and 2004, the number of Aboriginal people in prison had risen 22% from 1996. (www.nupge.ca/print//1553, 2006, quoting Howard Sapers,

---

[9]   Due to missing data for some categories, the Newfoundland and Labrador statistics were excluded by Statistics Canada from the original chart.

[10]   This would have been worded as the percentage rather than the number of Aboriginal inmates.

Table 5.1
Percentage of Adult Admissions to Provincial/Territorial Sentenced Custody Accounted for by Aboriginal People by Jurisdiction, 2003-2004[9]

Jurisdiction	Aboriginal People Sentenced (%)	2001 Adult Percent of Population	Percent Over-Represented
P.E.I.	2.0	0.8	1.2
Nova Scotia	7.3	1.5	5.8
New Brunswick	8.9	2.0	6.9
Quebec	2.4	0.9	1.5
Ontario	8.8	1.5	7.3
Manitoba	68.2	10.6	57.6
Saskatchewan	80.2	9.9	70.3
Alberta	38.7	4.2	34.5
B.C.	19.8	3.6	16.2
Yukon	72.9	19.9	53.0
NWT	87.5	44.7	42.8
Nunavut	97.1	78.5	18.6

Source: Adapted from Statistics Canada, 2006.

Federal Correctional Investigator) during the same period the general prison population dropped by about 12%. Further, the percentage of Aboriginal women in these institutions rose quite dramatically, climbing some 74% during the same period.

While statistics of prison over-representation are easy to arrive at and are readily available to the criminologist, more difficult to establish numerically (but recognized as existing by the federal ombudsman or Correctional Investigator for federal prisons, Howard Sapers in his report of 2006) is another over-representation factor: over-classification of Aboriginal offenders in terms of the security risk that they pose. It is easy for non-Aboriginal members of the justice system to over-estimate how violent they perceive Aboriginal offenders to be. While this doesn't constitute evidence, more personal reflection, as a non-Aboriginal who has worked for over three decades with Aboriginal people, I have been guilty of this over-estimation myself. Sapers (2006) recommended in this area that in the next year the system should:

1. implement a security classification process that ends the over-classification of Aboriginal offenders;
2. increase timely access to programs and services that will significantly reduce time spent in medium and maximum security institutions;
3. significantly increase the number of Aboriginal offenders housed at minimum security institutions.[10] (www.oci-beg.gc.ca/text/pblct/ci05-06.response-eng.shtml)

Learning Activity 2 - Journal Entry

In your course journal or notes, discuss the following questions.

1. Discuss several reasons why you think Aboriginal's are more over-represented in the prison systems in Manitoba, Saskatchewan, Alberta, Yukon and the Northwest Territories?

2. Do the concepts of racial profiling, prejudice and discrimination hold any possible explanation beyond the fact that there are a greater proportion of Aboriginals in these areas?

Court Initiatives

Gladue Courts

Since 2001, a new court initiative has had an impact on Aboriginal offenders. They are called Gladue Courts, named after the ground-breaking Supreme Court decision in the case of *R. v. Gladue* (1999). The case involved Jamie Tanis Gladue, a 19 year old Cree woman who, under the influence of alcohol, and verbal abuse from her partner, stabbed her common law husband to death. They lived in an off-reserve, urban area.

The relevant part of the Criminal Code of Canada that relates to this case and to Gladue Courts is Section 718.2(e), part of amendments made in 1996. This section:

> …mandatorily requires sentencing judges to consider all available sanctions other than imprisonment and to pay particular attention to the circumstances of aboriginal offenders…It is remedial in nature and is designed to ameliorate the serious problem of overrepresentation of aboriginal people in prisons, and to encourage sentencing judges to have recourse to a restorative approach to sentencing…
>
> Section 718.2(e) directs judges to undertake the sentencing of such offenders individually, but also differently, because the circumstances of aboriginal people are unique. In sentencing an aboriginal offender, the judge must consider: (a) the unique systemic or background factors which may have played a part in bringing the particular aboriginal offender before the courts; and (b) the types of sentencing procedures and sanctions which may be appropriate in the circumstances for the offender because of his or her particular aboriginal heritage or connection. (http://scc.lexum.umontreal.ca/en/1999/1999scr1-688/1999scr1-688.html)

---

[11]   Beginning in the 1960s and ending in the 1980s thousands of Canadian Aboriginal children (3,400 in Manitoba alone) were taken from their homes and fostered out to or adopted outside by non-Aboriginal people in Canada and the United States. While there were some positive stories arising from this experience, the general practice, known usually as "The Sixties Scoop" had an overall devastating effect on Aboriginal individuals, families and communities. See Steckley and Cummins (2008:196-201).

[12]   See Knockwood (1992) and Miller (1996).

Leading the way in the setting up of what were to become known as Gladue Courts were Aboriginal Legal Services of Toronto, and a number of Toronto judges, (most notably Mr. Justice Patrick Sheppard) who together established the first court so dedicated in October 2001. Although, it should be noted that there had existed prior to that the Tsuu T'ina First Nation Court in Alberta, which began operation the previous year. The Gladue Court so established would be the first of five such courts developed in Ontario, three in Toronto, one in Sarnia and one in Brantford.

Part of the process that Aboriginal Legal Services of Toronto (ALST) and other Aboriginal caseworker providers engage in is the development of what are called Gladue Reports. As well as the usual background information for a case, these caseworkers also place "the offender's situation into the Aboriginal context by describing the systemic issues affecting Aboriginal people, e.g., history of adoption or foster home,[11] impact of residential schools,[12] on the offender or offender's family, homelessness, factors leading to a separation from Aboriginal traditions" (Campbell Research Associates, 2008).

In the above study of 37 clients who had Gladue Reports filled out on them by these caseworkers, 11 had been fostered or adopted, 16 had experienced childhood physical abuse, 16 had experienced childhood sexual abuse, one had been at residential school, and 11 had had family members that had been at residential school.

Those who successfully went through the Gladue Courts would have alternative sentencing based on Aboriginal community programs.

Problems Concerning Gladue Courts

In their 2005 to 2007 evaluation of ALST, entitled "Evaluation of the Aboriginal Legal Services of Toronto Gladue Casework Program," Campbell Research Associates' were generally positive about the effects of the program. However, the report expressed concern about the length of time involved in making the reports, and the high caseload of the workers, especially as their work took them farther and farther out of the city of Toronto. This is of special significance given that this program is generally considered the "gold standard" of Gladue programs in Canada.

In less developed circumstances there are a number of clear problems with the Gladue Courts. First, it should be noted that they are only one part of the system, and cannot be expected to overcome all the problems in the system. This is one reason (along with four other problems mentioned here) why despite the existence of these courts, the incarceration of Aboriginal people has not gone down (see the section on statistics). Secondly, there are problems for and with judges. While the relevant part of the Criminal Code is good in the abstract, it can be considered to be lacking in specific instructions to judges. More significantly, perhaps, many judges are skeptical of the process, not wishing to issue punishment-free "get out of jail" cards. Thirdly, prosecutors are even more resistant to the process, not wanting the Aboriginal people they prosecute to "get off." Fourthly, even defense attorneys can pose a problem, as they may know little about the process, and are unsure about seeking out alternatives to prison. Finally, Aboriginal communities may want to es-

---

[13]   Dene here refers to the language associated with the Chipewyan people. The term "Dene" comes from a word meaning "people" in languages in the Athabaskan language family. This family includes the Tsuu T'ina, of the court mentioned earlier, with the "T'ina" their version of Dene.

tablish programs that serve as alternatives to sentencing, but then have problems finding adequate funding for such programs.

Circuit Courts and Language Problems

There are other similar courts that have been established during the same period, and these are circuit courts. In October 2001, the Cree-speaking Circuit Court, based in Prince Alberta, Saskatchewan, but travelling to a number of communities in northern Saskatchewan, opened its proverbial doors (see Whonnock, 2008). This was followed in December 2006 by the Dene-speaking[13] Court based in Meadow Lake in northern Saskatchewan. Also, in November of that year, the First Nations Court was established in New Westminster, British Columbia.

The introduction of these Aboriginal language circuit courts is an important first step because a good number of reserves are located far from the nearest courtroom. Sometimes the reserves can only be reached by plane. A consistent complaint during the Manitoba Justice Inquiry was of mainstream circuit courts flying into a community, dispensing "justice" quickly, and then leaving. The first time that a client would meet his or her lawyer would be just after the plane arrived. And none of the key players (e.g., judge or opposing lawyers) spoke an Aboriginal language.

The significance of this latter point should be noted. While precise numbers are difficult to establish, it can be said that there are still tens of thousands of people who speak Aboriginal languages. Cree and Inuktitut lead the way in numbers. There are still elders who speak no English or French, and many who are much more fluent in their Aboriginal language than they are in either of Canada's two official languages.

The Concept of Guilt

Criminal justice systems are built on the presumption of shared psychological and philosophical concepts. The concepts of "guilt" and "innocence" are integral to the European-based justice system of Canada. How do you deal with people who do not have such words in their vocabulary, thus strongly suggesting that the concepts themselves are fuzzy? The author recently translated for a movie English dialogue into Wendat (Huron). One problem encountered was translating the word "guilty," as no such word exists in the language. The same can be said for other Iroquoian languages (such as Mohawk, Oneida, Onondaga, Cayuga, Seneca and Tuscarora) and the Algonquian family of languages, the largest Aboriginal language family in Canada, and in North America. In Canada this includes, from east to west, Mi'kmaq, Malecite, Abenaki, Innu, Attikamek, Cree (spoken in every province from Quebec to Alberta), Ojibwe (spoken in various dialects, such as Odawa, Algonquin and Saulteaux from Quebec to Saskatchewan), Delaware, Siksika (Blackfoot), Peigan and Kainai (Blood).

If you look up "guilty" in Richard Rhodes' Ojibwe dictionary, the closest word you can find is naammendaagzid, "be considered guilty" (Rhodes, 1985:269) is derived from a verb root meaning "to accuse or to blame." In John O'Meara's extensive dictionary of Delaware, under "guilty" you

---

[14]   For a book-length telling of this story read Cowboys and Indians: The Shooting of J. J. Harper, by Gordon Sinclair Jr., Toronto: McClelland & Stewart.

will only find **maashiingwéexiin**, meaning to "have a guilty look on one's face, look guilty of something" (O'Meara, 1996:482). The literal meaning is "to have a strange face." In Frantz and Russell's Blackfoot dictionary, there is again no entry under the English word "guilty," but there is a verb otóí'm, meaning "accuse/blame" (Frantz and Russell, 1995:176). It is probable, but beyond the author's knowledge, that there would be a similar situation with Dene, which belongs to the Athabaskan language family, as well as in other Aboriginal language families spoken in Canada.

■ Winnipeg: J.J. Harper, Racism and the Winnipeg Police Service

Winnipeg has one of the largest Aboriginal populations in Canada; it also has had (in 2004) the highest crime rate in a city over 500,000 in Canada. In 1969 it was estimated that Aboriginal people made up about 1% of the population of Winnipeg (Frideres, 1998:240-241), but that they

> ...accounted for 23 per cent of the 5,472 people involved in a variety of offences in the city and 19 per cent of the 4,302 held in Headingly Jail, half of whom were being held for failing to pay fines. (Comeau and Santin, 1990:130)

> Headingly Jail, which houses prisoners serving sentences of two years less a day, had a 25% status Indian population in 1987, 41% Aboriginal if you include Métis prisoners. (ibid)

In 1988, when the following story took place, there were an estimated 40,000 to 50,000 Aboriginal people in Winnipeg, urban statistics on Aboriginal people being very difficult to establish precisely. At the time, the 1,140 member police force in Winnipeg had only nine Aboriginal constables.

The J. J. Harper Story[14]

It was roughly 2:30 in the cold morning of March 9, 1988. An Aboriginal man was walking alone. He was John Joseph Harper, of the mixed Saulteaux-Cree community of Wasagamack, 36, father of three, and a leader in the Indian Lake Tribal Council. He had had a few drinks in a local tavern.

Unknown to him, elsewhere in downtown Winnipeg, a 22 year old Aboriginal man had stolen a car and had been apprehended. Several officers were still patrolling the area. One such officer walked toward Harper and asked him to show identification. He did this despite the fact that Harper was "a poor match for the suspect in other respects [i.e., other than being 'Indian']" (see www.majic.mb.ca). Harper refused. He had committed no crime. The officer asked him again, and Harper proceeded just to walk away. The officer grabbed him by the arm and they fought. A few minutes later Harper was dead, killed by the officer's weapon.

The investigation was hastily and sloppily done. The scene of the crime had been hosed down before dawn, washing away any clues that there might have been there. In court, the officer claimed that Harper had pushed him down and tried to grab his holstered weapon. There is evidence now suggesting that the gun was already drawn and had been when he approached Harper. The gun

---

[15]   See Lisa Priest Conspiracy of Silence, Toronto: McClelland & Stewart, 1989 and Cummins and Steckley 2003:75-78.

had not been dusted for fingerprints. Within 36 hours of the crime, the Winnipeg police chief publicly stated that his officer was innocent, and the mayor agreed with him.

Justice A.C. Hamilton, reporting on what he encountered in the Manitoba Justice Inquiry that followed this incident and the Helen Betty Osborne case that took place in northern Manitoba[15] (see below), wrote:

> Our hearings in Winnipeg brought out the wrath of Aboriginal city residents as they described their personal experiences with police brutality, the courts' indifference and the oppression of bigotry and discrimination they encounter on a daily basis. (Hamilton, 2001:61)

Some incidents that Hamilton described were as follows, which can be called DWA (Driving While Aboriginal) and RWA (Running While Aboriginal):

> A Winnipeg native told us that he drove a large car. If he was in blue jeans and an old sweater, the police regularly stopped him, questioned why he was driving such a big car, and how he could afford it. He wasn't allowed to go on his way until he proved he owned the car. On the other hand, he said that if he was wearing a suit and tie and driving the same care, he was never stopped or questioned.

> A young Aboriginal man told of being arrested and taken to the police station, for running down a city street. He explained to the police that he was late, and was running to meet his girlfriend, but he was not believed. He asked us to consider whether, if he had been white, he would have been apprehended. (Hamilton, 2001:62)

The Manitoba Justice Inquiry, headed up by Saulteaux judge Murray Sinclair and A.C. Hamilton, reported in 1990:

> It is our conclusion that the City of Winnipeg Police Department did not search actively or aggressively for the truth about the death of J. J. Harper. Their investigation was, at best, inadequate. At worst, its primary objective seems to have been to exonerate Const. Robert Cross and to vindicate the Police Department.
>
> We believe that evidence was mishandled and facts were obscured by police attempts to construct a version of events which would, in effect, blame J. J. Harper for his own death. Our review of the taking of Cross' statements leads us to conclude that he was assisted in its compilation rather than being questioned. We have found that at least one officer rewrote his record of events. (see www.majic.mb.ca)

The representation of individuals within the Winnipeg Police Service has remained an issue well after the Manitoba Justice Inquiry into the death of J.J. Harper. At the time of the inquiry, 133 Winnipeg were officially reported as coming from Aboriginal decent. As well, only 5% of the civilian members (or 21 of 411 civilian members) were of Aboriginal decent. By 2006, the number of Aboriginal police officers in Winnipeg had increased to 148 (or 11% of the 1,382 sworn officers). While official statistics suggest that a roughly equivalent percentage of Winnipeg's population is

Aboriginal, Frideries wisely warns us that urban counts of Aboriginal people taken by Statistics Canada are typically underestimated in the thousands (Frideres, 1998:240 - 241). Given this "under counting," the true percentage of Winnipeg's Aboriginal population is likely closer to 15% to 20%.

This under-representation of Aboriginal employees within the Winnipeg police service may have ramifications beyond the J.J. Harper case. Specifically, this chapter will explore the notion of Aboriginals as "disposable persons" and how this idea may have been a factor in the tragic handling of the 911 emergency case by the Winnipeg police service in 2000.

Learning Activity 3 - Online Research

In Canadian criminal justice, the case of John Joseph (J.J.) Harper is an important one as it documents one instance where a person's Aboriginal identity negatively influenced the practice of justice in Canada.

All students of justice in Canada should be familiar with this important case. The final report of the Aboriginal Justice Inquiry into the death of J.J. Harper is available at the following link:

http://www.ajic.mb.ca/volumelll/chapter1.html

Saskatchewan, Aboriginal Youth, and the Justice System

In 2001, Craig Nyirfa Saskatoon Police Service's Aboriginal Liaison Officer (now with the Professional Development Centre for Aboriginal Policing, Canada Police College), uttered a bold, and probably not too far from accurate statement when he claimed: "An Aboriginal kid in Saskatoon today stands a better chance of ending up in the criminal justice system than finishing high school" (in Stackhouse 2001:F2-F4). While we don't have the necessary statistics to effectively back him up or challenge his claim, the situation in Saskatchewan for Aboriginal youth is clearly problematic. Table 5.2a shows figures for 2003-2007 for admission to secure custody, admissions to open custody and admissions to probation (www40.statcan.gc.ca/101/cst01/legal42a-eng.htm):

Table 5.2a
Saskatchewan Youth Correctional Services

	2003	2004	2005	2006	2007	Change
Admissions to secure custody						
Aboriginal	178	116	87	118	87	-91
Non-Aboriginal	60	43	29	40	28	-32
Admissions to open custody						
Aboriginal	208	165	116	108	147	-61
Non-Aboriginal	41	47	35	45	36	-5
Admissions to probation						
Aboriginal	841	831	763	851	887	+46
Non-Aboriginal	452	395	400	402	471	+19

The only province with comparable numbers, specifically with Aboriginal youth outnumbering non-Aboriginal youth is Manitoba, as can be seen in Table 5.2b:

Table 5.2b
Manitoba Youth Correctional Services

	2003	2004	2005	2006	2007	Change
Admissions to secure custody						
Aboriginal	76	114	76	99	79	+3
Non-Aboriginal	23	22	19	12	17	-6
Admissions to open custody						
Aboriginal	194	205	240	238	187	-7
Non-Aboriginal	44	38	31	29	32	-12
Admissions to probation						
Aboriginal	440	511	586	561	603	+63
Non-Aboriginal	348	420	350	351	387	+39

Data published in Statistics Canada's *Police-Reported Aboriginal Crime in Saskatchewan*, 2000, with data from Prince Albert, Regina and Saskatoon, illustrate that accused Aboriginals are generally younger than accused non-Aboriginals:

Table 5.3
Age of Accused Aboriginals and non-Aboriginals, 1997

	<12	12-17	18-24	25-34	35-44	45-54	55+
Aboriginal	2%	31%	28%	24%	11%	3%	1%
Non-Aboriginal	1%	23%	27%	23%	16%	6%	4%

Source: Statistics Canada, Police-Reported Aboriginal Crime in Saskatchewan, Prince Albert, Regina and Saskatchewan. Adapted by the author.

We see in this that one third (33%) of Aboriginal accused are 17 or younger, compared with one quarter (24%) of non-Aboriginal accused. For 24 and younger, the comparison is 61%, as opposed to 51%. It should be kept in mind, however, that the average age of Aboriginal people is also younger than that of non-Aboriginal people, so these figures exaggerate the difference somewhat.

The Starlight Tour of Neil Stonechild

The term 'starlight tour' was coined by police officer and journalist Brian Trainer in 1997 to refer to the practice of police officers of driving drunk Aboriginal people beyond the city limits of Saskatoon, and leaving them there to find their way back home.

The most famous Saskatoon starlight tour is the one taken by Neil Stonechild (see Reber and Renaud, 2005). He was 17 years old, an Aboriginal youth. It was Saturday night, November 24, 1990. He and his friend Jason Roy had been drinking and caused some kind of disturbance at a *711*. At some point he separated from Roy and knocked on the door of apartment where his ex-girlfriend was visiting with her sister, and her sister's white boyfriend. The boyfriend called the police and Stonechild left.

Stonechild was picked up by two officers and put into the backseat of a cruiser. Roy was stopped by the police and asked to identify the person sitting in the back of the cruiser. Not wanting to be arrested, Roy said that he didn't know who that was.

Stonechild was found the next Thursday, his frozen body discovered on the northern outskirts of the city. He was wearing a light jacket, jeans, and only one running shoe. Across his face were parallel cut marks, that and other injuries consistent with being hit with and wearing handcuffs. A police investigation followed, but it resolved nothing, and appears to have been superficial.

Over the next decade, a number of other similar cases came to light (see Steckley and Cummins, 2008:229-231). In 2000, there was established a Commission of Inquiry into Matters Relating to the Death of Neil Stonechild. A 380 page report came out in 2004, which verified the interpretation that Stonechild had been in the cruiser, was handcuffed, and was then taken on a starlight tour. Eight recommendations were put forward. Along with recommendations on training on anger management and race relations among officers, and suggestions to generally improve the complaint process concerning police matters, there were recommendations aimed a recruiting Aboriginal officers into the police force. Significantly, the fifth recommendation was:

> That Municipal Police Services in larger centres should designate an Aboriginal peace officer with the rank of Sergeant, where possible, to act as a liaison person for First Nation persons and as an informal ombudsman to deal with complaints and concerns from Aboriginal and persons from minority communities. (p.213)

As of February 2010, the Saskatoon Police Services (SPS) has a Cultural Resources Unit, with a sergeant and three constables, whose job it is to "provide assistance to cultural community groups, the Federal of Saskatchewan Indian Nations, Saskatoon Tribal Council, Métis Society, Open Door Society and the gay/lesbian/bisexual/transgendered community" (www.police.saskatoon.sk.ca).

The SPS has been served by their first Aboriginal Liaison Officer, Sergeant Craig Nyirfa. While he was praised and awarded for his work with Aboriginal people in the 2005 Annual Report of the

---

[16]   When specific crimes are mentioned in the Report, they tend to be significantly higher on the reserve than in the other categories.[16] There are a number of categories in which the rural and urban area crime rate is higher. Theft is one such example.

SPS (www.police.saskatoon.sk.ca/pdf/annual_reports/2005_Annual Report.pdf), such reports are suspected as being public relations communiqués. More significant is the praise given in the March 13, 2000 edition of the Aboriginal newspaper, *Saskatchewan Sage*, article "Year starts with an 'uproar' in the Aboriginal community," written by the paper's youth columnist, Chris Tyrone Ross. In discussing the Neil Stonechild story, Ross wrote:

> The only thing I have left to say before next month's column (as the story unfolds) is that there are some good cops in the police force as well. One fine example is Constable Craig Nyirfa, the Aboriginal liaison officer for the Saskatoon City Police. Craig Nyirfa has earned the respect from the Aboriginal community with his positive initiatives for Aboriginal young offenders. Every summer he takes a group of kids on a camping trip that includes canoeing, swimming, sports and recreation. He says spending time with youth is better than sending them to the correctional centre, which is one thing the Aboriginal community respects him for.

Reserves and Crimes

Taken on average, reserves have a higher crime rate than do urban or rural areas. This point is made clear in the following chart adapted from the *Police-Reported Aboriginal Crime in Saskatchewan*, (2000), which looks at the rate per 10,000 population in Saskatchewan in 1997.[16]

Table 5.4
Saskatchewan 1997: Crime Rate Based on Area

Offence Type	Saskatchewan	Reserve	Rural	Urban
Violent Offences	164	678	135	149
Sexual Assault	19	82	16	17
Serious Assault	33	131	21	35
Minor Assault	99	456	94	76
Property Offences	833	1,124	713	917
Break and Enter	194	391	149	219

Source: Statistics Canada, Police-Reported Aboriginal Crime in Saskatchewan, 2000. Adapted by the author.

Aboriginal People as Disposable People

A relatively new concept in the social scientific literature is that of "disposable people" (see Bauman, 2004 and Vehitelle, 2006). One of the recent uses of the term relates to the Black people of New Orleans after Hurricane Katrina (Giroux, 2006). Many were abandoned by federal, state and municipal agencies, and forced to stay in virtual concentration camps at the football stadium. The term disposable people refers to those that the law, social services and society in general treats as if they have no value. A good argument could be made to say that oftentimes historically and currently, Aboriginal victims of crimes are treated as they were disposable people. Here is some of the evidence and key cases that were pivotal to initiating inquiries into the teatment of Aboriginal peoples.

Learning Activity 4 - Watch and Listen

The Canadian Broadcasting Corporation (CBC) has developed a valuable online archive of many contemporary and historical television and radio clips covering a wide range of Canadian topics. You can visit the online archive at: **http://archives.cbc.ca/index.asp?IDLan=1**

The CBC's online archive has several important items related to the case of Donald Marshall, perhaps the most infamous case of "wrongful conviction." A public inquiry into Marshall's wrongful conviction for first-degree murder concluded that racism was at the core of the police's targeting Marshall for a crime he did not commit.

Follow the link below and watch a brief television clip from 1990 discussion Marshall's release from prison after 11 years for a crime he did not commit:

http://archives.cbc.ca/society/crime_justice/clips/12858/

Disposable Indians: Case Studies

Helen Betty Osborne (see Lisa Priest, 1989, Conspiracy of Silence)

On November 12, 1971, Helen Betty Osborne, a 19 year old Cree woman was killed on a rural road outside of The Pas, in northern Manitoba. Four young White men, under the influence of alcohol, and following the then local practice of "cruising for Indian women" forced her into their car, drove away from prying eyes and tore her clothes off. At least one of the men sexually assaulted her. One of the men, a teenager, murdered her by stabbing her 56 times with a screwdriver. For 12 years little was done about this crime, although at least two of the young men were not shy about telling the story of Helen's last night.

In 1983, Constable Bob Urbanoski of the Thompson, Manitoba detachment of the RCMP took up the case, and was able to gather up enough information to be able to lay charges on two of the young men in 1986.

Interestingly, of 104 prospective jurors considered for the trial, the 20 that were Aboriginal were rejected by the lawyers. This flowed from the flawed idea that Aboriginal jurors would be more biased than White ones would be. In the case of an interracial crime, there can be bias on both sides. This has generally been insufficiently recognized in the past when members of visible minorities are involved.

In December 1987, one of the young men was convicted of murder and sentenced to life in prison, but would serve only 10 years. Of the two of the others who had been involved with the trial, one was acquitted, and the other had received immunity from any charges because he had assisted the prosecution in making its case.

---

[17]   When the officer phoned in that Minnie had changed her mind about calling a taxi, one of the officers said "Cancel the taxi now. The squaw decided otherwise "(Nihmey 1998:84).

Minnie Sutherland (see John Nihmey, 1998, Fireworks and Folly:
How We Killed Minnie Sutherland)

Forty year old Cree woman, Minnie Sutherland died on January 11, 1989 of a cardiac arrest resulting from a blood clot in the back of her brain caused by her being hit by a car 10 days before.

At about 3:30 a.m., New Year's Day, Minnie was hit by a car in downtown Hull, Quebec. Officers, noticing that cars were backed up on the road, arrived at the scene. Hearing from Minnie's cousin that she had been drinking, they treated her case lightly. The woman who had driven the car that had hit Minnie was a nurse. She wanted to make sure that Minnie was okay. John Nihmey (1998) had access to the transcripts from the hearing that followed. In his view the police officers:

> ...were perplexed by what seemed to be an overreaction to a drunk woman [read drunk Indian woman][17]who had either slipped on an ice patch and fallen, or walked into a car that couldn't have been going very fast given all the traffic. (Nihmey, 1998:82-83)

After Minnie and her cousin were left by the officers, and by three young male university students who had taken an interest in what was going on, they were picked up by two men "looking for some action" and drove them to Ottawa. However, after seeing the state that Minnie was in, they called 911 and dropped the two women off at a restaurant. A female officer and an ambulance responded. Quickly aware of the fact that Minnie had been drinking, the paramedic suggested that Minnie be taken to a detoxification centre. The staff there would not admit her, as she was unconscious. The officer then drove her to the police station, where the police sergeant in charge suggested that Minnie be taken to a hospital. She was driven and left there, no one telling the hospital staff of the history of the incident.

On January 17, a doctor from the hospital sent a letter to the Hull police, in which he wrote:

> There is no doubt that the lack of information about the traumatic event was of great significance in making the initial diagnosis of the abnormality and in following this up to a logical conclusion which may have been able to prevent her demise...[I]f the allegations of the conduct of the Hull police are correct, then a serious error of judgment has been made by the officers concerned and this should be investigated. (Nihmey 1998:163)

In March, four out of the five jurors of a coroner's jury declared that they felt that racism was not a factor in the case. The next year the Quebec police commission cleared the officers involved of racism charges.

Death by Neglect: The 911 Case (see The Provincial Court of Manitoba, 2002)

It was Friday evening, around nine o'clock, February 15, 2000. Métis sisters Doreen Leclair and Corrine McKeown, aged 51 and 52 respectively, made five 911 calls to the Winnipeg police con-

---

[18]   "'Intimate violence' refers to any and all forms of maltreatment committed in relationships of intimacy, trust, and dependence" (McGillvray and Comaskey, 1999:xiv).

cerning the threatening presence of a former boyfriend. Eight hours later, they were found stabbed to death.

What happened? Regarding the first call there is some dispute. Either the police didn't come, or they felt that nothing was amiss when an officer arrived there. No matter which version is truth, but the third call, the women were seriously threatened. The tapes reveal that the women were telling the operator that a man violating a restraining order had stabbed Corrine. In response, the operator told the women that they were partially responsible for the situation in allowing the man into the house in the first place. Further, they should resolve the situation themselves.

A fourth call was made. The operator promised to send a squad car, but no such car was dispatched. Finally, by the fifth call, the operator was becoming concerned, hung up the phone and dialled the number back, with no luck. When a police car was finally sent, it was too late.

A police run investigation was held, during which four 911 operators and a duty inspector were suspended with pay. The resulting report was five volumes long, but short in addressing questions that local Aboriginal groups wanted answered. The next year, Manitoba's Chief Medical Examiner called for an inquest. This was opposed by the Police Association. The local police union president said that the main problems were there were too many 911 calls and too few officers hired to patrol the streets. The police chief admitted that the case was mishandled, but denied that racism or the lack of Aboriginal officers played a part.

Aboriginal Women: The Most Disposable People

Several of the statistics presented above point to a situation in which Aboriginal women are the people worst served by the justice system. Many reserves have violence. Aboriginal victims of violence are more likely to know those who assaulted them. The justice situation for Aboriginal women on reserves is inequitable for several reasons. One is that spousal abuse primarily that of males abusing females, is not just between the man and the woman but between their families as well. If a woman accuses a man of spousal abuse on the close knit hard to escape world of the reserve, she has to deal with his family as well. And his family may include band chiefs, band councillors, or even tribal police if such exist. Also, in that tiny world that is a reserve, reserve based alternatives to prison can readily put the woman in a dangerous, very threatened position.

The most accessible look at the way in which the differential impact of the justice system in this regard comes from Anne McGillvray and Brenda Comaskey's *Black Eyes All of the Time: Intimate Violence, Aboriginal Women, and the Justice System* (1999). The material presented in that book is an analysis based interviews with 26 women in Winnipeg in the summer of 1995. It is an expanded version of the 1996 report, *Intimate Violence, Aboriginal Women and Justice System Response: A Winnipeg Study*. A key concept in this book is the notion of "resistance to resistance," which is explained in the following passage:

> Where culture itself provides the excuse for perpetrating intimate violence and for failures in the system's response, silencing those who try to speak out, the violated become another 'dark rock' in the political system, offering a small but tenacious resistance to resistance. (McGillvray and Comaskey, 1999:4)

The cultural excuse includes reserve based diversions from prison time. It is a form of resistance to the inequities of mainstream justice, but it can be applied in a way that is oppresses female victims, for example, in terms of "intimate violence."[18] Aboriginal women victimized in this way are resisting the introduction of forms of diversions from prison that could further the victimization process. The authors' interpretation of one of their interviewees goes a long way in explaining the complex situation that these women find themselves in:

> Her partner's violence brought her into contact with the criminal justice system. He pleaded guilty and received a short sentence – not enough, in her view, to 'pay' for what he did to her, not long enough to give her a period of safety to rebuild her life. Despite having racist and insensitive encounters with police and with lawyers, who did little for her and did not understand her situation, and no input into his sentence, she believes that the justice system is there to protect the innocent and to punish wrongdoers, even if it did neither very well in her case. She knows that jail does not help the guilty party but believes that he needs to be taught a lesson. She values punishment and wants longer jail terms for such crimes. She thinks that counselling and treatment should be available in jail. She is not particularly impressed with diversion from the justice system or with alternative measures, given the politics of reserve communities, but feels that they might be worth a try as long as the sentencing process is fair, he learns a lesson and gets effective treatment, and she is kept safe from him. (McGillvray and Comaskey, 1999:6-7)

Learning Activity 5 - Discussion

Using the course's discussion board, post your thoughts on the following questions.

1. How does the concept of racial profiling (see Chapter 3) link to the concept of being a "disposable person" in Canadian society?

2. Why are Aboriginals in Canada considered at higher risk of being considered "disposable"? 3. Why Aboriginal women in particular?

Conclusion

So what can we conclude from this? Changes have been made, changes are being made, and changes still need to be made. The answers are not simple. Simply "following traditional principles" is not enough, and definitely a justice system without structures and practices directed specifically at Aboriginal people will not work. It certainly hasn't in the past. And Aboriginal people are not going to "disappear" as was commonly thought one hundred years ago, nor are they going to assimilate as is believed by many today. We can return to the example we gave at the beginning of this Chapter, the Aboriginal spiritual elder. Adapting the justice system so that it recognizes Aboriginal equivalents and parallels, while maintaining a well-measured distinctiveness, is what would seem to work best.

■ References

Baumann, Z. (2004). *Wasted lives.* London: Polity Press.

Clutesi, G. (1969) *Potlatch.* Victoria, B.C.: The Morriss Printing Company.

Comeau, P. and Aldo S. (1990). *The first Canadians: A profile of Canada's native people today.* Toronto: James Lorimer and Company.

Cummins, B. and Steckley, J. (2003). *Aboriginal policing: A Canadian perspective.* Toronto: Prentice-Hall.

Frantz, D. and Russell, N. (1995). *The Blackfoot dictionary of stems, roots and affixes.* Toronto: University of Toronto Press.

Frideres, J. (1998). *Aboriginal peoples in Canada: Contemporary conflicts.* 5th ed. Toronto: Prentice-Hall.

Frideres, J. (2002). *Aboriginal peoples in Canada: Contemporary conflicts.* 6th ed. Toronto: Prentice-Hall.

Giroux, H. (2006). *Stormy weather: Katrina and the politics of disposability.* Boulder, CO: Paradigm Publishers.

Goldman, I. (1975). *The mouth of heaven: An introduction to Kwakiutl religious thought.* New York, NY: John Wiley & Sons.

Hamilton, A. (2001). *A feather not a gavel: Working towards Aboriginal justice.* Winnipeg: Great Plains Publications.

Lee, J. (1983). "Controlling society." In J. Paul Grayson (ed.), *Introduction to sociology: An alternate approach.* Toronto: Gage Publications.

McGillivray, A. and Comaskey, B. (1999). *Black eyes all of the time: Intimate violence, Aboriginal women, and the justice system,* Toronto: University of Toronto Press.

National Union of Public and General Employees. (2006), *Systemic discrimination against native prison inmates.* Retrieved from www.nupge.ca/print/1553.

Nihmey, J. (1998). *Fireworks and folly: How we killed Minnie Sutherland.* Toronto: General Publishing Company.

Nowell, C. and Ford, C. (eds.). (1968). *Smoke from their fires: The life of a Kwakiutl chief.* Hampden, CT: Archon Books.

O'Meara, J. (1996). *Delaware English/English Delaware dictionary.* Toronto: University of Toronto Press.

Priest, L. (1989). *Conspiracy of silence.* Toronto: McClelland & Stewart.

Provincial Court of Manitoba. (2002). *The fatality inquiries act, report by provincial judge of inquest respecting the deaths of Doreen Leclair and Corrine McKeown.* Retrieved from www.manitobacourts.mb.ca/pdf/911_report.pdf.

Reber, S. and Renaud, R. (2005). *Starlight tour: The last lonely night of Neil Stonechild.* Toronto: Random House Canada.

Report of the Commission of Inquiry into Matters Relating to the Death of Neil Stonechild. (2004). Retrieved from www.justice.gov.sk.ca/stonechild.

Rhodes, R. (1985). *Eastern Ojibwa-Chippewa-Ottawa dictionary.* Berlin: Mouton de Gruyter.

Spradley, J. (1969). *Guests never leave hungry: The autobiography of James Sewid, a Kwakiutl indian.* New Haven, CT: Yale University Press.

Stackhouse, J. (2001). Welcome to Harlem on the prairies. *Globe and Mail*, November 3, F2-F4.

Statistics Canada. (2000). P*olice-reported Aboriginal crime in Saskatchewan*. Catalogue No. 85F0031.

Statistics Canada. (2006). *Aboriginal people as victims and offenders*. Retrieved from www.statcan.gc.ca/daily-quotidien/060606/dq060606b.eng.htm

Statistics Canada. (2009). *Youth correctional services, admissions to provincial and territorial programs*. Retrieved from www.40.statcan.gc.ca/101/cst01/legal42a-   eng.htm.

Steckley, J. (2003). *Aboriginal voices and the politics of representation in Canadian introductory sociology textbooks*. Toronto: Canadian Scholars' Press.

Steckley, J. and Cummins, B. (2008). *Full circle: Canada's first nations*. 2nd ed. Toronto: Pearson Education.

Stymeist, D. (1975). *Ethnics and Indians: Social relations in a northwestern Ontario town*. Toronto: Peter Martin Associates.

Vehitelle, L. (2006). *The disposable American*. New York: Knopf.

Whonnock, K. (2008). *Aboriginal courts in Canada, fact sheet*. Retrieved from www.scowinstitute.ca/library/documents/Aboriginal_Courts_Fact_Sheet.pdf.

PART TWO

Unit Two: Young Offenders

Chapter 6
An Overview of Justice and Canada's Young Persons

Learning Activity 1 - Fun Quiz

Take this fun quiz before you read the chapter. Answer "True" or "False":

1.   According to Canadian law, a young offender/youth at risk is a youth between the ages of 10 and 18 who has violated a criminal law.

2.   The 1908 Juvenile Delinquents Act (JDA) was the forerunner to the 1984 Young Offenders Act (JDA).

3.   Under the JDA, the Federal Government established the upper and lower age limits of a juvenile delinquent.

4.   The YOA held youths more criminally responsible than ever before in Canada.

5.   The current (2003) Youth Criminal Justice Act (YCJA) holds youths accountable to a different set of criminal laws.

6.   Under the YCJA, young offenders who commit any serious crime are tried in adult courts.

7.   The youth crime rate has been increasing in Canada since 1990.

8.   Youths have the highest crime rate among any other age group in Canada.

9.   Youths and young adults have the highest criminal victimization rates in Canada.

10. Ageism is the idea that youths are given an "easy ride" in Canada.

ANSWERS: 1F, 2T, 3F, 4T, 5F, 6F, 7F, 8F, 9T, 10F

Even though official crime statistics for Canada and the United States show that youth crime is the lowest it has been since 1987 (seeWinterdyk, 2006), around the world; crime is disproportionately still the activity of young adults and youths. Further, young adults and youths in Canada are more likely to be crime victims than other age groups (MacLaren, 2005).

Defining "Young Offender"

What is the legal definition of a "young offender"?

In Canada, the official use of the term "young offender" first appeared in the Federal Government's Young Offenders Act of 1984. It replaced the then-official term of "juvenile delinquent" that was found in the 1908 Juvenile Delinquents Act.[19]

By Canadian legal definition, a young offender is between 12 years of age and 17 years of age (inclusive). By law, anyone younger than 12 years of age cannot be charged with a criminal code offence. Persons 18 years of age and older are considered adults if they a charged with a criminal code offence—regardless of the "age of majority" in the province that the crime was committed (Fetherston, 2005).

Learning Activity 2 - Journal Activity

Using your course Blackboard/discussion board, address the following questions:

- Why do you think both the YCJA and YOA established the minimum age of criminal responsibility at 12 years of age?

- What do you think makes a 12 year old different from a child who is, say, 10 years old (a point which has been discussed at various levels)? What evidence do you have to support your answer?

- Take a look at the UN (Beijing Rules) declaration of standards on the minimum age of responsibility: **http://www.unhchr.ch/html/menu3/b/h_comp48.htm**

The Juvenile Delinquency Act–1908 (JDA)

The current Youth Criminal Justice Act (YCJA) of 2004 continues the focus of the Young Offenders Act (YOA) to hold young persons criminally responsible for their actions. This is very different from the approach found during the 75 years that the JDA was law.

---

[19]   The term juvenile delinquency is derived from Latin "juvenilis" meaning a young immature and undeveloped and "delinquent" meaning guilty of misdeed. Hence, a term carrying significant negative connotations. For an enriched discussion of the term see Maxim (1980:60-77).

Under the JDA, juvenile delinquency was considered a child welfare issue rather than a criminal justice issue. In the Act, it states that "every juvenile delinquent shall be treated, not as a criminal, but as a misdirected and misguided child" (Department of Justice Canada, 2005). The guiding principle of the JDA was the notion of **parens patriae**, which roughly translates as "kindly parent." In those instances where the parents of a child cannot or will not provide parental support, the government must become the parent (Fetherston, 2005). The underlying rational was based on the intent involved a *rehabilitative* focus. Therefore, the actors of the juvenile justice system were granted *bona fide* (based on good business norms), which essentially allowed a young offender to be dealt with in a manner deemed most beneficial to the young offender—without question.

What were the basic features of the JDA?

The following were the key provision of the JDA (Hogeveen, 2005:27-33):

1. Juvenile delinquency included what we now consider both criminal and non-criminal behaviour (e.g., underage smoking, truancy, underage alcohol consumption).
2. While the Act set the lower limit at 7 years of age, the upper limit was left to the discretion of the provinces. For example, in Quebec and Manitoba the upper limit was 18 while in BC, Alberta, and Newfoundland is was 17, and the remaining provinces it was 16.[20]
3. Provinces, municipalities, and in some instances individual judges, decided what actions could be considered delinquency.
4. Because of the child welfare focus of the JDA, juvenile delinquents were commonly sent to reformatory schools or juvenile detention houses.
5. In rare instances, a juvenile delinquent could be charged with a *Criminal Code* offence. It had to be a serious (i.e., indictable) and the youth had to be at least 14 years of age or older.

Learning Activity 3 - Summarize

In your own words, summarize the key provisions of the former JDA. Be sure you can define the notion of **parens patriae**.

---

[20]   Based on data from the Canadian Centre for Justice Statistics, in 1983, less than 1.5% of delinquent offences were committed by youth under the age of 11 of which only 3.4% involved acts of violence.

■ The Young Offenders Act (YOA) (1984-2003)

Perhaps because of the changing nature of Canadian society beginning in the 1960s, pressure to change the JDA began in the 1970s. And according to Maxim (1980:48), given that there was considerable "confusion and critical dissensus regarding juvenile delinquency" this prompted the Canadian government to revamp the Act. As early as 1970, there was a proposal to move away from the child welfare focus in the JDA (Fetherston, 2005).

What was "wrong'"with the JDA?

There were several reasons why the JDA was replaced (Fetherston, 2005:91-92):

1.   Significant differences between provinces in terms of what actions were classified as "juvenile delinquency."
2.   Provincial differences regarding who could be a juvenile delinquent and how they should be treated.
3.   Concerns about the lack of legal rights that youths had in the legal hearing.
4.   Pressure to hold youths criminally responsible if they committed a criminal code.

Passed in 1982 and then becoming effective in 1984, the YOA replaced the *child or social welfare/rehabilitative* approach found in the JDA with a criminal justice approach.

What were the key provisions of the YOA?

1.   Regardless of the province, a young offender was a youth between the ages of 12 and 17 (inclusive).
2.   A young offender was someone who commits a *Criminal Code* offence (non-criminal behaviour does not fall under the YOA).
3.   Criminal courts trials were used to determine criminal responsibility.
4.   Accused youth had all the legal rights of an accused adult.
5.   The range of sentences for criminal offences was uniform across Canada.
6.   Youth were expected to take responsibility for their actions.
7.   Society had a right to be protected against any harms committed by young persons.
8.   Young offenders have legal rights and freedoms.
9.   Parents had the right to be notified of all court proceedings.

While youth were held criminally responsible for their actions under the YOA, the range of sentences for young offenders differed from sentences given to adult offenders. Judges were given a broader range of sentencing options with greatly reduced minimum and maximum punishments compared to adult sentences for the same offence. Especially in the case of very young first time offenders who commit less serious crimes, the YOA shifted its focus to one of greater accountability for a young person's actions and did away with the paternalistic aspects and treatment of young persons under the JDA.

Learning Activity 4 - Right to a Jury?

Given that the YOA and now the YCJA hold young offenders more accountable for their behaviour and given that transfer to adult court has been made "easier"; should young offenders who commit a serious crime be eligible to have their case tried before a jury?

In comparison to the JDA, the YOA established clearer procedures to transfer some suspected young offenders into adult court; thereby allowing them to be sentenced to the same punishment as an adult offender. Only youths over the age of 16 who were suspected of committing the most serious offences (violent offences, property and some drug) could be transferred to adult court (Fetherston, 2005).

Learning Activity 5 - Discuss

Using the course's discussion board or in class, post/discuss your thoughts on the strengths and weakness of the approach to criminal behaviour of 12 to 17 year olds in the YOA compared to the child welfare approach found in the JDA.

The Youth Criminal Justice Act (YCJA) (2003 – present)

Why was the YOA replaced?

After several years of debate and different suggestions for a new name of the Act, the YCJA was passed into legislation on April 1st, 2003. While some within the general public were pushing for more adult-like sentences for young offenders, many within the youth justice system saw positive results from treating younger first time offenders of less serious crimes differently from the multiple offenders of serious crimes (Fetherston, 2005).

Once finally approved, the YCJA retained most of the key provisions in the YOA (e.g., age of young offender, criminal responsibility, criminal process and rights).

What makes the YCJA different from the YOA?

There are several important changes in the new Act (Fetherston, 2005:103-105):

1.   The YCJA outlines a list of serious that presumes a youth will receive an adult sentence.
2.   In addition to the serious offences outlined in the former YOA, youths who are repeat offenders of additional serious offences can receive adult sentences. Now, youths as

young as 14 can receive adult sentences.

3. Young persons are no longer transferred to adult court for trial. Instead, Youth Courts can impose an adult sentence for the offences of the above list.

4. There is less emphasis on incarceration as a sentence for first time young offenders of less serious offences.

5. Youths who plead guilty to committing less serious criminal offences for the first time can be "diverted" away from a criminal court and into an "extrajudicial programs."

Learning Activity 6 - Online Research

Follow the link below to the Department of Justice Canada's website. It provides valuable information on the basic aspects of the YCJA. In particular, review the information on the "Preamble and Declaration of Principle" for the Act. It explains the basic approach the Federal Government adopted when writing the new law:

http://www.justice.gc.ca/en/ps/yj/repository/2overvw/2010001a.html

Young Offenders' Crime in Canada

As Doob, Marinos and Varma (1996) observed: while the general public has a passing understanding of youth crime, there is a tendency to overestimate the extent and gravity of their behaviour. However, there seems to be two popular myths about youth crime in Canada. (Both myths are false.)

Myth 1: The rate of youth crime in Canada is higher today than it has ever been.

Myth 2: Youths between the ages of 12-17 commit more crime than any other age group in Canada.

Total Youth Crime Rate

Has the Youth Crime Rate Changed?

As can be seen in the graph below, the highest youth crime rate in Canada was experienced in 1991 and then declined throughout the 1990s. The rate increased slightly between 2000 and 2003, but has declined since then.

Youth Crime as a Percent of All Crime

Goff (2004:15) estimates that only 22% of all reported crime results in a person being charged. This fact makes it difficult to say precisely how much crime in Canada is committed by young offenders. Furthermore, as Maxim (1980) noted in his dissertation, given the prevailing difficulty in how we define youth crime (outside of its legal definition) poses a major challenge to ensuring reliable data (see Warling, 2001).

Youth Crime Rate in Canada (1985 - 2005)

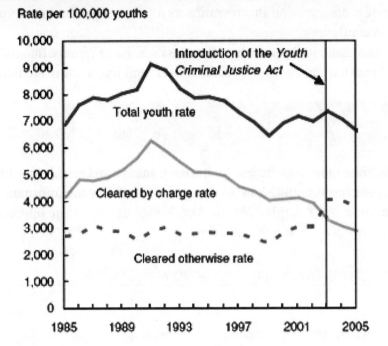

Rate per 100,000 youths

Don't Young Offenders Commit Most of the Crime in Canada?

Look at the age of those who are charged with a criminal offence in Canada:

Age Group	% of Criminal Cases*	% of Canadian Population*
12-17	13.9%	7.0%
18-24	26.4%	9.2%
25-34	24.2%	13.3%
35-44	21.6%	17.0%
45-54	9.9%	14.7%
55 +	4.1%	22.3%

* *Sources*:   Statistics Canada, 2004a, Juristat, Catalogue no. 85-002-XPE, Vol. 24, No. 12.

Statistics Canada, 2006, Juristat, Catalogue no. 85-002-XPE, Vol. 25, No. 4.

As seen in the above table, the accused in 13.9% of all criminal cases in Canada are young offenders. By comparing this number to the proportion of 12-17 year olds in Canada (7.0% of Canada's population is between 12-17 years of age), we can see that young persons are over-represented in *Criminal Code* cases.

However, adults between the ages of 18-24 are even more over-represented. About 26% of all criminal cases involve young adults, but they make up only 9% of the Canadian population. Those between the ages of 25-34 are also over-represented in *Criminal Code* cases.

However, we must be mindful of the fact that the "dark figure" of unreported and, hence, unrecorded crime among youth (especially for property crime) is significant. Skogan (1977) noted that in addition to complicating our understanding of the extent youth crime, it also limits the capacity of the youth justice system. This in-turn raises another interesting dilemma in that we should separate "youth crime" from "youth justice" (see Doob and Cesaroni, 2004). And while it is beyond the scope this text to address these issues, they represent part of the challenge of how to respond and interpret youth offending. However, a brief illustrative example from the doctoral work of Sandra Bell (1992) who, referring to the seminal work by Robert Emerson in 1969 in terms of what is being judged in the courtroom, posed the question: "what is being judged is whether the juvenile's family corresponds to the ideal family model." She found that "judicial decisions themselves are influenced by gender, agency, and family factors, in all cases except that of status offenders with an unstable family class background" (p.186).

Young Persons as Victims of Violence

Children and youth can become victims of violence at the hands of their parents, siblings, acquaintances, friends and strangers. This violence takes place in their homes, at school and in their community. According to a report by Statistics Canada, children and youth under the age of 18 represent about 21% of Canada's population (Statistics Canada, 2005b:3). Further, they are 22% of the reported victims of violent crime in our country. Here are some startling statistics from the report:

- 58% of young victims were physically assaulted
- 23% were victims of threats of violence
- 19% were victims of sexual assaults
- In 2003, there were 48 homicides against children and youths in Canada.

What makes these statistics more disturbing is the reality that a significant portion of violence against Canada's children and youth goes unreported. Often due to fear, inexperience or lack of knowledge, children and youth can be hesitant to report being victimized by family members, friends and even strangers.

In Terms of Age, Who are the Victims of Crime in Canada?

As much as there appears to be a growing concern about youth crime and youth violence, there has been in recent years a growing awareness and interest in youth as victims of crime. Among one of the first such studies to draw attention to this in Canada was Frank (1992) and Ryan, Mathews and Banner (1883). Although using relatively small sample sizes their findings were generally consistent with the larger study by Allen-Hagen and Sickmund (1993) that used data from the American National Crime Victimization Survey. They found that although those under the age of 20 only comprised 14% of respondents surveyed, they accounted for 30% of the victims. This works out to a rate of 67 per 1,000 teens who were victimized compared to 26 per 1,000 for those over the age of 20. Subsequently, Paetsch and Bertrand's (1999) survey of 962 students across Calgary found that not only had self-reported delinquency increased, but so had self-reported incidents of victimization.

According to data provided by Statistics Canada (2005a), the age groups that are over-represented as accused in *Criminal Code* cases are also over-represented in terms of being victims of crime. For example, persons between the ages of 15-24 are 1.5 to 1.9 times more likely to be a victim of violence than other Canadians.

Some of the risk factors that have been to be associated with risk of victimization have been divided into several categories including: individual factors, family factors, peer/school risk factors, and community risk factors. They include, among other indicators: antisocial beliefs and attitudes, authoritarian childrearing attitudes, low parental involvement, associating with delinquent peers, poor academic performance, diminished economic opportunity and certain lifestyle habits such as how frequent someone participates in night-time activities such as going to bars, movies and restaurants (see Mercy et al., 2002).

Learning Activity 7 - Reflect and List

What do you think are the biggest misunderstandings most Canadians have about the amount of youth crime today? List several reasons why you think these misunderstandings exist.

A Question of Ageism

What is "ageism"?

Ageism was first coined in 1968 by Robert Butler in his book *Why Survive? Being Old in America.* The terms refers to stereotyping and discrimination or prejudice against an individual or groups based on their age. Ageism reflects a social attitude. Similar to racism, a core aspect of ageism is to treat everyone of a particular age group on the basis of a negative stereotype. For example, when referring to senior groups one might hear: "I'm young, I deserve it more," "old foggy," "dirty old man," to more pejorative phrases and expressions.

Not only can an individual engage in ageism but ageism can be "systemic." Systemic ageism exists when laws, policies, procedures, customs and traditions discriminate against individuals on the basis of their age. Palmore (1990) has written extensively on the meaning ageism and how it no longer just applies to seniors but also to other age groups.

Unfortunately, very little empirical research has been conducted on the possible impact that ageism plays within the Canadian criminal justice system. Certainly, there is a vocal portion of both the general public and criminal justice practitioners that are calling for more adult-like punishment for young offenders. Indeed, some are advocating that the age of criminal responsibility be reduced from the current 12 years of age to 10 as is the case in Australia, England, New Zealand, and Wales (Winterdyk, 2004).[21] The question remains—Is *the over-representation of youth and young adults*

---

[21]   See http://www.canadiancrc.com/Youth_Justice_webpage/Youth_Criminal_Justice.htm (Accessed June 15, 2010).

a consequence of ageism within the criminal justice system and/or Canadian society or it is a product of the traditional desire to control youth at risk?

While there is no clear, or obvious, answer to the question, the issues presented above reflect that youth at risk represent a diverse group who are not always treated in a fair and equitable manner because of their "differences."

Learning Activity 8 - Summarize

What evidence is there that ageism as it relates to young persons is a factor in Canadian society? Is it at play in how we address criminal responsibility in Canada? Why or why not?

Ever since the legal conceptualization of "juvenile delinquency" at the end of the 1800s, efforts to address the problem of youth at risk have remained something of an enigma. As illustrated in the chapter, youth continue to both commit offences and be victims. As an identifiable group they are often overlooked as representing a diversity group. However, the history of how society has dealt with young offenders is filled with confusion and contradictions, and usually under the guise of good intentions.

This chapter is supported by the following reading by John Winterdyk. In Chapter 7 "Understanding Youth-at-Risk Behaviour," the author reviews several of the major criminological explanations of youth crime and victimization.

References

Allen-Hagen, B. and Sickmund, M. (1993). "Juveniles and violence: Juvenile offending and victimization." *Office of Juvenile Justice and Delinquency Prevention, Fact Sheet No. 3.* Washington, DC: United States Department of Justice.

Anderson M, Kaufman J, Simon T, Barrios L, Paulozzi L, Ryan G, et al. (2001). "School-associated violent deaths in the United States, 1994-1999." *Journal of the American Medical Association* 286:2695–702.

Bell, S. (1992). "Controlling delinquents: An analysis of the role of the family in the young offenders court." Unpublished doctorial dissertation, Department of Sociology, University of Toronto. (Available through University Microfilms International, Ann Arbor, Michigan).

Butler, R.N. (1975). *Why Survive? Being Old in America.* New York: Harper & Row.

Department of Justice Canada. (2005). *The evolution of juvenile justice in Canada.* Retrieved June 15, 2010, from http://www.justice.gc.ca/en/ps/inter/juv_jus_min/sec02.html

Doob, A. and Cesaroni, C. (1994). *Responding to youth crime in Canada.* Toronto, ON: University of Toronto Press.

Doob, A., Marinos, V., and Varma, K. (1996). *Youth crime and the youth justice system in Canada: A research perspective.* Toronto, ON: University of Toronto Press.

Fetherston, D. (2005). "The law and young offenders." In J. Winterdyk (ed.), *Issues and perspectives on young offenders in Canada.* 3rd ed. Toronto, ON: Thomson Nelson.

Frank, J. (1992). "Violent youth crime." *Canadian Social Trends* Autumn:2-9.

Goff, C. (2004). *Criminal justice in Canada.* 3rd ed. Toronto, ON: Nelson.

Hogeveen, B. (2005). "History, development, and transformations in Canadian juvenile justice, 1800-1984." In K. Campbell (ed.), *Understanding youth justice in Canada.* Toronto, ON: Pearson Education Canada.

Maxim, P. (1980). "Some trends in juvenile delinquency in Canada: 1958-1973." Unpublished doctoral dissertation. University of Pennsylvania. (Available through University Microfilms International, Ann Arbor, Michigan).

Mercy, J., Butchart, A., Farrington, D., and Cerdá, M. (2002). "Youth violence." In E. Krug, L. Dahlberg, J. Mercy, et al. (eds.). *The world report on violence and health.* Geneva (Switzerland): World Health Organization.

Palmore, E. (1990). *Ageism: Negative and positive.* New York: Springer.

Paetsch, J.J. and Bertrand, L.D. (Summer, 1999). "Victimization and delinquency among Canadian youth." *Adolescence.* Retrieved June 15, 2010, from http://findarticles.com/p/articles/mi_m2248/is_134_34/ai_55884920/pg_1

Ryan, C., Mathews, F., and Banner, J. (1993). *Student perceptions of violence: Summary of preliminary findings.* Toronto, ON: Toronto Youth Services.

Skogan, W. (1977). "Dimensions of the dark figure of unreported crime ." *Crime & Delinquency* 23(1):41-50.

Statistics Canada. (2004). *Adult criminal court statistics, 2003/04.* Catalogue no. 85-002-XPE, vol. 24, no. 12. Retrieved June 15, 2010, from http://www.statcan.ca/bsolc/english/bsolc?catno=85-002-X20040128431

Statistics Canada. (2005a). Children and youth as victims of violent crime. Catalogue no. 85-002-XIE, vol. 25, no.1. Retrieved June 15, 2010, from http://www.statcan.ca/english /freepub/85-002-XIE/0010585-002-XIE.pd.

Statistics Canada. (2005b). *Youth court statistics, 2003/2004.* Catalogue no. 85-002-XPE, vol. 25, no. 4. Retrieved June 15, 2010, from http://www.statcan.ca/bsolc/english/bsolc?catno=85 -002-X20050047948

Statistics Canada. (2006). *Crime statistics in Canada.* Catalogue no. 85-002-XIE, vol. 26, no. 4. Retrieved June 15, 2010, from, http://www.statcan.ca/Daily/English/040601/d040601a.htm

Warling, D. (2001). Are juveniles getting a fair trial? The jury is still out. Unpublished doctorial dissertation. Department of Applied Psychology, University of Toronto. (Available through University Microfilms International, Ann Arbor, Michigan).

Winterdyk, J. (ed.). (2004). *Juvenile justice systems: International perspectives.* 2nd ed. Toronto, ON: Canadian Scholars' Press.

PART TWO

Unit Two: Young Offenders

Chapter 7

Understanding Youth-at-Risk-Behaviour

John Winterdyk

▮ Learning Activity 1 - Fun Quiz

Take this fun quiz before you read the chapter. Answer "True" or "False":

1. Most social scientists have concluded there is a single reason why young persons are at greater risk of participating in delinquent and criminal behaviour.

2. Most social scientists believe that punishment is the best way to deter criminal behaviour among young persons.

3. Some social scientists argue that youths from lower-class families have a greater chance of participating in youth gangs.

4. The theory of Differential Association suggests that youth delinquency is a product of an under-developed sense of guilt and remorse among some young people.

5. One social science theory suggests that the impact of labelling a young person delinquent can influence him/her to accept the label and engage in more delinquent actions.

6. Sigmund Freud's theory has informed many psychological theories that focus on childhood development.

7. Gottfredson and Hirshi's "General Theory of Crime" isolate parental child-rearing practices as important in a young person's future delinquency and criminality.

8. Biological explanations of delinquency and criminality by some young persons have only recently been advanced.

9. There is some evidence to suggest that the effects of legal and illegal drug use may be at play in explaining some young person's delinquency.

10. Instead of focusing on a single "cause" for youth delinquency, it is probably better to look for multiple factors.

ANSWERS: 1F, 2F, 3T, 4F, 5T, 6T, 7T, 8F, 9T, 10T

Introduction

Perhaps one of the most perplexing issues we face in attempting to understand youth-at-risk or youth crime is that, strictly speaking, "young offender" is not a sociological or psychological term. Rather, this term was coined by the legal system to identify those young persons who, within the framework of our social values, engage in behaviour that is considered inappropriate or illegal. For example, the lower and upper age of criminal responsibility for young offenders throughout the world from is as low as 7 in India to 21 in such countries as Finland and even 25 in China (Winterdyk, 2002). However, given the wide range of behaviour that our legal system must contend with, we need to examine the issue of causation in order to explain the frequency, perceived seriousness, and social impact of youth crime, and in order to deter, control, or prevent such behaviour. Or as Robert Hoge (2001:49) suggests, to satisfy our "natural curiosity about a significant social issue." Yet, what a particular society defines as "at-risk" or "deviant" changes with time and place. That is, the construct of "offending" is both relative and evolutive. For example, under the 1908 Juvenile Delinquents Act, truancy was a delinquent offence. While truancy is no longer consider an offence, it has still been linked to future anti-social conduct (see, for example, Loeber et al., 2003).

For the purpose of this chapter, I have grouped the explanatory models according to their disciplinary orientation. In addition, attention is given to integrated or bridging theories, which use aspects of the main approaches to create hybrid theories that are intended to reflect the complexity of human behaviour. First, however, we should familiarize ourselves with how it is that most people formulate their perspectives of reality as opposed to how research attempts to construct reality.

Epistemology: Methods of Knowing

Students and lay persons, in general, are often question the merits of using theory study and explain human behaviour. After attending my first theory course, I was left with the impression that theories are "common sense" models used to describe something. For example, stress prompts reactive behaviour. As a youth, I was "picked on" (i.e., labeled) by one of my high-school teachers, which affected my behaviour. As we'll see below, explanations of behaviour are also rooted in one or more theories.

What separates theories from common-sense knowledge is that conventional ways of knowing are not bound by rules of objectivity. Conventionally, we tend to learn through the media, friends, teachers, intuition, and so on. While such sources tend to allow us to function with comparatively few complications in our life, they are not necessarily the best means for predicting and or formulating justice policy. Without research based on evidence, there are considerable risks to formulating intervention, prevention or suppressions strategies when dealing with young offenders. Theories represent a set of interrelated propositions that allows us to test the assertions. That is, they require empirical verification (evidence) in order to be supported or rejected.

Williams and McShane (1999) describe four important aspects of a good theory. First, a theory must be logically sound and internally consistent. It should be able to make sense of conflicting positions (e.g., does stress play a more significant role than being "picked on" when trying to explain and predict anti-social behaviour among youth). Third, a theory should focus our attention of a concrete aspect of behaviour, the environment, or something else that can be observed and measured in order to test its veracity. Finally, a good theory should have a degree of social approval. Unless a theory has a degree of support it will not likely gain acceptance.

Broadly speaking, theories can be divided into micro (individualistic), macro (environmental), and micro/macro levels (integrated). Each level presents its own assumptions and actions. Although this chapter is not able to provide an exhaustive overview of the theories, we offer a cross-sectional review of some of the main and emerging theoretical perspectives.

■ Sociological Explanations of Youth Crime

Sociological approaches are primarily concerned with how *macro* issues (social forces) such as social organizations, social class, norms, values, race, ethnicity, and social stratification effect human behaviour. In general, sociological approaches are based on a consensus model that assumes human nature is palpable and that we learn primarily by observing and participating in the ever changing social environment. If we can understand the effects of certain social forces, we can then better address antisocial behaviour among our youth.

Consensus and conflict theories are two key sociological perspectives that have been used to explain social phenomena.

Consensus Perspective versus Conflict Perspective

The consensus perspective, the more traditional of the sociological theories of explaining delinquency, is based on the assumption that there is an agreement among people in society – that is, that people share common values, needs, and goals. Consensus forms the basis of structural-functionalist theories; led by the pioneering work of the French scholar Emile Durkheim (1858-1917). This perspectives stresses order and stability in society, and it depends on initiations such as the family, the school system, and the church to maintain social equilibrium. For Durkheim and subsequent functionalists, criminality was largely determined by a lack of social cohesion. Antisocial behaviour among young people is seen as dysfunctional, as is any potentially harmful conflict or lack of cohesion with a social system.

In contrast, the conflict perspective assumes that there is very little agreement in society and that people and institutions subscribe to different social, political, or economic values or interests. Within the context of this perspective, deviance is any behaviour that violates the status quo's rules, norms, and attitudes. These general assumptions have given rise to several varieties of conflict theory that can be viewed as part of a continuum.

Although the theoretical principles of social conflict theory can be traced back to the works of Karl Marx (1818-4883) and Friedrich Engels (1820;-1895), it was Dutch criminologist Willem Bonger (1876-1940) and later North American researchers Thorsten Sellin, Ralf Dahrendorf and George Vold who, between the 1903s and 1950s applied the perspective to the study of crime and criminality. In 1938, Sellin focused on the conflict of "conduct norms"—those cultural rules that we require or expect people to follow in specific circumstances (e.g., when dining out in a formal setting people are expected not to eat with their elbows on the table). However, as Anthony Platt observed in his 1969 classic *The Child Savers*, the creation of the legal category of delinquency is the result of the class consciousness that emerged during the later nineteenth century. Some noteworthy contributions that reflect the conflict orientation include the following:

■   1955: Drawing on the initial work of Robert Merton's *anomie theory* of 1938 (also generally referred to as strain theory – see below), Albert Cohen's work focused on youth male gangs as being largely products of culture conflict when the rules and norms of an individual's social setting conflict with those of conventional society. That is, boys from the lower socio-economic classes strive to increase their status through illegal means.

■   1960: Cloward and Lloyd Ohlin's *opportunity theory (*also drawing on the initial work of Merton and attempting to bridge the differences between the theories of Merton and Cohen) explains delinquency as largely a product of lower-class youth striving for, but being unable to attain, middle-class status. This lack of attainment leads to strain and ultimately the youth engage in antisocial acts as a way of expressing, or venting, their frustration. How often have you seen a young person lash out when unable to attain a goal through conventional means?

■   1973: William Chambliss observed two gangs for two years – one from a white upper-class setting (the Saints) and the other from a lower-class setting (the Roughnecks). Based on his observations, Chambliss concludes that despite engaging in similar activities, the Roughnecks received considerably more negative attention than did the Saints, even though the Roughnecks were less truant. Why? Chambliss attributes the difference in social reaction to class structure.

So, whether crime was seen as a general reaction to strain-stress and *social* disorganization, to a *weakening sense of* attachment to social order, or to some form of discrimination, under these conditions criminal behaviour among young persons seems almost intuitive or not vial!

Drawing in-part from self-report studies on young offenders that showed delinquency was more evenly distributed across the social structure; rather than blame the only lower-class youth, **conflict theorists** suggest that it is the justice system that perpetuates acts of delinquency by tending to target youth who come from less economically vibrant and socially mobile sectors of society. Falling under the general classification of "social process theories," which assert that delinquency is a function of how a person is socialized. More specifically, delinquency is in essence a form of social learning, a lack of social control, or the result of labelling by society (see Vold et al., 1998). Since the law embodies the values of those who control society (the status quo), it is more likely to criminalize those outside the controlling power group. Individuals who have turned to crime will now be caught. There is no end to this cycle; according to this general orientation, crime will persist as a social problem until society provides for the need of all its citizens. This perspective is referred to as pluralistic conflict model of criminal law, "arguing that conflict is normal and ubiquitous in society" (Cao 2004:145).

The contemporary approach to addressing the disparity in the needs of youth is through *restorative justice.* The rationalization is that if social conflict is the source of delinquency, then employing nonpunitive strategies for trouble youth may prove more effective than using conventional methods of control. The process involves trying to restore balance among the offender, the victim, and the community. This movement has gained considerable support in recent years and was even entrenched in the Youth Criminal Justice Act (YCJA). This perspective has served to de-mystify the roles of law and legal practices within the context of crime control. Yet supporters of the conflict-based orientation have never been able to verify adequately their assertions about the purpose of criminal law. For example, is the YCJA intended to address the needs of youth or to punish them for their transgressions? Why was the previous Act, the Young Offenders Act, relatively ineffective in accomplishing either objective? Hence, from a policy perspective, conflict advocates have not provided sufficient clarity on which to change legislation. The new wave of conflict-oriented theories has attempted, to varying degrees, to address this criticism. We will review some of these in the final section of this chapter.

Let us first examine in a bit more detail some of the key theories that are used to explain youth-at-risk and youth crime.

Human Ecology Theory

Have you ever noticed problem areas in your neighborhood? Have you noticed whether young persons are more likely to engage in antisocial behaviour when they have little to do? Why do city kids get into more trouble than country kids?

Among the first sociologically based explanations of delinquency to emerge were the ecologically oriented theories. Theodorson (1982) presents an array of early studies dating back to 1830 that attempted to link crime and delinquency to ecological factors. These early studies identified such factors as the weather, geography, urban and rural environments, population density and composition, economic stability, and social mobility as potential causes of social trends and behaviours. It was not until the early 1920s that Robert E. Park, Ernest W. Burgess, both from the University of Chicago, developed a theoretical scheme that could be applied to the study of human communities.

Today, most of these factors form the basis for tracking Canadian population demographics, as well as predicting and explaining social trends such as crime and delinquency. Numerous contemporary researchers have found strong correlations between social and environmental factors and delinquency (see, for example, Shader, 2004). Although such factors do not assume a causal relationship, and are not capable of explaining all deviant behaviour, the role of the environment seems to be a powerful explanatory variable.

The Chicago School

A refinement of the early ecological work has been associated with the Chicago School, which arose during a period when juvenile delinquency was a growing problem in the United States, particularly in Chicago. In 1892, the University of Chicago established the first sociology department in North America.

The main principle of the school was that people are social creatures whose behaviour is the product of their social environment. In other words, our social environment provided the cultural values and definitions that govern our behaviour – a process referred to as *cultural transmission* whereby, for example, gang leaders recruit younger members in their community and ensure both the delinquent tradition and the survival of the gang in the neighborhood (see Shaw and McKay, 1969).

According to the Chicago School, increased urbanization and industrialization have created communities that contain a variety of competing cultures. It is these competing cultures (i.e., diversity), with their differing values and norms, that promote the breakdown of older, established value patterns. This culture conflict in turn causes the breakdown and impersonalization of our basic institutions, such as the family and social groups. Hence, delinquent behaviour occurs when the less dominant individual values and norms conflict with the more dominant cultural values and norms. Various supporters of the Chicago School, especially throughout the 1950s and 1960s, believed that these forms of social disorganization and social pathology are most prevalent in the city-centre area and that they decrease with distance from that area (see Miller, 1962).

Today, interest in environment and cultural influences on delinquency has evolved into more sophisticated models whose principles remain relatively intact. This perspective is now commonly referred to as environmental criminology. For example, see the Canadian website: http://www.ecricanada.com/ based at Simon Fraser University. It is one of the leading institutes whose focus is on studying crime through environmental factors.

Anomie Theory

The term anomie was first used by the famous French sociologist Emile Durkheim (1858-1917) to describe social behaviour that discards traditional values and norms for the new value system that has not yet been embraced by the greater society. Do you ever remember thinking, *"I don't give a f____ what others think. I'll just do it my way"*? In short, youth experiencing anomie when collective social conscience no longer exists. When this occurs, individuals exist in a state of normlessness, lacking moral convictions and failing or refusing to comply with the formal and informal means of social control.

Robert Merton's (1910-2003) refinement of Durkheim's theory in 1938 helped to broaden the framework of anomie theory and it helped to indentify conditions of anomie that could be linked with crime and deviance. Merton theorized that two elements in every culture interact to produce potentially anomie conditions: culturally define *goals* and socially approved *means* for obtaining the goals.

Ordinarily, goals and means fit together within the confines of the law. For example, in Canada, young persons value the goal of attain material wealth, so socially prescribed hard work, education, and saving money become the acceptable means. However, all youth may not have an equal opportunity to attain certain goals or an equal capability to follow the preferred means. These inequalities may produce what sociologist call *strain*. When this occurs, legitimate means of obtaining success become limited and anomie may prevail.

Merton (1938) identified five forms of individual adaptation that may or may not lead to delinquent behaviour:

- Conformity. This occurs when individuals adopt mainstream social goals and have the means with which to attain them.
- Ritualism. This occurs when goals become less important, but the means are still closely adhered to. For example, a young person might go to school despite the fact that he or she has no interest in education.
- Innovation. This occurs when individuals adopt social goals but reject or are unable to attain these goals through legitimate means. For example, a youth who wants, but cannot afford, a skateboard might obtain it by stealing.

- Retreatism. This occurs when individuals do not participate in society. People who are retreatists reject both goals and the means of society. Merton describes these individuals as being "in society but not of it." Drug addicts, alcoholics, squeegee kids, and social outcasts *can* be described as retreatists.
- Rebellion. This occurs when individuals reject both the culturally defined goals and the institutionalized means to achieve these goals. Instead, they attempt to substantiate an alternative set of goals and means. Gang members can be described as being rebellious.

One of the major early policy applications of strain theory was the War on Poverty, introduced in the early 1960s by US President Lyndon Johnson, proved not to be a very effective strategy (see Parsons, 1969). More recently, Robert Agnew (2006) has advanced the theory in his "general strain theory."

Social Learning Theory and Differential Association

Social learning (SL) theory specifically isolates social factors from environmental factors that affect individuals. This theory claims that we learn by listening to people and witnessing events unfolding around us. The SL perspective maintains that behaviour is learned based on a system of positive and negative reinforcements. Note that although social learning is the manner in which the individual learns, the process by which the individual learns is given another name: *differential* association – a concept developed by the esteemed sociologist Edwin Sutherland (1883-1950) (see the next subsection). Meanwhile, psychologists use such terms as *observational learning* and *modeling* or *frustration induction* to describe the learning process.

Differential association asserts that since human behaviour is flexible (i.e., it changes based on the situation), anyone can learn antisocial attitudes and behaviours, depending on who he or she associates with and the nature of that association. As an example of social learning, a young person who witnesses a role model or hero doing something illegal or socially inappropriate (e.g., athletes using steroids) is very likely to copy or imitate the behaviour of the role model. In essence the theory implied that societies did not approve of diversity even though today we have numerous forms of legislation that protect and support diversity.

Symbolic Interactionism

Gabriel Tarde (1843-1904) was among the first scholars to investigate social learning (i.e., human behaviour is a product of interaction) in his book, *Penal Philosophy* (1890/1912). In 1947, Edwin Sutherland developed a broader theory that was more specifically aimed at explaining crime and delinquency. Some of Sutherland's key assumptions are as follows:

- Criminal behaviour is learned through interaction with intimate personal groups in a process of communication.
- Deviant behaviour occurs when favorable definitions of delinquent (and criminal) acts are given more credence that unfavorable ones.
- The specific direction of criminal motives and drives depends on the frequency, duration, priority, and intensity of contacts with deviant or criminal associates.

■ Learning includes the skills required to commit the crime, the motives or rationalizations for the crime, and the attitudes associated with the crime.

Sutherland (1947) argued that whether learned behaviour becomes ingrained depends on the situation. Positive and negative reinforcement, over the long term, will determine whether the behaviour will become permanent. Positive reinforcement may take the form of praise from others, financial gain, or a sense of accomplishment, while negative reinforcement involves such unpleasant events or experiences as punishment or social rejection. In essence, differential association asserts that, since human behaviour is flexible, and changes based on the situation, and learning antisocial behaviour is based on how (i.e., peer pressure) and with whom one associates with.

Several sociologists have more thoroughly investigated the role of reinforcement in determining human behaviour. Ronald Akers (1985) developed the *differential reinforcement theory*, which stresses the importance of reinforcement. Akers believes that behaviour is the direct result of social interactions or exchanges in which the words, responses, presence, and behaviour of other persons make reinforcement available and provide the setting for reinforcement. Other sociological theories that have been influenced by Sutherland's work and that focus on crime as learned behaviour include Skyes and Matza's *neutralization theory* (1957) and Glazer's (1965) *differential* anticipation/identification *theory*. Each theory is based on social learning principles but offers a slightly different interpretation of how the leaning process occurs. It is important to recognize that no single view can adequately explain all criminal delinquent acts.

Although the sociological variation of social learning theory remains popular because of they explain how young people come to engage in crime, this perspective has also had its detractors. For example, the *labelling* perspective views behaviour as a byproduct of how and why laws are made and the effect that the stigma of crime has on someone (see "Social-Reaction Perspective" below). Some critics argue that social learning theory adds little to what is already well known and explainable (see, for example, Cao, 2004). For example, key concepts such as frequency, duration, priority, and intensity are too broad to quantify and empirically test. Similarly, critics have pointed out that this theory does not adequately acknowledge genetic or psychological factors, and it overlooks the relationship between the offender and the victim.

Nevertheless, researchers continue to attempt a clearer definition of the time-and-order relationship between the effects of association and delinquency.

Meanwhile, the field of psychology takes a slightly different approach to social learning theory. In his famous bobo-doll studies, Bandura (1973) demonstrated that children who viewed violent television programs in a controlled setting display more aggression towards the dolls then did children who had viewed less violent or nonviolent programs. This form of observational *learning* or *modeling*, accounts for how and why when young people witness violence as an acceptable means of resolving conflict, they are likely to imitate or copy this behaviour in similar situations. It has often been said that prisons and youth detention centres are ideal settings for learning how to commit crimes and resolve disputes ineffectively. Singer, Slovak, Freirson, and York (1998) report that children who view six hours or more of television per day display higher levels of anxiety and violent behaviour than children who view fewer than six hours per day. According to those who subscribe to the social learning model, whether or not behaviour becomes ingrained depends on the situation and the expected potential gain. Such potential gains may come in the form of praise from others, such as financial (external) regards, or, from within, for example, as self-reinforcement for a job well done. In other words, it is not just modeling that is important; the quality of parenting appears to be more directly linked to antisocial acts by young persons.

Social Reaction Perspective

Rather than investigating the root cause of crime, some sociologists have investigated the effects of criminal lifestyle–that is, criminals being in constant contact with some aspect of the criminal justice system. Franklin Tannenbaum (1893-1969) is credited with developing the social-reaction theory in his 1938 book, *Crime and the Community*. He believed that once a young person had been identified as having committed a delinquent act, the person becomes the thing he or she is described as being (cited in Jacoby 1994:259). In other words, once labeled as a criminal, an individual has a difficult time escaping (criminal) stereotypes. Worse, the individual begins to think of himself or herself as criminal. Tannenbaum (1979) referred to this process as the *dramatization of evil*. Deviance, therefore, does not describe the act committed by an offender, but rather is a consequence of applying rules, sanctions, and labels to the offender. This approach has its roots in *symbolic interactionism*, which focused on the process by which people come to see and define themselves as being deviant or criminal, and then behaves as such.

The social-reaction perspective has provided some unique contributions to the study of delinquency. It drew attention to the detrimental effects of official labelling of young offenders. This perspective was instrumental in promoting more humane policies such as nonpunitive diversion programs, decriminalization of status offences, deinstitutionalization practices, and, more recently, *reintegrative* shaming. It is believed that, by diverting delinquent youth from the criminal justice system and by using minimal formal intervention, minor offenders will be helped to retain their normal identities. However, as many have noted, deviance is not entirely society's responsibility, and young offenders are not passive victims of their own criminal activities. Furthermore, this theory does not explain how labels are internalized or why society adopts specific labelling repertoires. Nevertheless, the various expressions of societal reaction based theories would appear to have some evidentiary support as certain ethnic and racial youth groups in society tend to be labeled in a pejorative context. This appears to be more so the case when examined within the context of local spatial areas as opposed to larger geographic areas (see MacDonald et al., 2004).

Learning Activity 2 - Summarize

In your own words, summarize the key provisions of the following sociological explanations of youth delinquency and criminality:

- Anomie
- Differential Association
- Social Learning
- Social Reaction

Can you identify any similarities between these sociological explanations?

Psychological Explanations of Youth Crime

Unlike classical sociological theories, psychological explanations follow what is referred to as a positivistic tradition and focus on micro, or individual factors. That is, they concentrate on faulty developmental issues such as youth's psychological makeup (i.e., a disturbed mind or personality-based disorder) that lead to irrational and inappropriate behaviour.

Sigmund Freud and Psychoanalytic Theory

Even though Sigmund Freud (1856-1939) did not write extensively about crime, his ideas have often been used as a starting point for explaining youth crime. According to Freud's psychoanalytic theory, delinquency is the result of conflict among the three aspects of the unconscious mind: the *id*, which controls our biological and psychological drives and instinctual urges; the *superego*, which controls our unconscious sense of mortality; and the *ego*, the conscious part of our personality that acts as a referee between the id and the superego. This *psychodynamic* approach has also been described as a theory that explains intrapsychic conflict within a person. According to Freud's theory, delinquency can be viewed as a personality disorder resulting from some inner conflict.

Although his work has met with varying criticism, Freud continues to have a strong following and many of his followers have tested and modified psychoanalytic theory:

- Alfred Adler (1870-1937), credited as the founder of individual psychology, focused on inner conflict related to an inferiority *complex*, which compels us to strive for superiority or the need to control others. Examples include by bullying and sexual assault.
- Kai Erichson (1902-1984) developed his stage theory (1959), which suggests that as we mature from childhood into adulthood, we go through stages of development. Adolescents try to forge their identity, but may experience role confusion—they don't feel as if they fit in. When this happens, they risk losing control of their role identity and may turn to drugs as an expression of, and escape from, their identity crises.
- August Aichorn (1878-1952), a neo-Freudian and author of *Wayward Youth* in 1935, coined the term *latent delinquency* to define those youth who, as a result of an immature personality, exhibit a desire for immediate gratification and place a greater emphasis on personal desires over the ability to have good relationships with other people. He believed in using unconditional love and constructive education to assist wayward youth rather than relying on punishment or institutionalization.

In 1989, Ontario psychologist E.T. Baker started to use effectively the traditional *egostate therapy*, which is derived from the psychologist approach, with young offenders (see Watkins and Watkins, 2004). More recently, Baker modified the theory to focus only on sharing current memories rather than past memories. An extension of the psychoanalytic approach has been the development models (see below).

The Family Factor

So far, the psychological theories we have discussed have emphasized individual factors, but as many psychologist have noted, family factors are also important. For example, the psychologists, Derzon and Lipsey (2000) found that family characteristics such as poor parenting skills, family size, home discord, child maltreatment, and antisocial parents are all risk factors found to be linked to juvenile delinquency. Similarly, Gottfredson and Hirschi in their influential book, *A General Theory of Crime* (1994) ascribe to parental child-rearing practices a primary role in the development of self-control (see Hirschi 2002). When a child fails at school, hurts other children, or takes illegal drugs, the almost-universal tendency is to blame the child's parents. Other key factors that have been viewed as fundamental for healthy psychological development include parental consistency in providing love, as it has been proven that a stronger relationship exists between parental rejection and antisocial behaviour; and discipline and adequate supervision. Darling (1999), for example, found that parenting styles are largely correlated with child well-being, social development, academic performance, psychological development, and problem behaviour. As well, numerous studies have linked violence within the family—especially abuse by one or both parents—to antisocial behaviour and delinquency (Finkeihor and Dzuiba-Leatherman, 1998; Wiebush, Freitage and Baird, 2001). In fact, even witnessing family violence has been shown to have a marked effect on the socio-emotional development of children. The Montreal Prevention Experiment is part of a longitudinal study headed by Richard Tremblay at the University of Montreal. The prevention program runs two years and combines parent training with social skills training for youth to reduce offending. Various evaluations indicate that the program is effective at mitigating risk behaviour (e.g., Brame, Nagin, and Tremblay, 2001). However, other family-based programs haven't proven as successful (see Huizinga and Mihalic, 2003). Hence, the significance of the family is still not clear. For example, in her 1998 ground breaking book *The Nature Assumption*, Judith Harris raises serious doubt about the role of family as playing a pivotal role in a young persons' personality development and also challenges the conventional wisdom that birth order matters. In her most recent 2006 book *No Two Alike: Human Nature and Human Individuality*, Harris presents three explanations for personality development. They include:

- Having a relationship system allows us to distinguish family from strangers. It also enables us to tell individuals apart.
- Having a socialization system or network enables us to become members of a group and absorb the group's culture.
- Having a status system enables us to acquire self-knowledge by measuring ourselves against others.

Harris's approach along with other psychologists generally speaks to social and/or interpersonal relations as representing the key factors that forge or influence human behaviour. Within this realm one can readily comprehend how and why differences in social status, culture, ethnicity, for instance, might be considered to account for diversity in youth crime.

Learning Activity 3 - Journal Entry

In your course journal or notes, discuss the following questions.

1. Discuss the key similarities and difference among the following explanations of youth-at-risk behaviour:

   ■   Applications of Freud's psychoanalytic model
   ■   Gottfredson and Hirshi's General Theory of Crime

2. Can you come up with your own "theory" as to how these two explanations could be related?

Biological Explanations of Youth Crime

Biological/Genetic Determinism

Most readers will probably be familiar with the 1859 work of the naturalist Charles Darwin (1809-1882) and his classic book *The Origin of Species* in which he argues that all species evolve in order to adapt to their changing environment. Although similar ideas can be traced back to ancient Greece, it was the work of Darwin that helped to spawn the concept of evolution to criminals. One of the major contributors to biological theories of crime was the Italian physician Cesare Lombroso (1835-1909). Lombroso adopted Darwin's idea of survival of the fittest, suggesting that humans can be categorized according to various levels of physical development. In his seminal work *The Criminal Man* (1876[1972]), Lombroso argued that criminals have "atavistic" traits (i.e., a "throwback" to an earlier stage of human evolution) that distinguish them from noncriminals. Lombroso also coined the term born criminal, which reflected his belief that some people will turn to crime because of their inherent physical traits.

Lombroso's ideas of physical anomalies being correlated to crime and delinquency have long since been dismissed because of their poor methodology and political sensitivity, but his assertion of determinism lives on in many theories. And in spite of the criticisms heaped on his ideas, his contribution was significant because he stressed the importance of scientific method. As Hirschi (2002, p. xxxviii) observed when commenting on Lombroso: "A lot of what we are reading now with the resurgence of biological perspective Lombroso said more clearly more than a century ago."

Despite resistance in some circles to research involving connections between crime and biology, those interested in this line of study have continued to improve their methodologies and capitalize on sophisticated technology such as brain mapping techniques. As a result, today we are witnessing a resurgence of literature based on hereditary biological factors (see Rowe, 2002). As Fishbein (1990) noted in her extensive review of the literature on biological explanations, biological factors can indeed play an equally significant role in the development of antisocial behaviour and should be considered accordingly. For a more recent accounting of the biological theories of delinquency, see Shoemaker (2009, Ch. 3). Shoemaker notes, however, that research in the area has been improved methodological with the use of control groups and replication of findings. Biological theories "are now emerging and plausible and worthy of continued investigation" (p.53).

Physical Factors

The interest in the relationship between physical features and delinquency or crime dates back to when Franz Joseph Gall (1758-1828) attempted to map the skull and relate the various lumps and bumps to 27 faculties or personality traits. Subsequent support came from Johan Spurzheirn (1776-1832) and Charles Goring (1870-1919), whose classic 1913 study report that criminals tended to be shorter and weigh less then noncriminals, and from William Sheldon (1898-1977), who associated body type (referred to as morphology) with distinctive temperaments (cited in Vold, Bernard, and Snipes, 1998).

Although many texts have dismissed Sheldon's initial work, the lives of 200 boys, now men, were followed for 30 years at the Biological Humanics Center. Hartl, Monnelly, and Elderkin (1982) present the follow-up results of Sheldon's original group. Among their key findings, they reported that "the one (factor) that has stood up most consistently is the association of mesomorphic body build with juvenile delinquency" (p.533). Benefiting from more refined methodology, they further add that it was also low ectomorphy and high andrornorphy that strengthened the association with delinquency. Yet as deterministic as their research may appear, they clearly point out such is not the case. Rather, in knowing our own somatotype, we "can profit from the insight it affords and take steps towards freedom" (p.557).

What is perplexing is that if physical types are predictive, then how do we explain the dramatic shift of our Aboriginal youth from their stable precontact societies into being disproportionately represented in our youth justice system?

Genetic Factors

In the early 1990s, a Dutch youth was found not culpable for a murder because evidence revealed that a mutation in a gene (monoamine oxidase A), which the family possessed had been shown to be associated with violent, antisocial behaviour (cited in Botkin, McMahon, and Francis, 1999). Since the work of Charles Darwin and Gregor Mendel (1822-1884), who essentially revolutionized our understanding about humankind and the nature of human evolution, genetics has been the focus of much research. Darwin's famous work *Origin of Species* (1859-1995) suggested that species evolved through a reciprocal interaction between the environment and the genetic makeup of a plant or animal. Countless studies have attempted to link criminality, delinquency, aggression, and anti-social behaviour to genetic abnormalities. Although these studies have shown that there are no genes directly responsible for crime, they have also determined that some genes, in combination with certain hot monal conditions (e.g., the onset of puberty, or low serotonin levels) or environmental factors can be strongly associated with certain forms of delinquency. Recent studies demonstrate not only the importance of genetic traits but also the significance of maturational and environmental processes. For example, drawing on a rich history of twin-based studies and using data from the ongoing Minnesota Twin Family Study Project, Doyle (1998:v) found in her study off 666 twins (aged 11-17) that there was higher "hereditary and reduced shared environmental influences for symptoms of antisocial personality disorder." Interestingly, the differences emerged around the age of 15 and reinforced the notion that cultural transmission from parents is negligible. In a more recent study by Arseneault et al. (2003), they found that young children expressing antisocial tendencies were heavily influenced by genetics, with a heritability estimate of 82 percent.

Today, the focus of attention has shifted toward not asking if genetics plays a role, but asking how genetics combines and interacts with cultural, environmental, and social factors to create a predisposition for antisocial behaviour. However, the evidence has not been compelling enough to prompt lawmakers to acknowledge the role of genetics in delinquent behaviour. As the science of such research improves we might expect to see a shift in the level of acceptance within the legal profession.

Psychophysiological Factors

A considerable number of studies have examined whether frontal brain dysfunction, traumatic head injury at an early age, reduced skin conductance, or a lower resting heart rate might differentiate violent young offenders from nonviolent ones. For example, certain imbalances in neurotransmitters such as acetylcholine, norepinephrine, dopamine, and serotonin have been found to increase aggression levels (Moffit et al., 1998) and nervous system irregularities (Fishbein, 1990). For this reason, Walsh (2002) and others believe that this area may hold new insight into certain types of delinquent behaviour, but much more research needs to be done. Using PET scans to examine the brains of several impulsive murders, Raine (1997) found that, when compared with those of noncriminals, the prefrontal areas of the murderers' brains were virtually inactive. In other words, the murderers' brains do not function in a normal manner. Another recent study in which brain scans were used to measure the brain-wave activity of both teenagers and adults found that emotional turbulence among young people may have a physiological basis. Yurgen-Todd (cited in Hotz, 1998) found that teenagers process emotions more intensely and indiscriminately than do adults. This pioneering study will likely spawn further research in the area, as well as in examining what role the environment plays in how young people respond to different environmental factors (e.g., family, television, school, and peers).

Psychopharmacological Factors

Since the mid-1970s, a number of studies have examined the effects of legal and illegal drugs on the brain. In the majority of these studies, drugs, including alcohol and caffeine, and even certain vitamin deficiencies, have been found to affect young persons both at a psychological and a behavioural level (see Marsh, 1981; Raine, 1993; Rowe, 2002). Moir and Jessel (1997) also note that certain drugs, particularly many illicit drugs, are reported to increase aggressive responses, although the actual expression of aggressive behaviour depends on the dose, the route of administration, genetic factors, and the type of aggression.

Drugs and alcohol are not the only mood-altering chemicals that relate to aggressive behaviour, particularly in young offenders. Surveys show that the majority of violent young offenders have consumed some form of mood-altering drug on the day they committed the crime. Of particular concern is the fact that the average age of onset for the use of mood altering drugs has fallen since the 1980s, and there has been a shift towards more illicit drugs (U.S. Department of Health and human Services, 1996). Seemingly harmless substances have also been linked to violence. In 1978, Leonard Hippchen was among the first theorists to suggest that dietary habits, vitamin and mineral imbalances, hypoglycemia, and even environmental toxins are related to the development of crime and delinquency. Bennett, McEwan, McEwan and Rose (1998) found that by correcting food allergies in young offenders, they were able to reduce antisocial tendencies. Similarly, one of the first studies undertaken to examine the effects of pesticides on children in Mexico found that children exposed to agricultural pesticides expressed significantly more aggressive and antisocial behaviour than children not living in that agricultural region (Guillette, Maza, Aguilar, Soto, and Garcia, 1998). Recently, Needleman, McFarland, Ness, Fienberg, and Tobin (2002), using sound methodology, found that convicted juveniles were nearly twice as likely as control subjects to have high levels of lead in their bones. Finally, Diplock, Cohen and Plecas (2009:1) present a careful review of the literature between 2000-2007 and found that contrary to popular opinion "there are many risks associated to marijuana use with regards to impairment, academic and social development, general and mental health."

As the scientific evidence involving the relationship between biology and delinquency grows, we must remember that correlations are not the same as causes. Before such conclusions can be drawn, more careful research is required. Ultimately, criminal justice policies must be based on well founded theories and findings that survive scientific scrutiny. Any policy regarding the handling of young offenders should be based on informed evidence.

Learning Activity 4 - Online Research

The case of a 13-year old girl from Medicine Hat, Alberta, who was convicted of murdering her own family was national and international news in 2006. In some ways, it is a case that illustrates that there is no single explanation for why some young people engage in violent behaviour.

Follow this link to the Canadian Broadcast Corporation webpage that describes the events and court verdict in the Medicine Hat, Alberta:

www.cbc.ca/Canada/story/2007/07/09/med-hat.html

Integrated and Interdisciplinary Explanation of Youth Crime

In the past, sociologists, psychologists, and biologists tend to formulate explanations for young offenders that relied on concepts unique to their particular disciplines. More recently, there have been attempts to bridge some of the disciplinary isolation (Cao, 2004). For example, in her 1998 Presidential Address to the American Society of Criminology, Zahn (1999:2) observed that criminology needs "to incorporate other disciplines that affect human behaviour such as biology and biochemistry ... [and] ... make better use of historical studies." It is anticipated that these new approaches will advance out understanding of youth crime and antisocial behaviour so that we might then be able to construct better policy.

Biosocial Theory

Although the foundation of biosocial theory can be traced to one of the first eugenicists, Francis Galton (1812-1911), more contemporary researchers have attempted to use biology to bridge our understanding of youth crime (see Walsh, 2002). Among the more notable efforts is the pioneering work of Mednick, Gabrielli, and Hutchings (1984). Some of the assumptions of the biosocial theory include the following:

- Not two people are genetically alike. Each person's unique genetic makeup contributes significantly to his or her behaviour, but it should also be noted that behaviour patterns are a combination of genetic traits and the environment.
- Social behaviour is learned, and each individual learns according to varying brain function and mental processing abilities. Learning is therefore fundamentally controlled by biochemistry (Raine, Brennan, Farrington, and Mednick, 1996), but individuals can learn to control their natural urges toward antisocial or delinquent tendencies.
- A wide range of biochemical factors can affect behaviour, from vitamin deficient and vitamin dependency to hormonal influences, allergies, and even premenstrual syndrome.
- Biochemical factors, when combined with social environment, can play a significant role in determining whether young people develop antisocial or delinquent behaviours.

Criticism of biosocial theory has focus on its alleged tendency to medicalize political issues such as gender, race, and marginalized groups. In spite of these concerns, however, an increasing number of researchers are exploring how the biosocial approach could explain chronic delinquent behaviour (see Walsh, 2002). Moffit, Caspi, Rutter, and Silva (2001) have been conducting a longitudinal study since the 1970s in Dunedin, New Zealand, and have found a significant correlate of persistent antisocial behaviour among young persons and an interaction of social and psychological factors with neuropsychological dysfunctions. In terms of prevention, the biosocial perspective subscribes to a proactive approach of detecting possible markers in individuals or their environment, and then targeting theses markers through strategies such as public health intervention.

Lifestyle and Routine Activities Theory

Routine activities or opportunity theory, another end-to-end integrated theory emerged during the 1970s. During the 1990s, it became one of the most commonly tested theories in criminology. While the biosocial theory focuses on the interaction between the brain and the environment, the lifestyle theory focuses on the interaction between social and environmental opportunities and the individual's motivation to attain certain goals. Developed by Lawrence Cohen and Marcus Edson (1979), this theory claims that in every society there are people who are willing to commit a crime. Both the motivation to commit a crime and the availability of targets are constant. For a criminal act to occur, however, certain variables must be present: the *availability of suitable targets*, such as unattended cars or homes, or helpless individuals; the *absence of capable* guardians for the offender; and the *presence of motivated offenders*, such as unemployed, drug-addicted, bored, or homeless youth. If all these factors are present, then a predatory crime will likely occur.

Canadian researches Kennedy and Forde (1990) found that lower-class young males were at greater risk of being either offenders or crime victims, based on their lifestyle behaviour (e.g., going to bars, walking or driving at night). However, these lifestyle variables still need to be more clearly defined, and some critics suggest that even greater attention must be paid to the situational context that motivates individuals.

Integrating Social Processes and Structural Conditions

One of the most cited integrated theories was conducted by Elliot, Huizinga, and Ageton (1985). They combined three popular theories of delinquency—social *control*, strain, and *social learning* theories—into one statistical model. Drawing on longitudinal data from the National Youth Survey, their model focuses on the socialization process in establishing social control. As a young person ages, he or she must contend with a wide variety of social stresses that may reduce social-control bonds. Furthermore, life experiences (such as the youth's network of peers) may create a dysfunctional learning environment. Collectively, the interaction of these factors can weaken conventional social-control bonds and predispose a young person towards delinquent behaviour. The model accounts for 52 to 55 percent of the variance in delinquency.

Although this model attempts to take into account a number of possible paths to delinquency, it has several methodological flaws. For instance, researchers have not been able to measure clearly the construction of social control and bonding, strain, or elements of learning.

The integrated theories continue to hold promise as they attempt to offer a more comprehensive explanation of delinquency and crime (see, for example, Wright, Caspi, Moffitt, and Silva, 1999). However, as Cao (2004) notes, additional research needs to be conducted before we can determine whether the theories hold true promise for the future study and control of crime and delinquency. Yet, depending on whose work you read or cite you might get a different interpretation of the integrated approach. For example, Anderson (2007), Walsh (2002) and Wikstrom and Sampson (2006) all provide compelling arguments and evidence that an integrated approach—especially one that includes the role of biology—may hold significant promise for explaining delinquency and anti-social behaviour.

We will next provide an overview of some of the different perspectives that can be categorized as integrated theories.

Feminist Theory

In the strictest sense, the feminist perspective is not an integrated theory, but it does represent an attempt to bridge male-dominate paradigms for explaining crime and delinquency. Some scholars suggest that feminist theory is part of the *critical criminology* and *postmodern* movement as it, like other theories associated with this period, represents an alternative to all aspects of positivism and attempts to deconstruct conventional ways of defining criminal behaviour (see Shawartz and Friedrichs, 1994).

Feminist theory began with the pioneering works of Freda Adler in 1975 and Carol Smart in 1976. More recently, Birgit Brock-Utne (1989) of Norway began in the 1980s to bridge feminist ideology with *peacemaking criminology*.

Numerous variations on feminist theory exists today, including *radical* feminist theories that emphasize the discriminatory treatment and oppression that women have experienced (e.g., sexual abuse) in the juvenile and adult justice system; *liberal* feminist theories that focus on different economic and social standards between males and females; and *marxist* feminism, which attributes women's deviance and crime to their social and economic marginalization.

Finally, phenomenological feminist theories focus on the regulators of juvenile justice and examine whether young females receive discriminatory treatment by the youth justice system and how the YCJA penalizes females.

Collectively, the feminist theories represent a comparatively new way of looking at the issues of youth crime, since, in the past, social issues were mainly studied from a male viewpoint. Collectively the feminist perspectives challenge the male biases and neglects of mainstream criminology (White, Haines, and Eisler, 2009). However, the perspective has been accused of offering little more than a Band-Aid solution and of sharing many of the same characteristics as labelling theory (see Boyd, 2004). Furthermore, there is insufficient evidence to demonstrate that since the emergence of feminist writing, crime rates among young persons have changed. Nevertheless, current explanations of female delinquency can be divided into two main categories:

- Developmental theories. These theories stress the important of psychological, development, and home environment factors facing females, which differ from those facing males. For example, differences in hormonal traits and genetic makeup have successfully explained differences between male and female violence rates.
- Socialization theories. These theories examine the socialization process surrounding females, since young girls tend to be brought up with different role expectations from those of young boys. Female socialization theories focus on the behaviours of delinquent girls who were not raised in a nurturing environment (see Chesney-Lind and Shelden, 1992).

Development and Life-Course Perspective (LCP)

The developmental and life-course perspective (LCP) is not so much an integrated theory as a way of thinking in an integrative manner that has become "increasingly prominent in criminology" (Akers and Sellers, 2004). It is based on earlier *developmental-based theories*, which assert that personal traits tend to direct our development and influence our behavioural choices. The life-course perspective is a broad interdisciplinary approach that includes history, biology, psychology, sociology, and other disciplines.

The contemporary variation of these early ideas is based on Glueck and Glueck's (1950) popular longitudinal research on young persons in the 1930s. They attempt to show a link between both physical and social factors of delinquent behaviour.

After their death, their theory and ideas went dormant until a University of Chicago criminologist, Robert Sampson, found their data in the basement of Harvard University Library and subjected this data to more recent sophisticated analysis along with his colleague John Laub (Laub and Sampson, 1993). Canadian criminologist Marc LeBlanc (2002) was among the first to rework the early ideas into what is now commonly called LCP. The perspective asserts that antisocial acts by young persons are the result of complex interaction of both social (e.g., social bonds) and personal factors (e.g., low verbal ability and hyperactivity) that express themselves in different ways at different ages. For example, most youths do not begin to experiment with sex until their early teens. The age of onset for certain behaviours (e.g., cheating, lying, stealing, and honesty) has somewhat predictable patterns pending the knowledge of certain antecedent experiences. Youth who were sexually abused as children may not become sexual promiscuous until their teens.

Subsequently, LCP continues to gather momentum and has seen a number of deviations of its model as the theory undergoes testing and refinement (see, for example, Benson, 2002). Researchers are attempting to identify the various *pathways* and *latent* traits that might offer clues as to how to prevent or mediate the risk of problem behaviours emerging.

In summary, the interdisciplinary approach of these new bridging theories marks the continuing evolution of research into crime and delinquency. In the 1994 edition of their theory text, Williams and McShane note that "[t]he field appears to be on the verge of a paradigm revolution." In their 1999 edition, they state that "contemporary criminology is now fermenting nicely," so although the direction new theories will take may be uncertain, it does appear certain that through improved methodology and testing of theories (see Cao, 2004), we will be better able to explain and ultimately reduce the rate of youthful misconduct.

■ Summary

This chapter has provided an overview of some of the theories and perspectives used to explain, or better understand youth crime. Although none of the explanations are "perfect," each theory offers some insight. As we saw, sociologists offer insight on social organization, ethnicity, social stratification, and environmental conditions. These factors can create strain, thereby encouraging deviation, undermining social cohesion, and predisposing a young person to delinquency.

Psychological perspectives shift the focus from social factors to individual traits. These explanations of delinquency fall into two main theoretical camps: those that use the role of learning (e.g., committing copycat crimes or hanging around with the wrong crowd), and those that emphasize psychodynamic factors, such as family conflict, inappropriate discipline, and other developmental experiences that can disrupt a young person's emotional development.

Biological explanations similarly focus on specific individual traits. They stress the importance of genetic influences, hormonal imbalances, nutrition, drugs, and even physical traits. The biological theories also suggest a possible heredity link in the case of some young offenders.

Newer integrated and interdisciplinary theories reflect the fact that crime and delinquency are complex issues, and any attempt to deal with them must consider a wide variety of factors and interpretations. However, as we begin to accept the fact that crime is a complex phenomenon, we must acknowledge that there are no simple answers or solutions for understanding delinquency. Therefore, any attempt to deal with the issue must be open to wide variety of interpretation and orientation.

Only through diligent testing, constant evaluation, and careful analysis can we begin to narrow the gap between simply describing the phenomenon of juvenile delinquency and explaining, predicting, and ultimately preventing youth crime.

References

Adler, E. (1975). *Sisters in me: the rise of the new female criminal*. New York: McGraw-Hill.

Agnew, R. (2006). *Pressured into crime: An overview of general strain theory*. Los Angeles: Roxbury.

Akers, R. (1985). *Deviant behaviour: A social learning approach*. 3rd ed. Belmont: Wadsworth.

Akers, R., and C. S. Sellers. (2004). *Criminology theories: Introduction, evaluation*, and *application*. 4th ed. Los Angeles: Roxbury.

Anderson, G.S. (2007). *Biological influences on criminal behavior*. Boca Raton: CRC Press.

Andrews, D.A., J. Bonta, and R.D. Hoge. (1990). "Classification for effective rehabilitation: Rediscovering psychology." *Criminal Justice and Behaviour* 17(1):19-52.

Arseneault, L., T.E. Moffitt, A. Caspi, A. Taylor, F.V. Rijsdijk, S.R. Jaffee, J.C. Ablow, J.R. Measelle. (2003). "Strong genetic effects on cross-situational antisocial behaviour among 5-year-old children according to mothers, teachers, examiner-observers, and twins' self-reports." *Journal of Child Psychology and Psychiatry* 44(6):832-48.

Axinn, W G., J.S. Barber, and A. Thornton. (1998). Determinants of *marriage and childrearing attitudes*. Ann Arbor: University of Michigan (Institute of Social Policy).

Bandura. W. (1973). *Aggression: A social learning analysis*. Englewood Cliffs: Prentice Hall.

Bennet, P. W., L.M. McEwan, H.C. McEwan, and E.L. Rose. (1998). "The Shipley project: Treating food allergy to prevent criminal behaviour in community settings." *Journal of Nutritional and Environmental Medicine* 8:77-83.

Benson, M.L. (2002). *Crime and the life course*. Los Angeles: Roxbury.

Berkowitz, L. (1962). *Aggression: A social-psychological analysis*. New York: McGraw-Hill.

Boodman, S. (1999, 16 January). "Unwanted children have no confidence." *Calgary Herald*, p. K24

Brame, B., D.S. Nagin, and R.E. Tremblay. (2001). "Development trajectories of physical aggression from school entry to late adolescence." *Journal of Child Psychology and Psychiatry* 42(4): 503-512.

Brock-Utne, B. (1989). *Feminist perspective on peace and peach education*. New York: Pergamon Press.

Cao, L. (2004). *Major criminological theories: Concepts and measurement*. Belmont: Wadsworth.

CBC News. (2004). *Home life linked to high school dropouts*. Statistics Canada. Retrieved April 28, 2004, from http://www.chc.ca/stories/2004/04/05kanada/dropouts_20040405.

Chambliss, W. (1973). "The saints and the roughnecks." *Society* 11(1): 24-31.

Chesney-Lind, M. and R.G. Shelden. (1992). *Girls, delinquency and juvenile justice*. Pacific Grove: Brooks/Cole.

Child and Family of Canada. (2004). *Teen suicide*. Retrieved from http://www.cfc-efc.ca.

Cloward, R.A. and L.E. Ohlin. (1960). *Delinquency and opportunity: A theory of delinquent gangs*. NY: Free Press.

Cohen, A.K. (1995). *Delinquent boys: The culture of the gangs*. New York: Free Press.

Cohen, U. and M. Edson. (1979). "Social changes and crime rate trends: A routine activity approach." *American Sociological Review* 44:588-607.

Darling, N. (1999). *Parenting style and its correlates.* ERIC Digest, Illinois, ERIC Clearinghouse on Elementary and Early Childhood Education. (ERIC Identifier ED427896).

Darwin, C. (1859/1993). *Origin of the species.* London: Gramercy Books.

Derzon, J.H. and M.W. Lipsey. (2000). "The correspondence of family features with problem, aggressive, criminal and violent behavior." Unpublished manuscript. Nashville: Institute for Public Policy Studies, Vanderbilt University.

Diplock, J., I. Cohen, and D. Plecas. (Summer 2009). "A review of the research on the risks and harms associated to the use of marijuana." *The Journal of Global Drug Policy and Practice* 3(2).

Doyle, A.F. (1998). "The familial transmission of antisocial behaviour: Evidence from the Minnesota twin family study." Unpublished Doctoral dissertation, University of Minnesota.

Durkheim, E. (1897/1964). *Suicide.* Glencoe, Free Press.

Elliot, D.S., D. Huizinga, and S.S. Ageton. (1985). *Explaining delinquency and drug use.* Beverly Hills: Sage.

Erikson, E.J. (1959*). Identity and the life cycle.* New York: International University Press.

Farrington, D. (1986). "Stepping stones to adult criminal careers." In D. Olweus, J. Block, and M. Radke-Yarrow (eds.), *Development of antisocial and prosocial behaviour: research, theories,* and issues. Orlando: Academic Press.

Einkelhor, D. and J. Dzniba-Leatherman. (1994). *Health Canada, the consequences of child maltreatment: a reference guide for health practitioners.* Ottawa: Health Canada, National Clearinghouse on Family Violence.

Goring, C. (1913). *The English convict. London*: His majesty's Stationary.

Gottfredson, M.R. and T. Hirschi. (1994). *General theory of crime.* Stanford: Stanford University Press.

Guillette, E.A., M.M Maza, M.G. Aguilar, A.D. Sow, and E. Garcai. (1998). "An anthropological approach to the evaluation of preschool children exposed to pesticides in Mexico." *Environmental Health Perspectives* 106(6):347-353.

Harris, J.R. (1998). *The nurture assumption.* New York: Free Press.

Harris, J.R. (2006). *No Two Alike: Human Nature and Human Individuality.* New York: W.W. Norton.

Hartl, D., E.P. Monnelly, and R. Elderkin. (1982). *Physique and delinquent behaviour.* New York: Academic Press.

Hippchen, L. (1978). *Ecological-biochemical approaches to the treatment of delinquents and criminals.* New York: Can Nostrand Reinhold.

Hirschi, T. (2002). *Causes of delinquency.* New Brunswick: Transaction Publishers.

Hoge, R.D. (2001). *The juvenile offender: Theory, research and application.* Boston: Kluwer.

Holz, R.L. (1998, 31 July). "Brian scans reveal teenagers think differently." *Calgary Herald*, p. G13.

Huizinga. D. and S. Mihalic. (2003). "Preventing juvenile delinquency." In H. Kury & K. Obergfell-Fuchs (eds.), *Crime prevention: New approaches.* Mainz, Germany: Weisser Ring.

Jeffrey, C.R. (1994). "Biological and neuropsychiatric approaches to criminal behaviour." In G. Barak (ed.), *Varieties of criminology: Reading from a dynamic discipline.* Westpot: Praegar.

Kennedy, L.W. and D.R. Forde. (1990). "Routine activities and crime: An analysis of victimization in Canada." *Criminology* 28(1):137-152.

Kerlinger, F.N. (1973). *Foundation of behavioral research,* 2nd ed. New York: Holt, Rinehart & Winston.

Labovitz, S. and R. Hagedorn. (1981). *Introduction to social research,* 3rd ed. New York: McGraw-Hill.

Laub, J. and R. Sampson. (1993). "Turning points in the life course: Why change matters to the study of crime." *Criminology* 31:301-325.

Latyon, E. (1979). *The myth of delinquency.* Toronto: McClelland & Stewart.

LeBlanc, M. (2002). "The offspring cycle, escalation and de-escalation in delinquent behaviour. A Challenge for criminology." *International Journal of Comparative and Applied Criminal Justice* 26(1):53-84.

Locher. R. and M. Stoutharner-Loebet. (1986). "Family factors as correlates and predictors of juvenile conduct problems and delinquency." In M. Tony and N. Morris (eds.), *Crime justice: An annual review of research,* 7th ed. Chicago: University of Chicago Press.

Loeber, R., D.P. Farrington, and D. Petechuk. (May 2003). "Child delinquency: Early intervention and prevention." *Child Delinquency Bulletin Series.* Washington, DC: Office of Juvenile Justice and Delinquency Prevention. Retrieved June 29, 2010 from http://www.ncjrs.gov/html/ojjdp/186162/contents.html.

Lombroso, C. (1876/1972). "The criminal man." In S.E Sylvester (ed.), *The heritage of modern criminology.* Cambridge: Schenkman.

MacDonald, J.M., G.P. Alpert, M.R. Smith, and A.R. Piquero. (2004). "A context study of racial profiling." *American Behavioral Scientist* 47(7): 943-962.

Marsh, T.O, (1981). *Roots of crime.* Newton., NJ: Mellen.

McCord, J. (1986). "Instigation and insulation: Family and later criminal behavior." In J. Block, D. Olweus, and M.R. Yarrow (eds.), *Development of Antisocial* and *Prosocial Behaviour.* New York: Academic Press.

McCord, J. (1991). "Questioning the value of punishment." *Social Problems* 38:1607-1679.

Mednick, S.A., W.E. Gabrielli, and H. Hutchings. (1984). "Genetic influence in criminal convictions: Evidence from an adoption cohort." *Science* 224:891-894.

Merton, R. (1938). "Social structure and anomie." *American Sociological Review* 3:672-682.

Miller. W.B. (1958). "Lower class culture as a generating milieu of gang delinquency." *Journal of social Issues* 14:15-19.

Miller. W.B. (1962). "The impact of a 'total-community' delinquency control project." *Social Problems* 10:168-91.

Mills, C. (1959). *The sociological* imagination. NY: Oxford University Press.

Moffit, T.F., G.L. Bramliner, A. Caspi, J.P. Fawcett, M. Raleigh, A. Vuwiler, and P. Silva. (1998). "Whole blood serotonin relates to violence in an epidemiological study." *Biological Psychiatry* 43(6):446-457.

Moffit, T.E., A. Caspi, M. Rutter, and P.A. Silva. (2001). *Sex differences in antisocial behaviour: Conduct disorder, delinquency, and violence in the Dunedin longitudinal study.* Cambridge: Cambridge University Press.

Moir, A. and D. Jessel. (1997). *A mind to crime.* New York: Signet.

Moore, D. (1998, 7 May). *Violence on the rise among native youth.* Retrieved May 1998 from http://interactive.cfra.corn/1998/05/07/26147.html.

Needleman, H.L., C. McFarland, R.B. Ness, S.E. Fienberg, and M.J. Tobin. (2002). "Bone lead levels in adjudicated delinquents: A case control study." *Neurotoxicology and teratology,* 24(6): 711-717.

Park, R.E.K., E.W. Burgess, and R.D. McKenzie. (1928). *The city.* Chicago: University of Chicago Press.

Parsons, T. *Politics and social structure.* NY: The Free Press.

Pinker, S. (2002). *The blank slate.* New York: Viking Press.

Platt, A.M. (1969). *The child savers.* Chicago: University of Chicago Press.

Rafter, N.H. (1999). *Creating born criminals.* Chicago: Chicago University of Illinois Press.

Raine, A. (1993). *The psychopathology of crime.* New York: Academic Press.

_____ (1997). "Antisocial behaviour and psychophysiology: A biosocial perspective and a pre-frontal dysfunction hypothesis." In D. Staff, J, Breiling, and J. Maser (eds), *Handbook of antisocial behaviour.* New York: John Wiley.

Rowe, D. (2002). *Biology and crime.* Los Angeles: Roxbury.

Schwarts, M.S. and D.O. Friedrichs. (1994). "Postmodern thought and criminological discontent: New metaphors for understanding violence." *Criminology* 32:221-246.

Shaw, C.R. and H.D. McKay. (1969). *Juvenile delinquency* and *urban areas.* Chicago: University of Chicago Press.

Simons, R.L., C. Johnson, and R. Conger. (1994). "Harsh corporal punishment versus quality of parental involvement as an explanation of adolescent maladjustment." *Journal of Marriage and the Family* 56:591-607.

Singer, M.l., K. Slovak, T. Freirson, and P. York. (1998). "Viewing preferences, symptoms of psychological trauma, and violent behaviours among children who watch television." *Journal of American Academy of Child and Adolescent Psychiatry* 37:1041-1048.

Smart, C. (1976). *Women, crime and criminology: A feminist critique.* London: Routledge & Kegan Paul.

Span, P. (1998, 25 November). "Nature vs. nurture: Brash author earns beefs, bouquets for discounting roles of parents." *Calgary Herald*, p. G4.

Sullivan, C., M.Q. Grant, and D. Grant. (1957). "The development of interpersonal maturity: Applications to delinquency." *Psychiatry* 20(11):373-385.

Sutherland, E. (1947). *Principles* of criminology. 4th ed. Philadelphia: B. Lippincott.

Skyes, G.M. and D. Matza. (1957). "Techniques of neutralization: A theory of delinquency." *American Sociological Review* 22:664-670.

Tannenbaum, F. (1938). *Crime and the community.* NY: Columbia University Press.

_____. (1979). Dramatization of evil. In J. E. Jacoby (ed.), *Classics of Criminology.* Prospect Heights: Waveland Press.

Tarde, G. (1890/1912). *Penal philosophy.* Trans. Rapelje Howell. Boston: Little Brown.

Theodorson, G. A. (ed.). (1982). *Urban patterns: Studies in human ecology* (Rev. ed.). University Park: Pennsylvania University Press.

U.S. Department of Health and Human Services. (1996, December), Monitoring the future. Washington, D.C.

Vold, G. (1981). *Theoretical criminology.* 2nd ed. Prepared by T.J. Bernard. New York: Oxford University Press.

Vold, G., T.J. Bernard, and J.B. Snipes. (1998). *Theoretical criminology.* 4th ed. New York: Oxford University Press.

Walsh, A. (2002). *Biosocial criminology: Introduction and integration.* Cincinnati, OH: Anderson.

Watkins, J.G., and H.H. Watkins. (2004). *Ego state therapy.* Retrieved June 1, 2004, from http://www.clinicalsocialwork.com/egostate.html.

White, R., E. Haines, and L. Eisler. (2009). *Crime and criminology: An introduction.* Don Mills, ON: Oxford University Press.

Wiebush, R., R. Freitage, and C. Baird. (2001, July). *Preventing Delinquency Through Improved Child Protection Services*, OJJDP, Juvenile *Justice Bulletin.*

Williams, F.P., and M.D. McCone. (1994*). Criminological* theory. 2nd ed. Upper Saddle River, NJ: Prentice Hall.

_____. (1999). *Criminological theory.* 3rd ed. Upper Saddle River, NJ: Prentice Hall.

Williams, F. (1984). "The demise of criminological imagination: A critique of recent criminology." *Justice Quarterly* 1:91-106.

Winterdyk, J. (ed.). (2002). *Juvenile justice systems: International perspectives.* 2nd ed. Toronto: Canadian Scholar's Press.

Wikstrom, P-O. and R.J. Sampson. (2006). *The explanation of crime: Context, mechanisms and development.* Cambridge: Cambridge University Press.

Wright, B.R.E., A. Caspi, T.F. Moffitt, and P.A. Silva. (1999). "Low self-control, social bonds, and crime: Social causation, social selection, or both?" *Criminology* 37(3):479-514.

Yablonsky, L. and M.R. Haskell. (1988). *Juvenile delinquency.* 4th ed. New York: Harper & Row.

Zahn, M.A. (1999). "Thoughts on the future of criminology: The American Society of Criminology 1998 Presidential Address." *Criminology* 37(1):1-16.

PART TWO

Unit Three: Older Adults

Chapter 8
An Overview of Justice and Canada's Older Adults

▪ Learning Activity 1 - Fun Quiz

Take this fun quiz before you read the chapter. Answer "True" or "False":

1. Traditionally, the term "seniors" referred to adults 65+ years of age and who have retired from the workforce.

2. The proportion of Canadian society that will be 65+ years of age is decreasing.

3. People are living longer than ever before.

4. The suicide rate among older adults is lower than for all other adults.

5. Older adults are as financially secure as other adults.

6. Less than 2% of older adults have experience elder abuse in the past 5 years.

7. Most elder abuse is perpetrated by a family member or friend of the victim.

8. Older adults have a higher rate of violent crime victimization.

9. Older adults have a much lower rate of property crime victimization.

10. We have a fairly accurate idea about the amount of elder abuse in Canadian society.

ANSWERS: 1T, 2F, 3T, 4F, 5F, 6F, 7T, 8F, 9T, 10F

As noted in an article by Rosenberg and Moore (1997), since the early 1990s there has been increasing policy debate and general rhetoric about the growing shift in demographics with regard to the elderly and the impact they are having and will continue to express upon Canadian society. They reported that in 1991, the elderly represented 11.7% of the Canadian population and by 2011 their representation would grow to 14.1% and 22% by 2030. These are trends that have very real implications and we are not alone. By comparison, between 1990 and 1994 the elderly population in the United States greatly exceeded the rate of growth among the rest of the population. In 1994 about 1 in 8 Americans was elderly and by 2030 it is projected that the ratio will be 1 in 5 (Hobbs, 2001). Catharine Brant's 1978 book title, *Forgotten people: Reaching out to the elderly,* no longer seems to apply. Perhaps the notion of "ageism" (discussed in Chapter 6) no longer applies as their presence becomes more visible. For example, consider some of the following facts:

- Data from the Canadian Council on Social Development shows that during the 1990s almost 20% of the elderly were living below the poverty line. But this is down from a high of 34% in 1980.
- The steady decline in the fertility rate since the 1970s is expected to accelerate the proportion of the "greying" population.
- Three areas of spending are particularly sensitive to demographic shifts:
    - Social security will accelerate from around 3% of the GDP in 2007 to almost 5% by 2031.
    - Health care will accelerate from around 7.7% of the GDP in 2007 to over 12% in 2031. For example, a growing issue is the problem of "self-neglect." Self-neglect occurs when older adults, by choice or by lack of awareness, live in ways that disregard their health or safety needs, sometimes to the extent that this disregard also becomes hazardous to others.
    - According to Statistics Canada projections, there will be no significant impact on the GDP in relation to education costs (see below for further details).
- Based on data from the 2004 General Social Survey (GSS) on victimization, 10% of seniors experienced at least one victimization in the 12 months preceding the survey.
- Fraud can express itself in many different forms (e.g., identity theft, credit card scams, bogus home improvement pitches, Nigerian letters, etc.) but the elderly are disproportionately targeted because of their generational mannerism towards being trustworthy of others and today more readily disposable income (Sharpe, 2004).

As we grow older, the likelihood that we will be involved in a criminal event, either as a victim or perpetrator, decreases. However, as reflected in the points above, Canadian's senior citizens are at risk of becoming victims of elder abuse. For example, in 2000, Cornwall described elder abuse as Canada's "hidden crime." However, referring to information obtained from the National Advisory Council on Aging, she points out that there are sufficient complaints to indicate that elderly abuse is a serious problem in our society. Furthermore, as a greater proportion of Canada's population are reaching "old age" each year, the incidents of elder abuse are likely going to increase.

Defining "Older Adults"

Unlike the for terms "young offender" and "adult," there is no *formal* justice-related definition for terms such as "older adults," "seniors" or "the elderly." While these latter terms are part of our everyday language, there are discernable differences between them.

- *Older Adults*
  This term is becoming increasingly popular in both academic and government literature. It is the simplest of the terms in that it refers to all adults who are 65-years of age or older.
- *The Elderly*
  Most commonly, this term refers to adults who are 65 years of age or more **and** have become more vulnerable in terms of their health, finances and personal support networks.
- *Seniors*
  Traditionally, this term referred to adults who are 65+ years of age and have retired from the workforce. In Canada, it is often associated with "Old Age Security" benefits to all those who are 65+ years of age. Today, the term is become less precise as many private business offer "seniors" benefits to some adults beginning at age 55.

Learning Activity 2 - Journal Entry

In your course journal or in-class, articulate/discuss your immediate personal response to the following three labels:

- Older Adult
- Senior
- Elderly

Which would you like to be used to eventually describe you? Why?

Canada's Aging Population

As noted at the outset of this chapter, one of the more important changes taken place in Canadian society is the ageing of our population. This was also reflected in the dramatic growth in services, interest and research in the area which grew dramatically in the 1980s when there was a notable increase in the number of gerontologists, geriatricians, geriatric nurses, geriatric social workers, and others (Crandell, 1980). Until then the entire field of gerontology was neglected by both academics and non-academics.

As can be seen in the chart below, older adults (65+ years of age) make up approximately 13% of Canada's population in 2007. Over the next 50 years, it is predicted that the proportion of older adults will nearly double to 25%–hence the colloquial saying of a "greying population."

There are several reasons for the ageing of Canada's population. First, Canadians are having fewer children than previous generations. In fact, without immigration into Canada, our population would actually shrink in time. Second, Canadians are living longer than in previous generations due to healthier lifestyles, better medical support and new medical discoveries.

Percentage of Canadians Aged 65 Years and Older (1921 - 2005 and Projections to 2056)

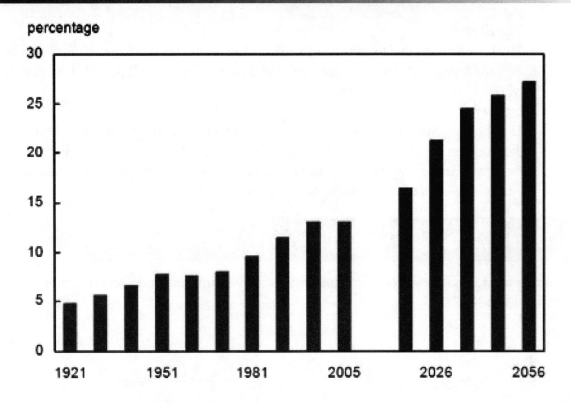

Source: Statistics Canada, 2007, *A Portrait of Canadian Seniors in Canada 2006*, Catalogue no. 89-519-XIE, p. 11.

Learning Activity 3 - Reflect

In what year will you turn 65 years of age? In reference to the chart above, about what percentage of Canadians will be 65 years and older when you turn 65? In comparison to today, what things do you hope are different in the way older adults experience life when you turn 65 years of age?

The Reality of Older Adults' Life in Canada Today

Although aging can represent a period of increasing freedom from previous lifestyle demands, it more often means increased susceptibility to financial hardship, health problems, social isolation and mental depression. To some extent, many of Canada's older adults face many of the challenges that Canada's First Nations people confront.[22] This is particularly true in regard to personal finances and health.

Personal Finances

- "The economic aspect of aging is one of the most important in the lives of the aging" (Crandell, 1980:506). On average, older adults are not as financially secure as other adult Canadians as the majority are retired and become dependent on social security benefits which is typically significantly lower than their preretirement income. In 2003, older adult couples had an average annual family income of approximately $43,000. This was approximately 27% less than other adult couples (Statistics Canada, 2007:64-65).

- Older adult females who live alone are at greater risk of living in poverty than older adult males and other Canadian adults. In 2003, older adult females who live alone had an annual income of $18,200–approximately 65% lower than other Canadian adults (p.67).

Physical Health

- The concept of "health" is not readily definable. For example, what constitutes "good" health at one stage of life may not apply in a different period. How we perceive our health can have a bearing on how we perceive ourselves. Hence, health is one of the most important aspects of old age.

- The average life expectancy for males who reach 65 years of age is 12.7 years; for women, average life expectancy is 14.1 years (p.44)

- Older adults are less likely to be in "excellent" or "good" health than other Canadians (p.46).

- Older adults are affected by more chronic health conditions, such as cancer, diabetes, heart disease and arthritis/rheumatism than are younger adults (National Advisory Council on Aging, 2006:5-15). The three top chronic problems are arthritis or rheumatism, high blood pressure, and lower back problems.

- Drawing on data from the National Population Health Survey, the most reliable source for health related information in Canada; elderly Canadians also experience more basic limitations to their daily lives that directly/indirectly affect their health. For example, mobility is the number one concern of those over the age of 65. It is followed by hearing problems and then vision (Rosenberg and Moore, 1999).

---

[22]   For marginal groups such as the First Nations people or other ethnic/racial minorities in Canada, being elderly can experience what Jackson et al. (1982) referred to as "double jeopardy." That is in addition to the challenges that aging brings on naturally, these group are often further jeopardized by their minority status.

Mental Health

- Unfortunately, having good mental health throughout life does not make one immune from the risk of depression, Alzheimer's disease, anxiety, or related mental health conditions as we age. At times such conditions can go undiagnosed and may eventually lead to severe depression and possible suicide (Elderly at higher risk…, 2007). The suicide rate among older adult males is higher than the average for older adult females and all other adults. The risk of suicide for older adult males increases by 50% between the ages of 65 and 85 (National Advisory Council on Aging, 2006:13).

- As older adults age, they become increasing more isolated from socializing with friends and relatives (50). As well, their rate of volunteering in community organizations drops as they grow older.

Learning Activity 4 - Discuss

Using the course discussion board or in-class, consider discussing what aspects of the above statistics related to the social conditions of older adults in Canada distresses you the most. Why? What do you think should be done about the social conditions of older adults?

Elder Abuse

It is apparent from the previous observations that as we age, we are confronted with an increasing number of personal issues, which to varying degrees requires, or involves, a degree of dependency on others. This unfortunately exposes the elderly to possible victimization and elder abuse.

Although elder abuse has been a part of societies for as long as there has been recorded history, the problem did not register on the radar of social scientists until the 1980s when the work of Suzanne Steimetz authored an article titled, *Battered Parents*. Her work seemed to trigger a proliferation of related work. At the time she suggested that since the 1960s and 1970s were the decades of awareness of child abuse and wife-beating, perhaps the 1980s marked the awareness (academically and politically) of elder abuse. Today, social scientists, criminal justice practitioners and health care officials are becoming increasingly concerned about the amount of elder abuse in Canadian society (see below).

Types of Elder Abuse

According to the Canadian Department of Justice website (2007), elder abuse can be broken down into three different categories.

- **Psychological Abuse** involves any actions that reduce an older adult's sense of self-worth or dignity and "threatens their psychological and emotional integrity"

(Department of Justice Canada, 2007:2). It includes such examples as threatening violence, threatening abandonment, insulting or demeaning comments and intentionally causing older adults to be concerned about their personal wellbeing.

■ **Physical Abuse** includes any act of violence, regardless of its resulting injury. Intentionally inflicting pain or injury that's results in bodily harm or mental distress is abuse (Department of Justice Canada, 2007:3). It includes such action as hitting, kicking, shoving, burning or scalding, using physical restraints, excessive medication and forcing older adults to remain in bed or in a room.

■ **Financial Abuse** involves the financial manipulation or exploitation of an older adult. This includes such actions as theft, fraud, and borrowing money with no intention of repayment, wrongful use of a Power of Attorney, removing personal items and unauthorized use of personal bank accounts, credit cards and lines of credit (Department of Justice Canada, 2007:3).[23]

Incidences of Elder Abuse

Data from the 1999 General Social Survey of 4,000 adults over the age of 65 provides some indication of the amount of elder abuse in Canada. The survey found that about 7% of those surveyed experienced some form of psychological, financial, and physical abuse in the 5 years prior to the survey (Department of Justice Canada, 2007:774-5). Psychological abuse was the most common type of elder abuse reported. Approximately seven percent said they had either been put down or called names. One percent reported experiencing physical or sexual abuse.

However, it is difficult to know how many older Canadian adults experience some form of elder abuse. Like other forms of abuse, experts feel that most instances of elder abuse go unreported to authorities. There are many reasons for unreported elder abuse. They include among others:

1. It is believed that most elder abuse is perpetrated by someone that the older adult trusts or relies upon (e.g., a family member, friend or care giver) but who may not have the skill set required to deal with an elderly person's needs.

2. Some abused elders do not know to whom they could report the abuse.

3. Some older adults are cognitively incapacitated to recognize they are being abuse.[24]

---

[23] Lau and Kosberg (1979) identified a fourth category of elderly abuse for which there continues to be a dearth of related research. They describe the "violation of rights" as the "forceful eviction from victim's residence and relocation in another setting." Human Rights groups regularly provide examples of the elderly being forced to relocate (especially in developing countries such as China and Egypt) to make way for new developments. See for example: http://www.cohre.org/store/attachments/GLOBAL%20SURVEY%202003-2006.pdf (retrieved Sept. 24, 2007).

[24] For a more detailed review of abuse of older adults visit the website on the "National Clearing House on Family Violence" at: http://www.phac-aspc.gc.ca/ncfv-cnivf/familyviolence/html/ageinstitutions_e.html.

Learning Activity 5 - Online Research

The Canadian Centre for the Prevention of Elder Abuse (CCPEB) has developed an interesting website. The website provides valuable information on the what to do if you are an older adult experiencing abuse, as well as suggestions on how to prevent elder abuse.

Follow this link to the CCPED website and explore its valuable information:

http://www.cnpea.ca/

Older Adults and Canada's Criminal Justice System

As was highlighted in our earlier discussion of youth crime (see Chapter 6), the amount of criminal activity associated with those over the age of 55 is very small (about 4%). The lack of criminal activity among the 65+ age group is even smaller.

It is equally interesting that older adults in Canada are at ***much less risk*** of being a victim of crime. Here are some highlights (Statistics Canada, 2007):

OVERALL CRIME VICTIMIZATION

↓ Older adults in Canada are **3 times less likely** to be a victim of a crime than other Canadians.

↑ Although older adults are much less likely to be victimized, 5 in 10 victimized seniors were victimized by a family member. Four in 10 non-senior victims were victimized by a family member.

VIOLENT CRIME VICTIMIZATION

↓ Older adults are almost **4 times less likely** to be a victim of violence than Canadians between 55 to 64 years of age. In comparison to 15 to 24 year olds, older adults are **20 times less likely** to be a victim of violence.

↑ The most common perpetrators of violence against older adults were their children or current spouse.

PROPERTY CRIME VICTIMIZATION

↓ The rate of personal property theft experienced by older adults is **one half of the rate** experienced by those between the ages of 55 to 64; and 8 times lower than the rate experienced by 15 to 24 year olds.

↓ Older Adults' homes are **3 times less likely** to experience a break and enter.

In this chapter, we have seen that older adults are not only growing in numbers but they are also being confronted with a wide host of problems and challenges that reflect a degree of diversity not given much attention until recently. As Canada's population continues to grow, it becomes ever more imperative that there needs to be more concerted efforts to develop public policy, allocate additional resources, and provide the training and support necessary to ensure the welfare of the elderly.

The reading that follows is comprised of selections from Health Canada's discussion paper entitled "Abuse and Neglect of Older Adults." We have provided the executive summary of the discussion paper, the paper's definitions of elder abuse, information on the characteristics of victims and perpetrators of elder abuse, theories of abuse and neglect and data on risk factors associated with abuse.

Learning Activity 6 - Online Research

In early 2005, the Ottawa Police Service (OPS) was the first police department in Canada to establish a specialized unit to address the issues of elder abuse in the community. Follow this link to see the Ottawa Police website information on this new unit:

http://www.ottawapolice.ca/en/serving_ottawa/support_units/elder_abuse.cfm

What do you think of this initiative by the OPS?

References

Brandt, C. (1978). *Forgotten people: Reaching out to the elderly.* Chicago: Chicago University Press.

Cornwall, C. (May 2000). Canada's hidden crime. *Reader Digest.* Retrieved September 20. 2007, from http://www.readersdigest.ca/mag/2000/05/think_crime.html.

Crandall, R. (1980). *Gerontology: A behavioral science approach.* Reading, MA: Addison-Wesley Publishing.

Department of Justice Canada. (2007). *Abuse of older adults: A fact sheet from the Department of Justice.* Retrieve May 6, 2007 from, http://www.justice.gc.ca/en/ps/fm/adultsfs.html.

"Elderly at higher risk of suicide in U.S." Retrieved September 22, 2007 from, http://www.ctv.ca/servlet/ArticleNews/story/CTVNews/20070918/elderly_suicide_070918/20070918?hub=Health.

"Forced Eviction." (2006). Retrieved September 24, 2007, from http://www.cohre.org/store/attachments/GLOBAL%20SURVEY%202003- 2006.pdf.

Hobbs, F.B. (2001). The elderly population. *U.S. Census Bureau, Population Division and Housing and Household Economic Statistics Division.* Age and sex statistics branch. Washington, DC.

Jackson, M., Kolody, B. and Wood, J. (1982). "To be old and Black: The case for double jeopardy on income and health." In R. Manuel (ed.), *Minority aging: Sociological and social psychological issues.* Westport, Conn.: Greenwood.

Lau, E., and Kosberg, J. (Sept./Oct. 1979). "Abuse of the elderly by informal care providers." *Aging* 299-300:11-15.

National Advisory Council on Aging. (2006). *Seniors in Canada 2006: Report card.* Retrieved April 21, 2007, from http://dsp-psd.pwgsc.gc.ca/Collection/HP30-1-2006E.pdf.

Rosenberg, M., and Moore, E. (1997). "The health of Canada's elderly population: Current status and future implications." *CMAJ* 157:1025-32.

Sharpe, C.C. (2004). *Fraud against the elderly.* Jefferson, N. Carolina: McFarland & Co.

Statistics Canada. (2005). *Criminal victimization in Canada, 2004.* Catalogue no. 85-002-XPE, vol. 25, no. 7. Retrieved April 10, 2007, from http://www.statcan.ca/bsolc/english/bsolc?catno=85-002-X20050078803.

Statistics Canada. (2006). *Crime statistics in Canada.* Catalogue no. 85-002-XIE, vol. 26, no. 4. Retrieved April 12, 2007, from, http://www.statcan.ca/Daily/English/040601/d040601a.htm.

Statistics Canada. (2007a). *A portrait of seniors in Canada, 2006.* Catalogue no. 89-591-XIE. Retrieved April 12, 2007, from http://www.statcan.ca/english/freepub/89-519-XIE/89-519-XIE2006001.pdf.

Statistics Canada. (2007b). *Seniors as victims of crime: 2004 and 2005.* Catalogue no. 85F0033MIE, no. 14. Retrieved May 2, 2007, from http://www.statcan.ca/english/research/85F0033MIE/85F0033MIE2007014.htm.

Steimetz, S.K. (July/Aug. 1878). "Battered parents." *Society* 54-55.

PART TWO

Unit Three: Older Adults

Chapter 9

Abuse and Neglect of Older Adults: A Discussion Paper
L. McDonald and A. Collins*

■ Learning Activity 1 - Fun Quiz

Take this fun quiz before you read the chapter. Answer "True" or "False":

1.   The amount of research into elder abuse in Canada is very extensive.

2.   We are confident that we know how much elder abuse is taking place in Canada.

3.   All provinces in Canada have enacted legislation aimed at protecting vulnerable older adults.

4.   The first major national survey into elder abuse in Canada was conducted about 20 years ago.

5.   Defining what we mean by the term "elder abuse" has proven to be a simple task.

6.   One of the symptoms of elder neglect is poor personal hygiene.

7.   Cognitive impairment puts older adults at greater risk of becoming a victim of elder abuse.

8.   Many of the perpetrators of elder abuse are family members.

9.   The most widely accepted explanation for elder abuse is that the perpetrator of the abuse is responding to an overly stressful situation.

10.   The incidence of elder abuse is increasing in Canada.

ANSWERS: 1F, 2F, 3T, 4T, 5F, 6T, 7T, 8T, 9T, 10T

▮ Executive Summary

As the decade comes to a close, it has become increasingly clear that abuse and neglect of older adults has come to be recognized as a problem worthy of serious academic inquiry and coordinated social action on the part of all Canadians. The purpose of this paper is to provide an overview of the important developments that have occurred in the field since the publication of the first discussion paper in 1989. Existing problems in defining abuse and neglect, issues surrounding data on incidence and prevalence, the lack of progress on the theoretical front and the related problems of identifying risk factors are revisited. Changes in adult protection legislation, along with advances in the creation of protocols for detection, intervention, and programming are described. We conclude by surveying some of the preventive strategies that have been adopted across Canada in recent years and by offering suggestions for future directions.

Issues related to definitions have historically generated considerable controversy in discussions about abuse and neglect of older adults, and these still persist today. Consequently, there continues to be a multitude of definitions available in the literature. Most would agree, however, that there are three major categories (domestic abuse and neglect, institutional abuse and neglect, self abuse and neglect) and three major types of abuse (physical, psychological and financial). Unfortunately, beyond this, little agreement exists. Stakeholders appear to be growing tired of the continued debate around definitions, nevertheless, this issue should not be shelved. It remains important because definitions determine who will be counted as abused and who will not; what the legislation does and does not cover; and who is and is not eligible for service. Thus, as Canada approaches the next millennium, the challenge will be to sharpen the definitions; seek agreement among practitioners, academics, legislators, and policy- makers about definitions; incorporate perspectives on abuse and neglect articulated by our ethnic communities and ensure the participation of those most affected by the definitions—the seniors themselves.

To date, a substantial number of studies have documented the existence and nature of abuse and neglect of older adults. However, only a few have provided data on the prevalence and incidence of the problem among non-institutionalized seniors. Accurate data has been difficult to obtain because of differences in definitions, methodologies and samples. Consequently, at this time, it is not possible, with any degree of confidence, to interpret the reported prevalence rates, which vary from 1 to 4% in Australia, Norway, the United States, and Canada to a high of 20% in France. Incidence rates are still unknown in most countries, including Canada. Therefore, there is no way of knowing whether abuse and neglect is getting better or worse. In Canada, we only have prevalence data from 1989 which, at best, offers a quick snapshot of the problem. From the standpoint of strategic planning, two priorities have emerged. The first is the need to know the actual dimensions of the problem so that interventions can be calibrated to meet them. This could be achieved through follow-up with the participants in the Ryerson study (1989). Additionally, an incidence study, comparable to the National Incidence Study on Child Abuse, is necessary to help plan for the future.

Canadians have been slow to investigate the abuse and neglect of older adults in institutions. Despite this, there is evidence to suggest that this is a widespread problem. In Canada, however,

---

*   Reprinted in part with permission from: Health Canada (2000). Abuse and neglect of older adults: A discussion paper. Ottawa, ON: Health Canada

there are currently no real incidence or prevalence studies of abuse and neglect in institutions. Additionally, few theories have been offered to explain this phenomenon. North American scholars have articulated a number of hypotheses. These include: the lack of comprehensive policies with respect to infirm seniors; financial incentives that contribute to poor- quality care are built into the long-term care system; poor enforcement of institutional standards; poorly trained staff; and work related stress.

The last decade had seen increasing pressure placed on Canadian institutions to establish protocols for detection, intervention, and prevention of abuse and neglect. While these are long overdue, no information is available on how many facilities have incorporated these strategies and no information is available on whether they work. It is argued, therefore, that at this time, prevalence studies are needed to quantify how many older adults are abused or neglected in institutions at any given point in time. This would document the extent of the current problem and, in turn, allow us to focus on where and how limited resources should be used. At the same time, incidence studies are needed to provide clues about the etiology of abuse. These would also provide us with the data to evaluate the efficacy of preventive programs. Finally, the *outcomes* of abuse need serious consideration because there appears to be some evidence that abuse is associated with increased mortality rates in institutions.

With respect to our current knowledge about the characteristics of victims and perpetrators, a decade and a half of research can be summarized in the following way: victims of psychological and physical abuse are often in good health but suffer from psychological problems, while their abusers often have a history of psychiatric illness and/or substance abuse, often live with the victims, and are financially dependent; patients with dementia who exhibit disruptive behaviour and who live with family caregivers are more likely to suffer physical abuse, while their abusive caregivers may have low self-esteem and may be clinically depressed; a typical financial abuse victim may not exist; and victims of neglect tend to be very old, with cognitive and physical incapacities, which serves as a source of stress for their caregiver. Importantly, race and ethnicity have emerged in the literature as two new risk factors, but most of the discussion to date has been based on speculation.

A review of the abuse and neglect literature suggests that there have been few new developments on the theoretical front. Because there is such a paucity of incidence studies in the world, it is not surprising that little headway has been made in this regard. At present, most people still rely on the same old theories with the same old flaws. Importantly, there is still a strong tendency to blur the boundaries between theoretical explanations and the individual risk factors related to abuse. For example, specific risk factors, like stress, are often treated as full theoretical explanations even though stress is a factor that could be incorporated into many different theories. At present, at least four distinct theoretical perspectives are available in the literature. They are the situational model, social exchange theory, symbolic interactionism, and the feminist model. Recently, there has been some suggestion that there may not be one all inclusive explanation for abuse and neglect of older adults. If this is the case, it is suggested that theorists will have to cast their nets wider than the current gerontological and family violence literature.

Investigations into the specific factors hypothesized to be associated with abuse and neglect remains limited and those that do exist suffer from significant methodological problems. The principal factors that have been associated with abuse include the personality traits of the abuser, the intergenerational transmission of violence, dependency, stress, and social structural factors such as ageism—all of which can be subsumed under any of the previously mentioned theories. At present, because the field has made such little progress. it is unwise to assume that we can predict who will he abused and/or neglected regardless of how many protocols exist or how elaborate they are. At the direct service level, there are few formal response protocols, policies, and procedures; those that do exist range from unsystematic assessments that rely on professional judgement rather than objective data, to checklists of risk indicators. Many of the screening and assessment tools currently in use are based on assumptions found in the domestic violence literature and, thus, contain the same weaknesses found in the field. Currently, there is a clear content bias toward issues related to physical abuse and neglect. As such, the instruments available today most likely catch only a small percentage of the total abuse cases.

Four major kinds of programs have been developed to respond to abuse and neglect: the statutory adult protection service programs; programs based on the domestic violence model; advocacy programs for seniors; and an integrated model. All fifty states in the United States and four Canadian provinces have dealt with the problem of abuse and neglect by enacting special adult protection legislation. This approach is influenced by child welfare models and is characterized by legal powers of investigation, intervention, and mandatory reporting. There has been, and continues to be, considerable controversy over adult protection legislation and programming. Proponents argue that such intervention means that the rights of older adults are safeguarded, and that attempts can be made to improve their quality of life while protecting them from harm. Opponents vigorously challenge this position and suggest that this system of care infantilizes seniors and violates their independence.

The domestic violence approach has gained considerable momentum in North America because it is not seen as violating people's rights, or as discriminating on the basis of age. This response consists of a multi-pronged approach that includes a whole range of health, social, and legal resources. This model is not without critics who are quick to point out problems with police response and restraining orders, poorly managed shelters, and a shortage of follow-up services. This model also fails to apply in eases of neglect.

Like the domestic violence model, an advocacy approach acknowledges that the older adult is potentially vulnerable and may be in a dangerous situation. Advocacy programs believe that the least restrictive and intrusive interventions should be used. Advocacy undoubtedly plays a role in protecting and furthering the rights of victims. However, knowing one's rights is one thing—acting on them is another. Those who can assert themselves are more likely to gain attention. Unfortunately, many victims are in need of help but, because of disability or isolation, may not get the assistance they require.

An observable trend at the direct service level has been the development of multidisciplinary teams using an integrated model. Although little research has established the efficacy of this approach, many believe that it enhances the quality and quantity of care. The main drawback appears to be that teams spend more time per case than professionals acting alone.

A glaring lack of program evaluation still exists in the field. At present, even the most fundamental questions about what types of services work, for whom, and under what circumstances, remain unanswered. This is an area that requires immediate attention. Evaluation is important, and thus, it has been suggested that deliberation by clinicians, researchers, and seniors about how to measure the effectiveness of interventions would be useful at this critical juncture.

At present, there appears to be three major types of roadblocks to the provision of services to abuse seniors. Some are associated with client variables, some are attributed to front-line practitioners and others exist as a result of broader systems level issues. The most obvious barrier is related to the hesitancy of victims to engage with services. At the system level, barriers include: agency mandates that do not specifically address abuse and neglect; inadequate funding of appropriate resources; and an overall lack of coordination among existing services. What is needed at this time is a broad-based community response that includes services that are available, affordable, accessible, known, and perceived as appropriate by the seniors themselves. It also appears that mainstream services do not appropriately address the needs of seniors from diverse backgrounds. This alone presents many challenges at the service delivery level.

Education and public awareness are critical elements in any comprehensive approach to abuse and neglect of older adults. This includes the education of older adults themselves, professionals, caregivers and the public. A number of exciting and innovative programs have developed within Canada in this regard.

Thus, when one reflects on the developments in the field of abuse and neglect of older adults in the last decade, there is reason to be proud because considerable progress has been made. This is not to suggest that there is nothing more to be done. Most of our progress has been made in the areas of prevention and intervention, with only small gains in the area of research. It seems that the next logical step for Canada would be the formation of a national organization devoted to the abuse and neglect of older adults that could pull together the strands of practice, education, and research. From this, a national strategy for action can be developed through the participation of all stakeholders, the most important of which being Canadian seniors.

Learning Activity 2 - Online Research

One type of evidence that our society is becoming more concerned about the incidence of elder abuse is the availability of on-line material related to its identification and prevention. One example of this on-line material is a site developed by the Government of Canada.

Follow this link and explore the information provided:

http://www.seniors.gc.ca/c.4nt.2nt3col@.jsp?cid=161

1: The Canadian Context

The purpose of this paper is to provide a general overview of the major developments that have occurred in the field of elder abuse and neglect since the publication of the first discussion paper in 1989. To this end, we revisit the problems of defining abuse and neglect; the issues about the incidence and prevalence of abuse; progress on the theoretical front; and related problems of identifying risk factors for abuse and neglect. Changes in adult protection legislation and related research are examined and advances in creating protocols for detection and intervention, as well as innovations in programming, are considered. The discussion concludes by surveying some of the preventive strategies adopted across Canada and setting out some ideas for future research.

The field of elder abuse has expanded dramatically since the appearance of the first federal discussion paper in 1989 (Gnaedinger, 1989). At that time, elder abuse had just been recognized as another form of family violence, similar in status to child abuse, "discovered" in the 1960s, and wife abuse, identified in the 1970s. Although the first reference to elder abuse was made in Britain in the 1970s (Baker, 1975; Burston, 1975), the issue had far greater prominence in the United States at that time, with Canada following suit in the 1980s. The first prevalence studies—by Belanger (1981) and Grandrnaison (1988) in Quebec, Shell (1982) and King (1984) in Manitoba, the G.A. Frecker Association on Gerontology (1.983) in Newfoundland, Haley (1984) in Nova Scotia, Stevenson (1985) in Alberta, and the Ontario Advisory Council on Senior Citizens (1985) in Ontario suggested that an appreciable proportion of Canadian seniors were being mistreated at the hands of their caregivers.

In the late 1980s, the first Canadian book on abuse, written by Schlesinger and Schlesinger (1988), served to formally alert the field to some of the more distressing issues practitioners and legislators had to face. The authors unearthed over 200 North American papers on the abuse and neglect of older adults, providing the first annotated bibliography for Canadians. During the 1980s, the need to respond to the problem prompted an examination of adult protection legislation and a consideration of the pros and cons of mandatory reporting of abuse. The initial debates, restricted to a small cadre of practitioners and academics, provided the impetus for reforms to adult guardianship and adult protection legislation—a process that had begun in 1973 in Newfoundland and 1976 in Alberta. At the same time, the federal and provincial governments of Canada began funding various research, educational, and intervention initiatives, all of which supported the drive to produce irrefutable evidence of the existence of abuse and neglect of older adults.

In 1989, the landmark national survey, by Elizabeth Podnieks, revealed that four percent of elderly Canadians living in private dwellings experienced some form of abuse and neglect (Podnieks, 1990). The publication of this study brought the first era of Canadian research on elder abuse to a favourable conclusion. A small but important group of enterprising practitioners, aided by an even smaller group of researchers, had succeeded in bringing the disturbing social problem of elder abuse and neglect to the attention of Canadians.

The 1990s saw a new era characterized by an ever-increasing commitment to research, education, and action on behalf of Canada's abused and neglected older adults. Today, numerous national, provincial, and local conferences directed toward professionals, the public, and seniors themselves, are offered to address the multitude of issues related to the abuse and neglect of older adults (e.g., *One Voice* 1995; Health and Welfare Canada, 1997). A wealth of educational materials is regularly produced, from the local to the national level, and governments, despite fewer resources, continue to fund innovative responses to the problem (e.g., British Columbia Seniors Advisory Council, 1992; Health and Welfare Canada, 1992; Health and Welfare, 1993; Mackenzie and Senechal, 1991; Wasylkewycz, 1993; Wigdor, 1991).

The early 1990s saw the introduction of a whole new generation of researchers who, moving beyond proving that elder abuse was a social problem, began to conduct research designed to guide practice and the formulation of policy, and, to a lesser extent, the reform of legislation (e.g., Beaulieu, 1992; Pittaway and Westhues, 1993; Poirier, 1992; Reis and Nahmiash, 1995a; Stones and Pittman, 1995; Sweeney, 1995), As the decade comes to a close, abuse of older adults has been recognized as a critical problem, worthy of serious' academic inquiry and concerted social action on the part of all Canadians. As Canada approaches the next millennium, we take stock of these developments, the new issues they raise, and their implications for the seniors of tomorrow.

Learning Activity 3 - Journal Entry

In your course journal or notes, discuss the following questions.

1. Why do you think that only a fraction of elder abuse is reported in Canada?
2. Why would a victim of elder abuse not report it to authorities?
3. Can you think of any other type of abuse that goes unreported to the police?
4. How are these types similar to elder abuse?

2: Defining Abuse and Neglect

2.1: Proposed Definitions

A leading researcher in the field of elder abuse observed that "from the very beginning of the scientific investigation into the nature and causes of elder abuse definitions have been a major issue" (Wolf, 1988:758). The lack of a generally acceptable definition has spawned a wide variety of definitions of abuse and neglect, which, to this day, still generates controversy and debate (Bennett, 1990; Council of Europe, 1.992; Decalmer and Glendenning, 1993; Kozma and Stones, 1995; Sanchez, 1996; Wallace, 1996). Nevertheless, most would agree on three basic categories of abuse and neglect: (1) domestic elder abuse; (2) institutional abuse; and (3) self- neglect or self-abuse. Most would also agree on the major types of abuse—physical, psychological, and financial abuse. Beyond this classification, however, there is little agreement (Decalmer and Glendenning, 1993; Hudson, 1994; Wolf, 1992).

Choosing definitions is obviously risky. For the purposes of this paper, the definitions of abuse will be based on those set out by the National Centre on Elder Abuse (NCEA) in the United States, mainly because there is some consensus on their utility. "Domestic elder abuse" generally refers to any of several forms of maltreatment of an older person by someone who has a special relationship with the senior, such as a spouse; a sibling, a child, a friend, or a caregiver, in the older person's own home or in the caregiver's home (NCEA, 1998). The abuse is called "domestic abuse" because it occurs in the community, rather than in an institution such as a nursing home. The abusive behaviour can cause physical, psychological, and material injury to the older person, resulting in distress and suffering (Hudson, 1991; McDonald, 1996).

"Physical abuse" is defined as the use of physical force that may result in bodily injury, physical pain, or impairment. Physical abuse may include, but is not limited to, such acts of violence as striking (with or without an object), hitting, beating, pushing, shoving, shaking. slapping, kicking, pinching, and burning (National Centre on Elder Abuse (NCEA), 1998; Stones, 1995; Wolf and Pillemer, 1989). Such maltreatment as the inappropriate use of drugs, and physical restraints and force-feeding are also considered physical abuse (NCEA, 1998).

Sexual abuse, which is sometimes subsumed under physical abuse (McDonald, 1996), is defined as non-consensual sexual contact of any kind with an older adult. Sexual contact with any person incapable of giving consent is also considered sexual abuse. It includes, but is not limited to, unwanted touching and all types of sexual assault or battery, such as rape, sodomy, coerced nudity, and sexually explicit photographing (NCEA, 1998).

"Psychological (or emotional) abuse" is defined as the infliction of anguish, pain, or distress through verbal or non-verbal acts. This type of abuse includes, but is not limited to, verbal assaults, insults, threats, intimidation, humiliation and harassment. Other examples of emotional abuse include treating an older person like an infant; isolating the person from his or her family, friends, or regular activities; giving the older person the "silent treatment"; and enforced social isolation.

"Material abuse," often referred to as "financial abuse," involves the illegal or improper exploitation of an older person's funds, property, or assets. Examples include, but are not limited to, cashing an elderly person's cheques without authorization, forging an older person's signature, misusing or stealing an older person's money or possessions, coercing or deceiving an older person into signing any document (e.g., a will), and the improper use of guardianship or power of attorney ((Jordon, 1992; Health and Welfare Canada, 1993; McDonald, 1996; NCEA, 1998). Acts such as theft, physical assault, rape, and burglary by a person *outside* of a trusting relationship with the older person usually would not be classified as elder abuse but rather as crimes. Crimes against the elderly include some, but not all, forms of elder abuse (Health and Welfare Canada, 1993; McDonald, 1996).

"Neglect" is intentional or unintentional harmful behaviour on the part of an informal or formal caregiver in whom the older person has placed his or her trust. Unintentional neglect involves a failure to fulfill a caretaking responsibility, but the caregiver does not intend to harm the older person; intentional neglect occurs when the caregiver consciously and purposely fails to meet the needs of the older person, resulting in psychological, physical, or material injury to the older person (McDonald, 1996). "Neglect" typically refers to the refusal or failure to provide an older person with the necessities of life, such as water, food, clothing, shelter, personal hygiene, medicine, comfort, personal safety, and other essentials (NCEA, 1998). Neglect is also difficult to ascertain, because the symptoms can easily be confused with illness (Filinson and Ingman, 1989). Some of the signs of neglect appear in Table 9.1.

Self-neglect" is characterized as behaviour by an older adult that threatens his or her own health and safety. "Self-neglect" usually means that the older adult refuses or fails to provide himself or herself with the necessities of life noted above. This newer definition of self-neglect excludes situations in which a mentally competent older person knowingly makes a voluntary decision to engage in acts that threaten his or her safety (NCEA, 1998). The signs and symptoms are similar to neglect by a caregiver. There is some question as to whether self-neglect should be included in a consideration of neglect and abuse of older adults, because no abusive caregivers are involved

Table 9.1 - Signs and Symptoms of Abuse

PHYSICAL ABUSE

- bruises, black eyes, welts,
- lacerations, rope marks
- bone fractures, broken bones, skull fractures
- open wounds, cuts, punctures, untreated injuries in various stages of healing
- sprains, dislocations, and internal injuries/bleeding
- broken eyeglasses, signs of being restrained
- laboratory findings of medication overdose or underutilization of prescribed drugs
- an older person's report of being hit, slapped, kicked, or mistreated
- an older person's sudden change in behaviour
- a caregiver's refusal to allow visitors to see an older adult

FINANCIAL/MATERIAL ABUSE

- sudden changes in bank account or banking practices
- the inclusion of additional names on older person's bank signature card
- unauthorized withdrawal of the older person's funds using the person's ATM card
- abrupt change in will or other financial documents, unexplained disappearance of funds or valuable possessions
- paid bills despite adequate funds
- discovery of forgery of older person's signature
- unexplained sudden transfer of assets to someone in or outside the family
- an older adult's report of financial exploitation

ABANDONMENT

- desertion of an older person at the hospital, nursing facility or institution
- desertion of the older person at a shopping centre or other public location
- an older person's report of being abandoned

SEXUAL ABUSE

- bruises around the breasts or genital areas
- unexplained venereal disease or genital infections
- unexplained vaginal or anal bleeding
- torn, stained, or bloody underclothing
- an older person's report of being sexually assaulted or raped

EMOTIONAL/PSYCHOLOGICAL ABUSE

- being emotionally upset or agitated
- being extremely withdrawn, non-communicative, non-responsive
- unusual behaviour usually attributed to dementia(e.g., sucking, biting, rocking)
- an older person's report of being verbally or emotionally abused

Table 9.2 - Signs and Symptoms of Neglect and Self-Neglect

NEGLECT
- dehydration, malnutrition, untreated bedsores, poor personal hygiene
- unattended or untreated health problems
- hazardous or unsafe living conditions (dirt, soiled bedding, smell)

SELF-NEGLECT
- dehydration, malnutrition, untreated bedsores, poor personal hygiene
- unattended or untreated health problems
- hazardous or unsafe living conditions (e.g., improper wiring, no heat)
- unsanitary or unclean living conditions (smell)
- inappropriate and/or inadequate
- clothing, lack of medical aids (e.g., eye glasses, hearing aid)
- grossly inadequate housing and homelessness

Note: Adapted from the National Centre on Elder Abuse (1998).

Most recently, abandonment has been added to the list of abuse. "Abandonment" is defined as the desertion of an older adult by an individual who has assumed responsibility for providing care for that person or by a person with physical custody of an older adult (NCEA, 1998). The most common signs and symptoms are listed in Table 9.1.

2.2: Definitional Disputes

Many elder abuse professionals are weary of the continuing search for definitions of elder abuse and neglect. However, the issue remains an important one: the definition determines who is counted as abused and who is not; the definition determines what the legislation does and does not cover; and it determines who is and is not eligible for service. The definition will also determine the type of treatment offered and, ultimately, the effectiveness of the treatment in stopping the abuse. Thus, accurate definitions of abuse and neglect ensure accuracy in screening, classification, and appropriate treatment.

In addition, the variations in the definitions of elder abuse make it impossible to pool or compare data collected from different provinces in Canada, or even social agencies in any given city. Without standardized definitions of abuse, cross-national comparisons are also out of the question. If Canada were to conduct another study to determine the prevalence of abuse as it did in 1989, we would have to retain the original definitions of abuse if we were to judge whether the problem had grown better or worse since that time (Podnieks, 1992).

The "definitional disarray" noted by Piliemer and Firikelhor (1988:52) can be attributed to a number of factors. One clear difficulty is that the definitions have been developed from different perspectives—the abused older person, the caregiver, the health professional, the lawyer, the police, the social worker and the policy-maker. So, while the behaviour of a police officer is probably affected by definitions of elder abuse found in the Criminal Code, a community worker will follow agency policy, which, more than likely, will encourage a broader definition of abuse, in order to cover all contingencies in the community. The difference in perspective is easily illustrated: for example, a Canadian study revealed that there was considerable difference between the public's view of physical abuse and that of abuse professionals (Gebotys, O'Connor and Mair, 1992). The legal definitions of abuse and neglect also vary across jurisdictions in Canada. For example, in Newfoundland, the legislation applies only to "neglected" adults, and makes no provision for cases of abuse, whereas the legislation in British Columbia provides a specific definition of abuse (Robertson, 1995).

A review of the earlier literature on the abuse of older adults indicates the tendency of researchers and practitioners to develop taxonomies or typologies (lists of types) of elder abuse and neglect (Block and Sinnot, 1979; Chen et al., 1981; Hickey and Douglass. 1981; Lau and Kosberg, 1979; McDonald et al., 1991: Pillerner and Finkelhor, 1988; Rathbone-McCuan and Voyles, 1982; Sengstock and Hwalek, 1987; Sengstock and Liang, 1983; Steinmetz, 1988) or to try to develop broad, all-encompassing conceptual definitions that capture the multi-dimensional nature of abuse (Filinson, 1989; Fulmer and O'Malley, 1987; Hudson, 1988; Johnson, 1986, 1991; O'Malley et al., 1979, 1983; Podnieks, 1985; Rathbone-McCuan, 1980; Wolf, 1988).

The problem with descriptive lists of different types of abuses is that there is no uniformity among the categories used by the experts or within the categories themselves. Some researchers, for example, include violation of rights as a category, while other researchers omit this category (Lau and Kosberg, 1979; Sengstock and Hwalek, 1987). As well, the categories contain such a wide range of abuses that they tend to become ineffectual in application because every act becomes abusive or neglectful. The conceptual definitions also suffer from problems. Typical examples include the definitions by Fulmer and O'Malley (1987) "...actions of a caretaker that create unmet needs for the eider person" (p.27) or the one by Johnson (1991) "...self- or other-imposed suffering unnecessary to the maintenance of the quality of life of the older person by means of abuse and neglect caused by being overwhelmed" (p.4). The first definition focuses on the outcome of abuse, while the second refers to the causal factors, the means, and the outcome of abuse (Johnson, 1991; Stones, 1995). The unevenness of the conceptual definitions and their imprecise nature cause confusion for researchers and workers alike.

2.3: The 1990s and Beyond

Even though the terminology of abuse remains in a state of flux, there has been a concerted effort in the 1990s to address the lack of consensus around definitions of abuse and neglect. Researchers have "researched" definitions themselves, with some interesting results. Canadian researcher Michael Stones (1995) finds three basic approaches to the meaning and definitions of abuse and neglect found in the professional literature. He shows that there are connotative definitions that emphasize the consequences of abuse, such as the two examples above from Johnson (1991) and Fulmer and O'Malley (1987). There are definitions based on structural criteria that highlight the criteria to be used to determine whether behaviour is abusive. Stones (1995) refers to his own definition as an example: "A misdemeanor against acknowledged standards by someone a senior has reason to trust" (p.114). The third approach is to use denotative definitions, which are the same as the descriptive lists noted above and which appear in Table 9.2. The examples in Table 9.2 are a result of the compilation of an abuse inventory created through several rounds of agreement about different types of abuses on the part of seniors and practitioners (Stones, 1995).

The conceptual framework by Stones brings a new clarity to the issue of definitions. The continuing attempt to include seniors and caregivers in the definitional process is crucial if all Canadians are to identify abuse (Beaulieu, 1992; Hudson, 1994; Johnson, 1995; Nandlal and. Wood, 1997).

Some Norwegian scholars use the science of meaning (semiology) to understand acts of abuse (Johns, Hydle and Aschjem, 1991) and have developed a model in which abuse of older adults is a social act, involving a witness with a clear understanding and a moral evaluation of the event. This reflects quite a different view from North American perspectives which, until very recently, did not emphasize the moral aspects of abuse.

Even as the weaknesses of existing definitions are being tackled, new issues are complicating the matter. The globalization of activities related to abuse and neglect of older adults brings new definitional challenges, as a result of the intellectual contributions made by various nations from around the world. This variety of perspectives has also helped to refocus our attention on the multicultural diversity of our own Canadian society. For example, in a recent review of cross-cultural perspectives on the abuse of older adults, the concept of abandonment was introduced into the definition of elder abuse in India (Shah, Veedon and Vasi, 1995) and in Hong Kong (Kwan, 1995). Abandonment has also now been included by the NCEA in the United States. In some countries, definitions of abase do not include age, often because the lower life expectancy of the population precludes most people from entering old age (Kosberg and Garcia, 1995a). Closer to home, Tindale (1994) rightfully laments the lack of research on ethnic differences in patterns of abuse and neglect of older adults in Canada. A few Canadian studies of ethnocultural communities by the Aboriginal Nurses Association of Canada (1992), Bergin (1995) and Spencer (1996), represent a step in the right direction, but they are only a beginning. The first national conference on understanding and combating elder abuse in minority populations was held as recently as 1997 in the United States, indicating that our knowledge in this area is, at best, preliminary.

The 1990s has also seen the "discovery" of another group of Canadians who are at risk for abuse: disabled persons, who in some quarters are included with the population of abused older adults under the more inclusive phrase "vulnerable adults" (Mickish, 1993; Health and Welfare Canada, 1997; Roeher Institute, 1995; Sobsey, 1994). The rationale for this classification is that more disabled persons are living into old age, and they share many of the needs and interests of abused older adults. There is also an implication that amalgamating the groups will help to maximize the effect of scarce resources for combating the problems of both groups (Health and Welfare Canada, 1997). While combining resources will undoubtedly benefit both groups, it remains to be seen how the merger will be viewed by the disabled and the elderly, and how they will respond to sharing the label "vulnerable adults"—another term that will require definition.

The challenge of the next century, then, will be to continue to hone the definitions of abuse and neglect; to continue to seek agreement among practitioners, academics, legislators and policymakers about the definitions; to incorporate perspectives on abuse that represent Canada's ethnic communities and, perhaps, the disabled communities; and to ensure and enhance the participation of those most affected by the construction of definitions—the seniors in Canada (McDonald, Hamick, Robertson, and Wallace, 1991).

Learning Activity 4 - Discussion

Read the following information about the rise of elder abuse in care facilities in Ontario: http://www.cbc.ca/canada/story/2007/10/17/violence-nursing-homes.html#skip300x250

Discuss your thoughts on the following questions:

1. What ideas do you have on some ways to minimize the amount of elder abuse that is taking place in care facilities across Canada?
2. Are there more solutions than enacting a criminal law? If so, what might they be?

5: Characteristics of Victims and Perpetrators

The first wave of research on elder abuse, which began in the late 1970s in the United States, concluded that the typical victim was over 75 years of age, a female with debilitating physical and psychological impairments, and dependent upon a family caregiver, usually a daughter (Douglass, Hickey and Noel, 1980; Hwalek, 1989; Kosberg, 1988; O'Malley et al., 1983; Rathbone-McCuan, 1980; Sengstock and Hang, 1983; Shell, 1982; Stevenson, 1985; Wolf, 1986). Research at the end of the 1980s, based on sounder methodologies and more clinical experience, cast some doubt on early observations and indicated that the situation was far more complicated than originally presumed (McDonald, 1996). The focal point shifted from classifications of the victims to classifications of the perpetrators, and to profiles of different combinations of victims, perpetrators, and types of abuse (Bendik, 1992; Hocking, 1994; Homer and Gilleard, 1990; Pillemer, 1993; Spencer, 1995; Wolf, Godkin and Pillemer, 1986). Today, more and more researchers are uncovering the *interactive* aspects of elder abuse, and distinctions between patient- directed, patient-generated, and mutual abuse (Coyne, Reichmann and Berhig, 1993; Grafstrorn, Nordberg and Winblad, 1993; Homer and Gilleard, 1990; Nolan, 1993; Pillemer and Suitor, 1992).

A decade and a half of research can be distilled into four major observations:

1. Victims of psychological and physical abuse usually have reasonably good physical health, but suffer from psychological problems. Their abusers have a history of psychiatric illness and/of substance abuse, live with the victim, and depend on them for financial resources (Anetzberger, Korbin and Austin, 1994; Bristowe and Collins, 1989; Cooney and Mortimer, 1995; Greenberg, McKibben and Raymond, 1990; Homer and Gilleard, 1990; Paveza et al., 1992).

2. Patients with dementia, who exhibit disruptive behaviour and who live with family caregivers, are more likely to be victims of physical abuse. Their abusive caregivers may suffer from low self-esteem and clinical depression (Compton, Flanagan and Gregg, 1997; Coyne, 1991; Coyne et al., 1993; Homer and Gilleard, 1990; Paveza et al., 1992; Pillemer and Suitor, 1992).

3. There may not be a "typical" victim of financial abuse; however, when the abused person is dependent on the abuser, the financial abuse may be more serious (Rowe et al., 1993; Spencer, 1996).

4. Victims of neglect tend to be very old, with cognitive and physical incapacities. Their dependency on their caregivers serves as a source of stress (Bennett and Kingston, 1993; Wolf, 1992).

Race and ethnicity are two "new" risk factors considered in the elder abuse literature but most of the discussion is based on speculation (Bergin, 1995; Browne, 1989; Dunn, 1992; Cider, 1989; Griffin, 1994; Lachs et al., 1994; Longres, 1992; Maxwell and Maxwell, 1992; Moon and Williams, 1993; Spencer, 1996; Tomita, 1994). A study by Lachs et al. (1994) of 2,800 men and women in Connecticut showed that adults with minority status were more likely to undergo official investigation for alleged mistreatment than adults with non-minority status. In smaller studies that examined cases of abused minority older adults and non-minority adults, the results are contradictory (Hail, 1987; Longres, 1992). The national exploratory study by the Canadian Association of Social Workers (Bergin, 1995) found no compelling differences in the circumstances associated with elder abuse in ethnocultural communities, except for the obvious difficulties related to language barriers and the problems associated with adapting to life in Canada.

Although some ground has been gained in identifying the characteristics of victims of abuse, the emphasis in current research has shifted to an examination of the interactional aspects of abuse. This approach appears to bold some promise for accurately identifying abuse. Investigators now focusing on the abused older adult are also more interested in the consequences of abuse, a topic that is surprisingly absent in the research literature. Depression, mortality, learned helplessness and post-traumatic stress are some of the outcomes that are currently being investigated (Wolf, 1997).

6: Theories of Abuse and Neglect

A survey of the elder abuse literature suggests few new developments on the theoretical front (McDonald and Wigdor, 1995; McDonald, 1996). As noted above, an incidence study would be the most effective mechanism for examining the causes of abuse and neglect of older adults; and, because there are so few incidence studies anywhere in the world, it is no surprise that there has been little headway in theory building. Without fresh evidence, most professionals still rely on the same theories, with the same flaws. The very few theoretical advances are offshoots of a political economy approach (Riggs et al., 1995) and the growing influence of postmodernism on all aspects of gerontology (Katz, 1996).

At the outset, it is important to note that much of the literature on elder abuse does not make an essential distinction between theoretical explanations and the individual risk factors related to abuse (McDonald., 1996; McDonald et al., 1991). Typically, a theory provides a general, systematic explanation of how sonic part of the world works. In the elder abuse literature, a particular risk factor, such as stress, is often treated as *the* theoretical explanation even though stress is only one factor, and could be subsumed by a number of divergent theories. The relationships between the various risk factors and elder abuse should, in fact, form the crucial scaffolding upon which theories are built.

In the short history of elder abuse, different accounts of the relationships among the risk factors have led to at least four distinct theoretical perspectives, all of which have been "borrowed" from other disciplines and fields of study, usually, with few modifications being made in the transfer to the field of elder abuse.

6.1: The Situational Model

The first and most widely accepted perspective on the cause of elder abuse is the situational model, which has its roots in the mainstream perspectives on child abuse and family violence (McDonald et al., 1991; Phillips, 1986). A well-known premise of the situational model is that stressful situations cause the caregiver to abuse the older person, who is usually viewed as the source of the stress because of his or her physical or mental impairment. This approach implies that mistreatment is an irrational response to stressful situations. The situational variables that this theory associates with abuse include factors related to the caregiver, to the older person, and to the social and economic conditions of both parties (McDonald, 1996). An unemployed caregiver who has an alcohol problem may abuse an older parent who is financially secure but mentally impaired. Interventions grounded in this perspective attempt to reduce the stress of the caregiver by providing more support services and support groups (Seogin et al., 1992).

One major flaw of this perspective is that it fails to account for the fact that some caregivers, who experience the same stresses as abusers, do not abuse their elderly. The perspective has also been criticized for being dangerously close to blaming the victim, because it identifies the older person as the source of the stress. This is not an idle criticism, if one remembers that in one study, 7 out of I 0 nurses perceived the patient as the primary cause of the abuse (College of Nurses of Ontario, 1993). One might also wonder why general stress theory is not drawn upon to expand this model (Kahana and Young, 1990). More to the point, more rigorous case-comparison studies have produced little convincing evidence to support this model (see Pillemer, 1993, for reviews of these studies). The lack of evidence to support this model leads Pillemer (I 993) to marvel at its persistence in the elder abuse literature. In Canada, Pittway and Westhues (1993), in a secondary analysis of data from health and social service providers in London, Ontario, found modest support for this model as a means of predicting physical abuse. However, their study is hampered by the constraints of a secondary data analysis, which inevitably does not have all the required information.

6.2: Social Exchange Theory

Social exchange theory is founded on the assumptions "...that social interaction involves an exchange of rewards and punishments between at least two people, and that all people seek to maximize rewards and minimize punishments" (Glendenning, 1993:25). In most relationships, people have different degrees of access to resources and different capabilities to provide services to others, which makes some people more powerful than others. In the social exchange perspective, it is argued that, as people age, they become more powerless, vulnerable and dependent on their care-givers; it is these characteristics that place them at risk for abuse (Phillips, 1986). In essence, older adults remain in the abusive relationship only as long as the satisfaction of their needs exceeds the costs of the maltreatment.

There are many difficulties with this perspective, not the least of which is its ageist assump-tion: people do not automatically become dependent and powerless as they age. Indeed, several researchers have argued, and subsequently shown, that the dependency may lie elsewhere (Pillemer and Wolf, 1986). A number of investigations have found the abuser to be dependent on the older person; it is the abuser's sense of powerlessness that leads to maltreatment (Homer and Gilleard, 1990; Pillemer and Suitor, 1992; Pillerner and Wolf, 1986).

Interventions prompted by a social exchange analysis would first have to identify the dependent person. If the older person were assessed to be dependent, then sentences aimed at increasing independence would be in order, whereas a dependent adult child might need help from mental health services, or require vocational training or job placement in order to become self-reliant (McDonald, 1996).

6.3: The Symbolic Interactionist Approach

The symbolic interaction approach has been adopted from the family violence literature and focuses on the interactive processes between the older adult and the caregiver. This perspective emphasizes not only the behaviours of the elder and the caregiver, but also both persons' symbolic interpretations of such behaviour. Such an analysis of elder abuse centres on the different meanings people attribute to violence and on the consequences these meanings have in certain situations (McDonald, 1996). An example is the finding of Steinmetz (1988) that a subjective interpretation of stress by the caregiver is a better predictor of burden than the actual level *of* burden. The fact that many researchers have been unable to find an association between the *degree* of cognitive impairment of the abused person and the level of the abuse (Cooney and Mortimer, 1995) may sim-ply be a matter of overlooking the caregivers' interpretation of the situation.

Social learning, or modelling, is part of this perspective: the theory posits that abusers learn how to be violent from witnessing or suffering from violence, and the victims, in suffering abuse, learns to be more accepting of it. Treatment based on this approach would focus on changing family values and norms regarding abuse and attempt to change the interpretations of the situation. The difficulty with this approach is that it does not consider the social or economic factors that might influence the abusive process, nor does it account for the fact that not all caregivers who were abused as children abuse their elders. In fact, recent research comparing child abusers and elder abusers finds that child-abusing parents are more likely than elder abusers to have experienced severe violence in their childhood (Korbin, Anetzberger, Thomason and Austin, 1991). The authors conclude that the intergenerational transmission of family violence may be more applicable in the context of child abuse.

6.4: Feminist Models

Current prevalence studies indicate that spouse abuse is a significant dimension of elder abuse (McDonald et al., 1997; Podnieks, 1992). Despite the research findings, elder abuse experts have clung to the situational model; as a result, only limited theoretical advances have been made to explain this type of abuse (Aronson, Thornewell and Williams, 1995; McDonald and Wigdor, 1995). Most scholars have assumed that spouse abuse is a form of wife abuse "grown old." As a result, it has been explained by a handful of feminist scholars as one consequence of family patriarchy, which is identified as one of the main sources of violence against women in society (Jack, 1994; Pittaway and Gallagher, 1995a; Vinton, 1991). Some scholars have belatedly questioned whether spouse abuse is ever first-time abuse in old age (Eckley and Vilakazi, 1995; Knight, 1994; Neysmith, 1995).

A patriarchy is seen as having two basic elements: a structure in which men have more power than women, and an ideology that legitimizes this power (Miller, 1994). The family is considered to be the most fundamental unit of patriarchy in society, and traditional sex-role expectations for wives provide ideological support for the less powerful position of women in the household hierarchy. This power imbalance makes women vulnerable and open to abuse whether they are young or old. Feminist interventions generally include consciousness raising and mutual problem solving within a caring and equal relationship. The shortcoming of this approach is that, to date, there is little empirical evidence to support the claims of the theory. And, it is, at best, a partial account of *elder* abuse, because older men are just as likely as older women to be abused (Podnieks, 1992). Pittaway and Gallagher (1995a) in their study find that the feminist model is one of the stronger explanatory models explaining physical abuse and, interestingly enough, that the quality of the marital relationship is the most important risk factor in predicting physical abuse of older adults across all the models.

The application of feminist theories to all forms of spouse abuse is a hotly debated issue in the mainstream family violence literature (Miller, 1994; Renzetti, 1994). The small, but growing, body of research on gay and lesbian domestic violence has seriously thrown into question gender-based theories of partner violence (Coleman, 1994; Letellier, 1994) as has the growing evidence of women using violence against men (Genes and Loseke, 1993). The real issue, it is argued, is the power imbalance between partners (Jack, 1994; Miller, 1994). Feminist theories, then, might be extended to explain both female and male spouse abuse, if the theme of power imbalances is developed. These measures may also have some potential to explain sexual abuse, which, according to a British study, is mainly perpetrated by sons, husbands, son-in-laws and grandsons on older women on whom the perpetrator is dependent (Holt, 1993). In a convenience sample in the United States, Ramsey-Klawsnik found similar results, except that the abused older women were dependent on their abusers (Ramsey-Klawsnik, 1991).

As the 1990s come to a close, most scholars have realized that there are many manifestations of abuse and neglect of older adults on many levels and have come to question the search for a comprehensive, all- inclusive explanation of the phenomena (Pillemer, 1993). Most of the theorizing has been done at the individual level, not at the societal level, and most theories ignore the history of relationships across time, as would be found in a life-span view of elder abuse (Tindale, 1994).

In the future, new theories of abuse of older adults may continue to emphasize only *some* of the dimensions of elder abuse and neglect at any given time. Theoreticians may have to cast their theoretical nets wider than the current gerontological and family violence theories that have been the mainstay of the elder abuse literature. Some attempts have been made. For example, the political economy approaches to elder abuse describe abuse as a function of the forced dependency of older persons, which results from their exclusion from society through retirement, poverty, and institutionalization (Biggs et al., 1995; Phillipson, 1993). This perspective helps to locate abuse within the larger socio-political context, and urges a consideration of the role of the structural factors of race, gender, poverty, and ageism in abuse. Postmodernism, which has just made its debut on the gerontological stage, addresses elder abuse as a "problematization" (Katz, 1996:134) that entails an examination of how the gerontological enterprise turned abuse into a crisis (Katz, 1996:9). These and other theoretical initiatives are welcomed. With more theories, practitioners will have a wider array of interventions at their disposal, which will facilitate the provision of more effective care for mistreated older people (McDonald, 1996).

References

Aboriginal Nurses Association of Canada. (1992). *Annual General Meeting Report for 1992: Abuse of the Elders in Aboriginal Communities.* Fort Qu'Appelle, SK: Indian and Inuit Nurses of Canada.

Anetzberger, G.J., Korbin, J.E., and Austin, C. (1994). "Alcoholism and elder abuse." *Journal of Interpersonal Violence* 9(2):184-193.

Aronson, J., Thornewell, C., and Williams, K. (1995). "Wife assault in old age: Coming out of obscurity." *Canadian Journal on Aging* 14(2):72-88.

Baker, A.A. (1975). "Granny battering." *Modern Geriatrics* 5(8):20–24.

Beaulieu, M. (1992). "La formation en milieu de travail : L'expression d'un besoin des cadres en ce qui concerne les abus à l'endroit des personnes âgées en centres d'accueil." *Le Gérontophile* 14(3):3-7.

Bélanger, L. (1981). "The Types of Violence the Elderly are Victims of: Results of a Survey Done with Personnel Working with the Elderly." Paper presented at the 10th Annual Meeting of the Canadian Association on Gerontology–Scientific and Educational Meeting. Toronto, Ontario.

Bendik, M.F. (1992). "Reaching the breaking point: Dangers of mistreatment in elder caregiving situations." *Journal of Elder Abuse and Neglect* 4(3):39-59.

Bennett, G. (1990). "Action on elder abuse in the 1990's: New definitions will help." *Geriatric Medicine* 20(4):53–54.

Bennett, G., and Kingston, P. (1993). *Elder abuse: Concepts, theories and interventions.* New York, NY: Chapman and Hall.

Bergin, B. (1995). *Elder abuse in ethnocultural communities: An exploratory study with suggestions for intervention and prevention.* Ottawa, ON: Canadian Association of Social Workers.

Biggs, S., Phillipson, C., and Kingston, P. (Eds.) (1995). *Elder abuse in perspective.* Buckingham, England: Open University Press.

Block, M. R., and Sinnot, J. D. (1979). *The battered elder syndrome: An exploratory study.* Washington, DC: U.S. Dept. of Health, Education and Welfare.

Bristowe, E., and Collins, J.B. (1989). "Family mediated abuse of non-institutionalized frail elderly men and women living in British Columbia." *Journal of Elder Abuse and Neglect* 1(1):45–64.

British Columbia Seniors' Advisory Council. (1992). *A delicate balance: Assisting elderly victims of abuse and neglect.* Victoria, BC: British Columbia Seniors Advisory Council.

Browne, K.D. (1989). "Family violence: Spouse and elder abuse." In K. Howells and C. R. Hollin (eds.), *Clinical approaches to violence.* London, England: John Wiley and Sons.

Burston, G.R. (1975). "Granny- battering." (letter). *British Medical Journal* 6:592.

Chen, P.N., Bell, S., Dolinsky, D.L., Doyle, J., and Dunn, M. (1981). "Elderly abuse in domestic settings: A pilot study." *Journal of Gerontological Social Work* 4(1):317.

Coleman, V. (1994). "Lesbian battering: The relationship between personality and the perpetration of violence." *Violence and Victims* 9(2):139-152.

College of Nurses of Ontario. (1993). "Abuse of clients by registered nurses and registered nursing assistants: Report to council on results of Canada Health." *Monitor Survey of Registrants*, 1-11.

Cooney, C., and Mortimer, A. (1995). "Elder abuse and dementia: A pilot study." *International Journal of Social Psychiatry* 41(4):276-283.

Council of Europe. (1992). *Violence against elderly people.* Report prepared by Council of Europe Steering Committee on Social Policy, Strasbourg, France.

Coyne, A.C., Reichman, W.E., and Berbig, L.J. (1993). "The relationship between dementia and elder abuse." *American Journal of Psychiatry* 150(4):643-646.

Decalmer, P., and Glendenning, F. (eds.). (1993). *The mistreatment of elderly people.* Newbury Park, CA: Sage Publications.

Douglass, R. L., Hickey, T., and Noel, C. (1980). "A study of maltreatment of the elderly and other vulnerable adults." Unpublished manuscript, University of Michigan Institute of Gerontology. Ann Arbor, MI.

Dunn, J.L. (1992). "Elder abuse in reserve communities in the province of Ontario." *The Aboriginal Nurse* 7(2):17-19.

Eckley, S.C.A., and Vilakazi, P.A.C. (1995). "Elder abuse in South Africa." In J.I. Kosberg and J. L. Garcia (eds.), *Elder abuse: International and cross-cultural perspectives.* New York, NY: The Haworth Press.

Filinson, R. (1989). "Introduction." In R. Filinson and S.R. Ingman (eds.), *Elder abuse: practice and policy.* New York, NY: Human Sciences Press, Inc.

Filinson, R., and Ingram, S.R. (eds.). (1989). *Elder abuse: Practice and policy.* New York, NY: Human Sciences Press.

Fulmer, T.T. (1989). "Mistreatment of elders: Assessment, diagnosis, and intervention." *The Nursing Clinics of North America* 24(3):707-716.

Fulmer, T., McMahon, D.J., Baer-Hines, M., and Forget, B. (1992). "Abuse, neglect, abandonment, violence and exploitation: An analysis of all elderly patients seen in one emergency department during a six month period." *Journal of Emergency Nursing* 18(6):505–510.

Gebotys, R.J., O'Connor, D., and Mair, K.J. (1992). "Public perceptions of elder physical mistreatment." *Journal of Elder Abuse and Neglect* 4(1/2):151-171.

Gelles, R.J., and Loseke, D.R. (eds.). (1993). *Current controversies on family violence.* Newbury

Park, CA: Sage Publications.

Glendenning, F. (1993). "What is elder abuse and neglect?" In P. Decalmer and F. Glendenning (eds.), *The mistreatment of elderly people*. Newbury Park, CA: Sage Publications.

Gnaedinger, N.J. (1989). *Elder abuse: A discussion paper*. Ottawa: Health and Welfare Canada.

Grafstrom, M., Nordberg, A., and Winblad, B. (1993). "Abuse is in the eye of the beholder." *Scandinavian Journal of Social Medicine* 21(4):247-255.

Grandmaison, A. (1988). *Protection des personnes âgées : Étude exploratoire de la violence à l'égard de la clientèle des personnes âgées du CSSMM*. Montreal: Centre de Services Sociaux du Montréal Metropolitan (CSSMM).

Greenberg, J.R., McKibben, M., and Raymond, J.A. (1990). "Dependent adult children and elder abuse." *Journal of Elder Abuse and Neglect* 2:73-86.

Griffin, L.W. (1994). "Elder maltreatment among rural African- Americans." *Journal of Elder Abuse and Neglect* 6 (1):1-27.

Haley, R.C. (1984*). Elder abuse/neglect*. Halifax, NS: Department of Social Services.

Hall, P.A. (1987). "Minority elder maltreatment: Ethnicity, gender, age and poverty. *Journal of Gerontological Social Work (Special Issue on Ethnicity and Gerontological Social Work)* 9(4):53-72.

Health and Welfare Canada. (1997). *Adults With vulnerability: Addressing abuse and neglect*. Toronto, ON: Health and Welfare Canada.

Health and Welfare Canada. (1992). *A shared concern: An overview of Canadian programs addressing the abuse of seniors*. (Cat. H88–3/12– 1991E). Ottawa, ON: Health and Welfare Canada.

Health and Welfare Canada (1993). *Community awareness and response: Abuse and neglect of older adults*. Ottawa, ON: Health and Welfare Canada.

Hickey, T., and Douglass, R.L. (1981). "Mistreatment of the elderly in the domestic setting: An exploratory study." *American Journal of Public Health* 71(5):500-507.

Hocking, E. (1994). "Caring for careers: Understanding the process that leads to abuse." In M. Eastman (ed.), *Old age abuse: A new perspective*. 2nd ed. London, England: Chapman and Hall.

Homer, A.C., and Gilleard, C. (1990). Abuse of elderly people by their careers. *British Medical Journal*, 301 (6765), 1359-1362.

Hudson, J.E. (1988). "Elder abuse: An overview." In B. Schlesinger and R. Schlesinger (eds.*), Abuse of the elderly: Issues and annotated bibliography*. Toronto, ON: University of Toronto Press.

Hudson, M.F. (1994). "Elder abuse: It's meaning to middle-aged and older adults – Part II: Pilot results." *Journal of Elder Abuse and Neglect* 6(1):55-81.

Hudson, M.F. (1991). "Elder mistreatment: A taxonomy with definitions by Delphi." *Journal of Elder Abuse and Neglect* 3(2):1-20.

Hwalek, M. (1989). "Proper documentation: A key topic in training programs for elder abuse workers." *Journal of Elder Abuse and Neglect* 1(3):17-30.

Hwalek, M., Williamson, D., and Stahl, C. (1991). "Community based m-team roles: A job analysis." *Journal of Elder Abuse and Neglect* 3(3):45-71.

Jack, R. (1994). "Dependence, power and violation: Gender issues in abuse of elderly people by formal careers." In M. Eastman (ed.), *Old age abuse: A new perspective*. 2nd ed. London, England: Chapman and Hall.

Johns, S., and Hydle, I. (1995). "Norway: Weakness in welfare." In J.I. Kosberg and J.L.

Garcia (eds.), *Elder abuse: International and cross-cultural perspectives.* New York, NY: The Haworth Press.

Johnson, T. F. (1986). "Critical issues in the definition of elder mistreatment." In K. Pillemer and R. Wolf (eds.), *Elder abuse: Conflict in the family.* Dover, MA: Auburn House Publishing Company.

Johnson, I. M. (1995). Family members' perceptions of and attitudes toward elder abuse. Families in Society: *The Journal of Contemporary Human Services* 76(4):220-229.

Kahana, E., and Young, R. (1990). Clarifying the caregiving paradigm: Challenges for the future. In D. E. Biegal and A. Blum (eds.), *Aging and caregiving: Theory, research and policy.* Newbury Park, CA: Sage Publications.

Katz, S. (1996). *Disciplining old age: The formation of gerontological knowledge.* Charlottesville, VA: University Press of Virginia.

King, N. R. (1984). "Exploitation and abuse of older family members: An overview of the problem." In J.J. Costa (ed.), *Abuse of the elderly: A guide to resources and services.* Lexington, MA: Lexington Books.

Knight, B. (1994). "Homicide in elderly couples." In M. Eastman (ed.), "Old age abuse: A new perspective." 2nd ed. London, England: Chapman and Hall.

Korbin, J.E., Anetzberger, G., Thomason, R., and Austin, C. (1991). "Abused elders who seek legal recourse against their adult offspring: Findings from an exploratory study." *Journal of Elder Abuse and Neglect* 3(3):1-18.

Kosberg, J. (1988). "Preventing elder abuse: Identification of high risk factors prior to placement decisions." *The Gerontologist* 28(1):43-50.

Kosberg, J.I., and Garcia, J.L. (1995b). "Common and unique themes on elder abuse from a worldwide perspective." *Journal of Elder Abuse and Neglect* 6(3/4):183-197.

Kosberg, J.I., and Garcia, J.L. (1995a). *Elder abuse: International and cross-cultural perspectives.* New York, NY: The Haworth Press.

Kozma, A., and Stones, M.J. (1995). "Issues in the measurement of elder abuse." In M.J. MacLean (ed.), *Abuse and neglect of older Canadians: Strategies for change.* Toronto, ON: Thompson Educational Publishing, Inc.

Kwan, A.Y. (1995). "Elder abuse in Hong Kong: A new family program for the old east?" *Journal of Elder Abuse and Neglect* 6(3/4):65-80.

Lachs, M.S., Berkman, L., Fulmer, T., and Horwitz, R.I. (1994). "A prospective community-based pilot study of risk factors for the investigation of elder mistreatment." *Journal of the American Geriatrics Society* 42(2):169-173.

Lau, E., and Kosberg, J.L. (1979). "Abuse of the elderly by informal care providers." *Aging* 299:11-15.

Letellier, R. (1994). "Gay and bisexual male domestic violence victimization: Challenges to feminist theory and responses to violence." *Violence and Victims* 9(2):95-106.

Longres, J.F. (1992). "Race and type of maltreatment in an elder abuse system." *Journal of Elder Abuse and Neglect* 4(3):61-83.

MacKenzie, J.A., and Senechal, D. (1991*). First provincial seniors elder abuse conference: Final report and recommendations.* Halifax, NS: Senior Citizens Secretariat.

McDaniel, S.A., and Gee, E.M. (1993). "Social policies regarding caregiving to elders: Canadian contradictions." *Journal of Aging and Social Policy* 5(1/2):57-72.

McDonald, L. (1996). "Abuse and neglect of elders." In J.E. Birren (ed.), *Encyclopedia of gerontology: Age, aging, and the aged.* Volume 1. San Diego, CA: Academic Press.

McDonald, P.L., Hornick, J.P., Robertson, G.B. and Walace, J.E. (1991). Elder Abuse and Neglect in Canada. Toronto, ON: Butterworths.

McDonald, L., Pittaway, E., and Nahmiash, D. (1995). "Issues in practice with respect to mistreatment of older people." In M.J. MacLean (ed.), *Abuse and neglect of older Canadians: Strategies for change.* Toronto, ON: Thompson Educational Publishing, Inc.

McDonald, L., and Wigdor, B. (1995). "Editorial: Taking stock: Elder abuse research in Canada." *Canadian Journal on Aging* 14(2):1-6.

Meddaugh, D.I. (1993). "Covert elder abuse in the nursing home." *Journal of Elder Abuse and Neglect* 5(3):21-37.

Mickish, J.E. (1993). "Abuse and neglect: The adult and elder." In B. Byers and J.E. Hendricks (eds.), *Adult protective services.* Springfield, IL: Charles C. Thomas.

Miller, S.L. (1994). "Expanding the boundaries: Toward a more inclusive and integrated study of intimate violence." *Violence and Victims* 9(2):183-194.

Moon, A., and Williams, O. (1993). "Perceptions of elder abuse and help- seeking patterns among African- American, Caucasian-American and Korean-American elderly women." *The Gerontologist* 33(3):386-395.

Nandlal, J., and Wood, L. (1997). "Older people's understanding of verbal abuse." *Journal of Elder Abuse and Neglect* 9(1):17-31.

National Centre on Elder Abuse. (1998). *What is elder abuse: What are the major types of elder abuse?* http://www.interinc.com/NCEA/ Elder_Abuse/main.html.

Neysmith, S.M. (1995). "Power in relationships of trust: A feminist analysis of elder abuse." In M.J. MacLean (ed.), *Abuse and neglect of older Canadians: Strategies for change.* Toronto, ON: Thompson Educational Publishing, Inc.

Nolan, M. (1993). "Career-dependant relationships and the prevention of elder abuse." In P. Decalmer and F. Glendenning (eds.), *The mistreatment of elderly people.* London, England: Sage Publications.

O'Malley, T.A., Everett, D.E., O'Malley, H.C., and Campion, E.W. (1983). "Identifying and preventing family mediated abuse and neglect of elderly persons." *Annals of International Medicine* 98:998-1005.

O'Malley, T.A., Segal, H.D., and Perez, R. (1979). *Elder abuse in Massachusetts: A survey of professionals and paraprofessionals.* Boston, MA: Legal Research and Services for the Elderly.

One Voice—The Canadian Seniors Network (1995). *National action plan to reduce the abuse of older adults in Canada.* Ottawa, ON: One Voice.

Ontario Advisory Council on Senior Citizens (1985). *Report on survey of elder abuse in the community.* Toronto, ON: Ontario Advisory Council on Senior Citizens.

Paveza, G.J., Cohen, D., Eisdorfer, C., Freels, S., Semla, T., Ashford, J. W., Gorelick, P., Hirschman, R., Luchins, D., and Levy, P. (1992). "Severe family violence and Alzheimer's disease: Prevalence and risk factors." *The Gerontologist* 32(4):493-497.

Phillips, L.R. (1986). "Theoretical explanations of elder abuse: Competing hypotheses and unresolved issues." In K.A. Pillemer and R.S. Wolf (eds.), *Elder abuse: Conflict in the family.*

Dover, MA: Auburn House Publishing Company.

Phillipson, C. (1993). "Abuse of older people: Sociological perspectives." In P. Decalmer and F. Glendenning (eds.), *The mistreatment of elderly people*. London, England: Sage Publications.

Pillemer, K. (1993). "The abused offspring are dependent: Abuse is caused by the deviance and dependence of abusive caregivers." In R.J. Gelles and D.R. Loeske (eds.), *Current controversies on family violence*. Newbury Park, CA: Sage Publications.

Pillemer, K., and Finkelhor, D. (1988). "The prevalence of elder abuse: A random sample survey." *The Gerontologist* 28(1):51-57.

Pillemer, K.A., and Suitor, J.J. (1992). "Violence and violent feelings: What causes them among family caregivers?" *Journal of Gerontology* 47(4):165-172.

Pillemer, K.A., and Wolf, R.S. (eds.). (1986). *Elder abuse: Conflict in the family*. Dover, MA: Auburn House Publishing Company.

Pittaway, E.D., and Westhues, A. (1993). "The prevalence of elder abuse and neglect of older adults who access health and social services in London, Ontario, Canada." *Journal of Elder Abuse and Neglect* 5(4):77-93.

Pittaway, E., and Gallagher, E.M. (1995a). *Services for abused older Canadians*. Victoria, BC: British Columbia Office for Seniors.

Podnieks, E. (1988). "Définitions, facteurs et profils." *Vis-à-Vis* 6(3):4, 8.

Podnieks, E. (1985). "Elder abuse: Its time we did something about it." *Canadian Nurse* 81(11):36-39.

Podnieks, E. (1992). "National survey on abuse of the elderly in Canada." *Journal of Elder Abuse and Neglect* 4(1/2):5-58.

Podnieks, E. (1990). *National survey on abuse of the elderly in Canada*. Ryerson Polytechnical Institute. Ottawa, ON: Health and Welfare Canada.

Poirier, D. (1992). "The power of social workers in the creation and application of elder protection statutory norms in New Brunswick and Nova Scotia." *Journal of Elder Abuse and Neglect* 4(1/2):113-133.

Ramsey-Klawsnik, H. (1991). "Elder sexual abuse: Preliminary findings." *Journal of Elder Abuse and Neglect* 3(3):73-90.

Rathbone-McCuan, E. (1980). "Elderly victims of family violence and neglect." *Social Casework* 61(5):296-304.

Rathbone-McCuan, E., and Voyles, B. (1982). "Case detection of abused elderly parents." *The American Journal of Psychiatry* 139(2):189-192.

Reis, M.F., and Nahmiash, D. (1995a). *When seniors are abused: A guide to intervention*. North York, ON: Captus Press.

Renzetti, C.M. (1994). "On dancing with a bear: Reflections on some of the current debates among domestic violence theorists." *Violence and Victims* 9(2):195-200.

Robertson, G.B. (1995). "Legal approaches to elder abuse and neglect in Canada." In M.J. MacLean (ed.), *Abuse and neglect of older Canadians: Strategies for change*. Toronto, ON: Thompson Educational Publishing, Inc.

Roeher Institute. (1995). *Harms way: The many faces of violence and abuse against people with disabilities*. North York, ON: The Roeher Institute.

Rowe, J., Davies, K., Baburaj, V., and Sinha, R. (1993). "F.A.D.E. A.W.A.Y. The financial affairs of dementing elders and who is the attorney?" *Journal of Elder Abuse and Neglect* 5(2):73-79.

Sanchez, Y.M. (1996). "Distinguishing cultural expectations in assessment of financial exploitation." *Journal of Elder Abuse and Neglect* 8(2):49-59.

Schlesinger, B., and Schlesinger, R.A. (eds.). (1988). *Abuse of the elderly: Issues and annotated bibliography.* Toronto, ON: University of Toronto Press.

Scogin, F., Stephens, G., Bynum, J., Baumhover, L., Beall, C., and Grote, N.P. (1992). "Emotional correlates of caregiving." *Journal of Elder Abuse and Neglect* 4(4):59-69.

Sengstock, M.C., and Hwalek, M. (1987). "A review and analysis of measures for the identification of elder abuse." *Journal of Gerontological Social Work* 10(3/4):21-37.

Sengstock, M.C., and Liang, J. (1983). "Domestic abuse of the aged: Assessing some dimensions of the problem." *Interdisciplinary Topics in Gerontology* 17:58-68.

Shah, G., Veedon, R., and Vasi, S. (1995). "Elder abuse in India." *Journal of Elder Abuse and Neglect* 6(3/4):101-118.

Shell, D. (1982). *Protection of the elderly: A study of elder abuse.* Winnipeg, MB: Manitoba Council on Aging.

Sobsey, D. (1994). "An integrated ecological model of abuse." In *Violence and abuse in the lives of people with disabilities.* Baltimore, MD: Paul H. Brookes Publishing Co.

Spencer, C. (1996). *Diminishing returns: An examination of financial responsibility, decision-making, and financial abuse among older adults.* Vancouver, Gerontology Research Centre, Simon Fraser University.

Spencer, C. (1995). "New directions for research on interventions with abused older adults." In M. J. MacLean (ed.), *Abuse and neglect of older Canadians: Strategies for change.* Toronto, ON: Thompson Educational Publishing, Inc.

Steinmetz, S. (1988). *Duty bound: Elder abuse and family care.* Newbury Park, CA:Sage Publications.

Stevenson, C. (1985). *Family abuse of the elderly in Alberta.* Edmonton, AB: Alberta Social Services and Community Health.

Stones, M.J. (1995). "Scope and definition of elder abuse and neglect in Canada." In M.J. MacLean (ed.), *Abuse and neglect of older Canadians: Strategies for change.* Toronto, ON: Thompson Educational Publishing, Inc.

Stones, M., and Pittman, D. (1995). "Individual differences in attitudes about elder abuse: The Elder Abuse Attitude Test (EAAT)." *Canadian Journal on Aging* 14(2):61-71.

Sweeney, V. (1995). *Report on needs assessment for senior women as victims of violence.* Kentville, NS: Gerontology Association of Nova Scotia Valley Region.

Tindale, J.A. (1994). *Intergenerational conflict and the prevention of abuse against older persons.* Ottawa, ON: Health Canada.

Tomita, S.K. (1994). "The consideration of cultural factors in the research of elder mistreatment with an in-depth look at the Japanese." *Journal of Cross-Cultural Gerontology* 9:39-52.

Vinton, L. (1991). "Factors associated with refusing services among maltreated elderly." *Journal of Elder Abuse and Neglect* 3(2):89-103.

Wallace, H. (1996). *Family Violence: Legal, Medical, and Social Perspectives.* Boston, MA: Allyn and Bacon.

Wasylkewycz, M.N. (1993). "The elder abuse resource centre, a coordinated community response to elder abuse: One Canadian perspective." *Journal of Elder Abuse and Neglect* 5(4):21-33.

Wigdor, B.T. (1991). *Elder abuse: Major issues from a national perspective.* National Advisory Council on Aging. Ottawa, ON: Supply and Services Canada.

Wolf, R. (1997). "Elder abuse and neglect: Causes and Consequences." *Journal of Geriatric Psychiatry* 30(1):153–174.

Wolf, R.S. (1988). "Elder abuse: Ten years later." *Journal of the American Geriatric Society* 36:758-762.

Wolf, R.S. (1986). "Major findings from three model projects on elder abuse." In K.A. Pillemer and R.S. Wolf (eds.), *Elder abuse: Conflict in the family.* Dover, MA: Auburn House Publishing Company.

Wolf, R.S.(1992). "Victimization of the elderly: Elder abuse and neglect." *Reviews in Clinical Gerontology* 2(3):269-276.

Wolf, R.S., Godkin, M.A., and Pillemer, K. (1984). *Elder abuse and neglect: Final report from three model projects.* Worchester, MA: University of Massachusetts Medical Centre, University Centre on Aging.

PART TWO

Unit Four: Gender and Sexual Preferences

Chapter 10

An Overview of Gender and Justice in Canada

Learning Activity 1 - Fun Quiz

Take this fun quiz before you read the chapter. Answer "True" or "False":

1. The term "gender" has the same technical means as the term "sex."

2. Gender spheres describe those areas of Canadian society that are dominated by one gender or the other.

3. In Canada, women are over-represented in occupations such as retail sales, nursing and childcare.

4. The impact of gender spheres is seen less in education than in occupations.

5. Only about 5% of the women in Canada are foreign-born.

6. On average, women who are employed full-time make almost the same amount as men who are employed full-time.

7. Based on court data, women are accused of about 17% of all crime in Canada.

8. By a wide margin, women are accused of most prostitution-related offences.

9. The most frequent offence men are charged with is a crime of violence.

10. There is no occupation in the Canadian criminal justice system that women are over-represented.

ANSWERS: 1F, 2T, 3T, 4T, 5F, 6F, 7T, 8F, 9T, 10F

While there have always been differences between men and women, it wasn't until the 1900s when it became a theme of inquiry within criminology and criminal justice. Messerschmidt's *Masculinities and Crime* (1993) was one of the first texts to ask the question: "Why is crime predominantly a male activity?" Feminists generally looked to the concept of patriarchy and control. Followers of Messerschmidt's work focused on the social meaning of maleness and how it expresses itself.

Within the Canadian criminal justice system, although women are proportionately underrepresented in terms of criminal offences, they are disproportionately over-represented in terms of being victims of particular crimes (e.g., abuse). Hence, as noted by DeKeserdy (2000:29): "crime is clearly a gendered social problem and gender is consistently the strongest predictor of criminal involvement."

Criminologists, sociologists, psychologists and sociobiologists have attempted to explain these differences with no clear consensus other than the different perspectives attempt to link the cause of criminal behaviour to gender differences (see Balfour and Comack, 2006). Besides the amount of crime committed, there are differences in the *types* of crimes committed by men and women. And as noted above, similar gender differences exist in relation to criminal victimization rates. However, before we get too immersed into the topic, we will first define what is meant by "gender."

Defining Gender

Isn't "gender" the same as "sex"?

There are some important differences in meaning between the terms "sex" and "gender."

■ Sex

> This term is used in reference to biological and genetic differences within a species related to the capacity to reproduce. Female and male biological differences are determined at the time of conception. For example, females have 2X chromosomes while men have 1X and 1Y chromosome.[25] While it is possible to modify the sexual organs of individuals, their genetic makeup (e.g., DNA) cannot be modified.

■ Gender

> This term relates to the social identity and role that is determined by how a culture defines femininity and masculinity (Butler, 2007:217). The term gender is a social constructed notion of what it means to be feminine and what it means to be male. In other words, it reflects behavioural, psychological and sociological characteristics instead of biological and genetic qualities. Because masculinity and femininity are culturally bound, the characteristics associated with these terms can vary from culture to culture and over time (Robinson, 1988). Another term also found in the gender literature is **gender binary**, which assumes that there are distinct roles for each gender. Gender binary is sometimes seen as a means of bringing or maintaining order in a society. For example,

---

[25]   There are a number of genetic anomalies such as hermaphroditism or intersexuality in which the individual is neither male nor female. The incident rate according to the Intersex Society of North America is somewhere between 1 in 1,500 to 1 in 2,000. However, as noted on their website, the procedure for estimating is far from reliable or accurate (see: http://www.isna.org/faq/frequency (retrieved Oct. 03/07)).

certain religious groups identify the respective roles for men and women (see, for example, Numbers and Stenhouse, 2001).

Are there any other important gender-related terms?

▋ Gender Stereotypes

Within each culture, generalizations about how women and men are expected to behave are reinforced in society's social institutions (e.g., family, media, religion, economy, and education). These stereotypes are seen as "normal" and any variation from the stereotypes often results in some kind of negative response. The major theoretical model used to explain stereotyping is the "social cognitive approach." According to this approach, stereotypes represent belief systems that guide the way we process information (Matlin, 1999) and as Butler (2007) further notes, gender identity can help to enforce "proper" gender behaviour.[26]

▋ Learning Activity 2 - Recognizing Stereotypes

Gather 6 to 8 ads depicting men and women together and 3 to 4 ads with just men and 3 to 4 ads with just women. Discuss and describe how the respective ads "promote" gender stereotypes. What do you think about the depictions? Should that be changed? If so, in what way?

▋ Gender Spheres

Butler (2007) uses this term to describe those areas of "work, school or recreation that are dominated by one or the other gender" (p.369). For example, in the area of work, engineering occupations are within the man's gender sphere while nursing occupations are within the gender sphere of women. Gender spheres differ from society to society and over time, but they are supported by what Butler refers to as the "educational sphere." The existence of gender spheres, according to Butler (2007) raises the issues of equality between the sexes. Namely, are men and women different but equal, or different and unequal? Butler suggests they are both different and unequal.[27]

---

[26]   However, this implication may not always be positive. For example the idea that "big boys don't cry" or that a sexually aggressive woman is a "slut."

[27]   In a growing number of business sectors they are attempting to incorporate the concept of "inclusivity," which is intended to transcend diversity between the genders and reduce the tendency towards self-identification which then potentially allows for perceived discriminatory and/or prejudicial treatment based on self-identification.

Learning Activity 3 - Discuss

Using the course's discussion board or in class, discuss what role does our personal upbringing have on gender stereotypes? What social institutions (such as work, education, media and religion) have the most influence on reinforcing our gender stereotypes? What evidence do you have to support you opinion?

Gender Spheres in Canadian Society

Social science research demonstrates that gender is a factor in many aspects of Canadian society. Our social institutions (such as the economy, education, religion and family) tend to be divided along gender lines. Butler (2007) uses the term "gender spheres" to describe how our social institutions are differentiated by gender.

Gender Spheres in Canada's Occupation

Doesn't gender play a role in the workforce?

Distinct gender spheres are seen in Canada's occupations. It is interesting to note that "female-dominated" occupations tend to have a "helping" focus. As well, they tend to be not as well paid. For example, according to the Canadian "Gender Pay Equity" website:

Occupations in Canada

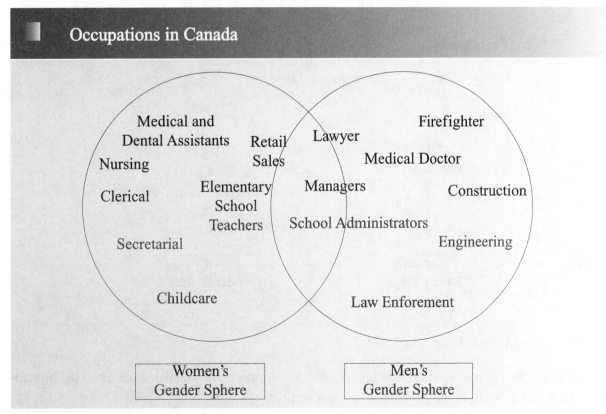

Source: Adapted from Butler, 2007:223.

- In 1999, 65.2 % of all teachers were paid according to the base pay scale, that is, 17 years or less of schooling (71.3% of women teachers are at this level, compared to 50.9% of male teachers)
- In 1999, there were twice as many male teachers than female teachers being paid at the 19-20 years of schooling pay scale (28.2% vs. 128%) (http://www.ei-ie.org/). While pay inequality still exists in many sectors, Altman and Lamontacne (1996) found that since the turn of the 1900s, the differences have diminished in most sectors.

Gender Spheres in Education

How is gender a factor in education?

It is not surprising that the gender spheres on education are similar to occupational gender spheres. Many occupations require a specific type of education (e.g., medical doctors must graduate from accredited medical schools).

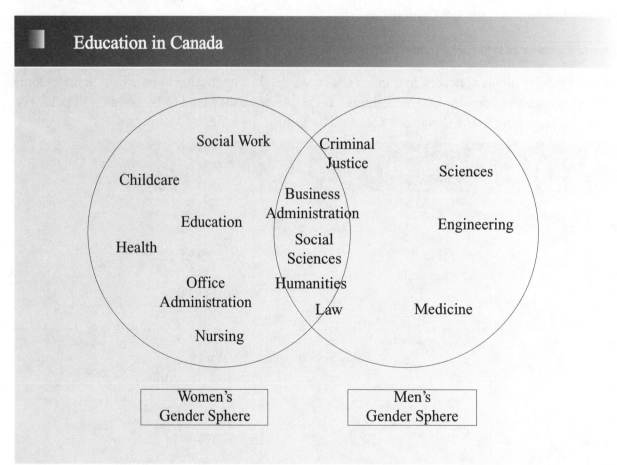

Education in Canada

Source: Adapted from Butler, 2007:223.

However, in educational areas such as business administration, the social sciences and the humanities, there is a more equal split between women and men.

Learning Activity 4 - Research

Make a list of some of the people you know. In terms of their occupation and education, do you see any similarities to the discussion of gender spheres in occupations? Why or why not?

The Realities of Being Female in Canada

Statistics Canada (2006) issued a comprehensive statistical analysis entitled "Women in Canada: A Gender-based Statistical Report" that provides many highlights of the role that gender plays within our society.

What did the analysis say?

Here are a few highlights from that report (pp.11-13).
   Population
   - Women make up slightly more than one half (50.4%) of Canada's population.
   - 19% of women in Canada are foreign-born.

   Birth Rate and Mortality Rate
   - The birth rate among Canadian women is 41 births per 1,000 women (between the ages of 15 to 49). This is 1/3 of the birth rate in 1959.
   - Females children born in 2001 can expect to live and average of 82 years compared to an average of 77 years for male children.

   Education
   - Women make up the majority of full-time students at Canadian colleges and universities. The rate of university graduation for women is 5 times greater than it was in 1971. Today, the number of males and females graduating from university is almost the same.
   - Women do not pursue graduate studies (Master or Doctoral degrees) at the same rate as men. For example, women represent 27% of those who are pursuing a doctoral degree.

   Employment
   - Women make up 47% of the paid workforce in Canada (up from 37% in 1976).
   - Women are more likely than men to be employed part-time (27% of working women compared to 11% for working men).
   - The average pre-tax income for women was $24,400. This is about 62% of the average pre-tax income of men.
   - For women working full-time, the average pre-tax income was $36,500 or about 71% of the average pre-tax income of men.

Learning Activity 5 - List and Summarize

1. How do the statistics related to females and employment compare to other minority groups discussed in this text? What about women and education as compared to other minority groups? Speculate on what similarities and differences might mean in the future?

2. Pick another English speaking country and gather comparable data for the four items covered above. How do their numbers compare to Canada's?

The Gender Spheres of Crime

Is crime in Canada shaped by gender?

Gender spheres shape criminal activity just like it does in other aspects of Canadian Society. In terms of those charged with a criminal offence, men represent an overwhelming majority in almost all categories of crime. In total, men represent 82.7% of all those charged with a criminal code offence (including traffic and drug related federal offences) (Statistics Canada, 2006:178).

As depicted in the diagram below, crime is predominately the activity of men in Canada. Only two offences are not male-dominated. Prostitution-related offences are almost equally split

Crime (charged individuals)

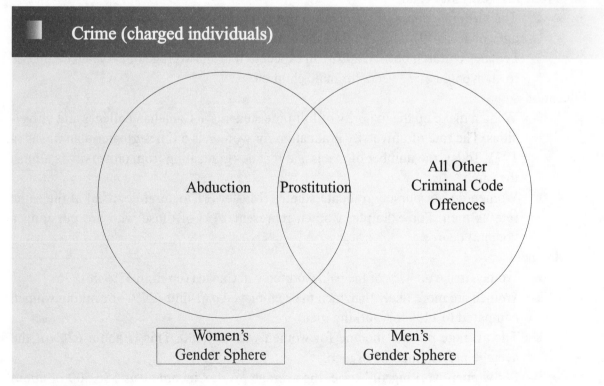

Source: Adapted from Statistics Canada, 2006, Women in Canada: A Gender-based Statistical Report, Catalogue no. 89-503-XIE, p. 178.

between women (47.2% of all offences) and men (52.8% of all offences) (p.178). Abductions are the only offence that women represent the majority of those charged – at 55.8% (p.178).

Is there such as thing as women's crimes and men's crimes?

It should be noted that compared to other crimes, there are relatively few individuals charged with abduction (less than 135 in 2004). The four most frequent charges against women are (p.178):

- Theft Under $5,000 (16,797 women charged)
- Assault (16,332 women charged)
- Bail Violations (12,908 women charged)
- Drug Offences (6,817 women charged)

The four most frequently occurring offences men face are (p. 178):

- Assault (76,864 men charged)
- Bail Violations (56,731 men charged)
- Theft Under $5,000 (40,545 men charged)
- Drug Offences (39,838 men charged)

Learning Activity 6 - Reflect

The difference between women and men in terms of crime rates has caused significant debate within the academic discipline of criminology (see Elliot, 1988 (Ch. 1); DeKeseredy, 2000 (Ch. 3); or for a more pointed discussion see Heindensohn, 1988 (Ch. 1). The theoretical explanations have run the gambit from biological explanations, to being socially troubled, to having personality flaws; to power-control issues within society; and more recently a range of feminist based perspectives which focus on gender related issues. And while there is no dominant perspective today, some argue that the lower crime rate for women likely to rise in time to become similar to the crime rate for men. This would mean that Canada's overall crime rate will likely increase significantly.

Others argue that the male crime rate is the one that may change. With the right approach, it may be possible to reduce the amount of crime men commit; thereby reducing the overall crime rate.

Which of the two "theories" do you think is likely to be more accurate? What evidence do you have to support your opinion?

Gender Spheres in Violent Crime Victimization

Is gender a factor in terms of who are the victims of violence?

In terms of violent crime victimization, women make up the greatest proportion of victims in sexual assaults (all levels), kidnapping/abduction and criminal harassment cases.

Crime (charged individuals)

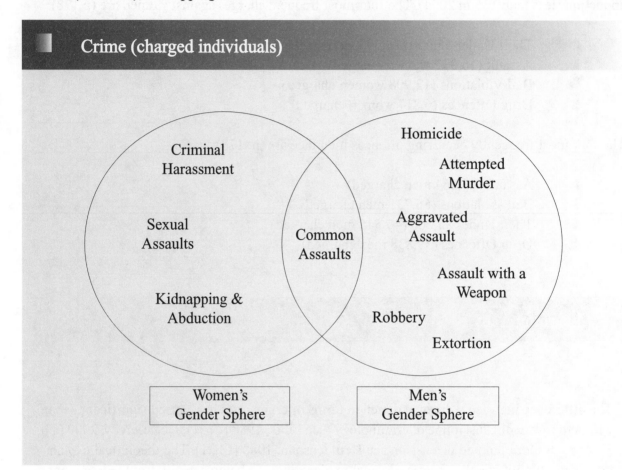

Source: Adapted from Statistics Canada, 2006, *Women in Canada: A Gender-based Statistical Report*, Catalogue no. 89-503-XIE, p. 178.

Learning Activity 7 - Discussion

Using your discussion board or in class, discuss the following questions:

1. Is it an accurate statement to say that "men own the means of violence in our society?"
2. Why do you think this is the case?
3. What evidence do you have to support your position?

Gender Spheres in Criminal Justice Employment

Women remain under-represented as employees within the Canadian Criminal Justice system. In 2001, about 65,500 of the 182,000 (or 36%) of the positions within Canada's criminal justice system were occupied by women (Statistics Canada, 2006:179). Excluding non-sworn employees, police agencies have the lowest proportion of female workers at approximately 15%. At the other end of the spectrum, 81% of paralegals in Canada are women.

Are some Canadian criminal justice jobs more open to women than others?

The diagram below depicts the gender spheres within criminal justice employment.

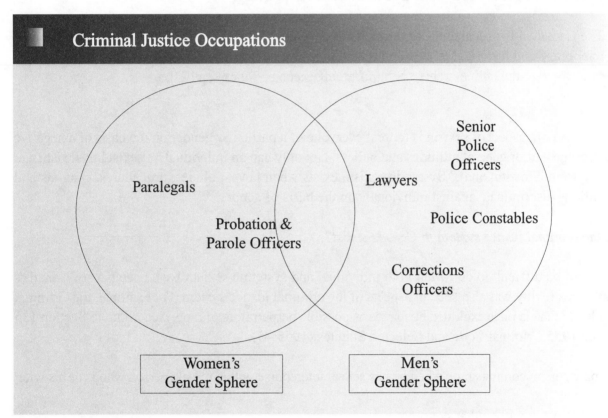

Source: Adapted from Statistics Canada, 2006, *Women in Canada: A Gender-based Statistical Report*, Catalogue no. 89-503-XIE, p. 178.

A Question of Sexism: How far have we come?

What is sexism?

Sexism is the discriminatory treatment and/or hatred directed towards individuals and groups on the basis of the group's gender rather than who they are as a person. It has very deep roots dating back to the Book of Genesis, which says that woman was created from the Adam's rib.

Learning Activity 8 - Watch and Reflect

Christine Silverberg was the first women to become Chief of Police of a large Police Service in Canada when she was appointed Chief of the Calgary Police Service in 1995.

Follow this link to watch a video clip from a 1997 interview with Chief Silverberg:

http://archives.cbc.ca/IDC-1-69-1737-11973/life_society/alberta_100/

Why did it take so long for a female Chief of Police to be appointed in Canada? Why does there continue to be are so few women senior officers in policing?

The Canadian Broadcasting Corporation has developed a valuable online archive of many contemporary and historical television and radio clips covering a wide range of Canadian topics. You can visit the online archive at **http://archives.cbc.ca/index.asp?IDLan=1**

A core aspect of sexism is to treat everyone of a particular gender on the basis of a negative stereotype and/or general attitudes and beliefs. Not only can an individual be sexist but sexism can be "systemic/institutional." Systemic sexism exists when laws, policies, procedures, customs and traditions discriminate against individuals on the basis of gender.[28]

Is the criminal justice system in Canada sexist?

It would be difficult to deny that both individual and systemic sexism have been part of Canada's past. This reality was also seen in aspects of the criminal justice system. For example, the Criminal Code of Canada once excluded husbands as possible perpetrators of rape. According to Section 135 of the 1955 Criminal Code and Selected Statutes (1955:45):

A male person commits rape when he has sexual intercourse with a female person who is or his wife:

(a)   without her consent, or
(b)   with her consent if the consent
    (i)   is extorted by threats or fear of bodily harm,
    (ii)   is obtained by personating her husband, or
    (iii)   is obtained by false and fraudulent representations as to the nature and quality of the act.

---

[28]   According to a 1998 Statistics Canada, the 10 most common jobs for women in 1996 were retail salesperson, secretary, cashier, registered nurse, accounting clerk, elementary teacher, food server, general office clerk, babysitter and receptionist. These account for 32 percent of all occupations held by women in that year (see Disability related support..., 2003). The report notes that women with disabilities are even further discriminated against than are men with disabilities.

However, the question remains: *Does the existence of gender spheres in occupations, education, criminal violence, criminal victimization and employment in the criminal justice system reflect sexism?* In a recent study by law professor Valerie Oosterveld from the law school at Western Ontario, she observed that international courts were still inconsistent in their approach when dealing with gender crime (see "Gender issues…", 2007). And while not directly dealing with gender, Denney, Ellis and Barn (2006:16) found that while the Canadian criminal justice system has introduced various measures to minimize gender bias and racial discrimination in the justice system, there remains "a gap between good intention and practice."

Learning Activity 9 - Watch and Reflect

The Canadian Broadcasting Corporation has developed a valuable online archive of many contemporary and historical television and radio clips covering a wide range of Canadian topics. You can visit the online archive at http://archives.cbc.ca/index.asp?IDLan=1

Two clips are particularly relevant to this topic.

- Follow this link to watch a 1967 video clip of several women discussing the impact that equality rights for women will have for them and Canadian society.

    http://archives.cbc.ca/IDC-1-69-1710-11759/life_society/day_care/

- The images in this next video clip may be disturbing to some of you. It is news coverage of the 1989 murder of 14 female at the Montreal's l'École Polytechnique.

Please feel free to skip viewing this video clip if you feel you will find it difficult to watch.

    http://archives.cbc.ca/IDC-1-70-398-2235/disasters_tragedies/montreal_massacre/clip1

In this chapter, we focused on gender as representing another area of diversity within the Canadian landscape. It was noted, that as a topic of interest, gender issues has gained considerable momentum since the 1960s and the emergence of feminism within criminology and criminal justice. Since then gender related issues and studies have been the subject of numerous articles and books authored predominately by women.

Issues reflected and covered in this Unit began with a brief description of the difference between gender and sex and how they relate to diversity. It was also noted how the use of different gender related terms are used to express prejudices, gender bias, and discrimination.

In the chapter, we also examined the concept of gender stereotyping and gender spheres. It was noted that in-spite of initiatives to support equality and "inclusiveness," stereotyping and genders spheres are still quite evident in Canadian society today.

From here we moved on to compare some of the statistical findings from Statistics Canada on the difference between men and women across four key social indicators (i.e., population, birth rate and mortality, education, and employment). The chapter also focused on "gender spheres" in crime and victimization. Again, it was noted that gender differences exist across a range of crimes and types of victimization and similar observations were made in relation to gender differences within the Canadian criminal justice system.

▌ References

Altman, M. and Lamontacne, L. (1996). "Gender pay inequality and occupational change in Canada." *The Journal of Socioeconomics* 25(3):285-309.

Balfour, G. and Comack. E. (eds.). (2006). *Criminalizing women.* Halifax, NS: Fernwood.

Butler, L. (2007). "Diversity and conformity: The role of gender." In P. Angelini (ed.), *Our society: Human diversity in Canada.* 3rd ed. Toronto, ON: Thomson Nelson.

Canadian Broadcast Corporation, Digital Archives Website. (2002). *Gunman massacres 14 women.* Retrieved May 8, 2007, from http://archives.cbc.ca/IDC-1-70-398-2235/disasters_tragedies /montreal_massacre/clip1.

Canadian Broadcast Corporation, Digital Archives Website. (2005c). *Top cop Christine Silverberg.* Retrieved May 8, 2007, from http://archives.cbc.ca/IDC-1-69-1737-11973/life_society/ alberta_100/.

Canadian Broadcast Corporation, Digital Archives Website. (2006). *Gay and lesbian emergence: Out in Canada.* Retrieved September 24, 2007, from http://archives.cbc.ca/IDD-1-69-599/life_soci ety/gay_lesbian/.

Canadian Broadcast Corporation, Digital Archives Website. (2007b). *The housewife and the working girl.* Retrieved May 8, 2007, from http://archives.cbc.ca/IDC-1-69-2495-11759/ life_society /mothers_day/.

Criminal Code and Selected Statutes, 1955. (1955). Ottawa, ON: The Queen's Printer.

DeKeseredy, W.S. (2000). *Women and crime and the Canadian criminal justice system.* Cincinnati, OH: Anderson.

Denny, D., Ellis, T. and Barn, R. (2006). "Race, Diversity and Criminal Justice in Canada: A view from the UK." *International Journal of Criminology.* Retrieved October 3, 2007, from http://www.internetjournalofcriminology.com/Denney,%20Ellis%20&%20Barn%20%20Ra ce,%2Diversity%20and%20Criminal%20Justice%20in%20Canada.pdf.

"Disability related support arrangements, policy options and implications for women's equality." (2003). Retrieved October 3, 2007 from, http://www.swc-cfc.gc.ca/pubs/pubspr/ 0662653238/200102_0662653238_18_e.html#endnote4.

"Gender issues in international criminal justice." (2007). Retrieved October 5, 2007, from http://law iscool.com/2007/08/21/gender-issues-in-international-criminal-justice/.

Matlin, M. (Winter 1999). "Bimbos and Rambos: The Cognitive Basis of Gender Stereotypes." *Eye on Psi Chi.* 3(2):13-14, 16.

Messerschmidt, J. (1993). *Masculinity and crime.* Boston, MA: Rowman and Littlefield.

Numbers, R. and Stonehouse, J. (2001). *Disseminating Darwinism: The role of place, race, religion and gender.* Cambridge, MA: Cambridge University Press.

Robinson, O.F. (1988). "The historical background." In S. McLean and N. Burrows (eds.), *The legal relevance of gender.* HoundmIll, England: MacMillan.

Statistics Canada. (2004). *Adult criminal court statistics, 2003/04.* Catalogue no. 85-002-XPE, vol. 24, no. 12. Retrieved April 12, 2007, from http://www.statcan.ca/bsolc/english/bsolc?catno= 85-002-X20040128431.

Statistics Canada. (2005). *Criminal victimization in Canada, 2004.* Catalogue no. 85-002-XPE, vol. 25, no. 7. Retrieved April 10, 2007, from http://www.statcan.ca/bsolc/english/bsolc? catno=85-002-X20050078803.

Statistics Canada. (2006). *Women in Canada: A gender-based statistical report.* Catalogue no. 89-503-XPE. Retrieved April 26, 2007, from http://www.statcan.ca/bsolc/english/bsolc?catno= 89-503-X 28, 2007, from http://www.statcan.ca/Daily/English/060606/d060606b.htm.

PART TWO

Unit Four: Gender and Sexual Preferences

Chapter 11

An Overview of Sexual Preferences and Justice in Canada

Learning Activity 1 - Fun Quiz

Take this fun quiz before you read the chapter. Answer "True" or "False":

1. The term "homosexual" has the same meaning as the terms "lesbian" and "gay man."

2. Same-sex marriages are legally recognized in Canada.

3. Lesbians and men are known as Canada's "hidden minority."

4. There is a significant amount of research related to Canadian gay men and lesbians.

5. Homosexual activity between men was once against the law in Canada.

6. Homosexuality activity between women was once against the law in Canada.

7. In 1967, Canada's Justice Minister Pierre Trudeau argued against the decriminalization of consensual homosexual activity between men.

8. The Canadian Charter of Rights and Freedoms explicitly states that sexual orientation is a prohibit grounds of discrimination.

9. In Canada, gay men and lesbians are the largest group of those who report being a victim of a hate crime.

10. Heterosexism is the same as homophobia.

ANSWERS: 1F, 2T, 3T, 4F, 5T, 6F, 7F, 8F, 9F, 10F

As described in the CBC Archives from 2006, the 1960s was marked by protests, legal fights, and social backlashes to many of the conventional norms of the day. The 1960s spawned a growing solidarity among gays and lesbians and throughout the 1970s and 1980s; homosexuality became more readily accepted ("Gay and lesbian…", 2006).[29] However, the first social movement to advance the civil rights of people was founded in Germany in 1897 (Adams, 1987).[30] It wasn't until around the early 1700s that various European countries began to accuse and frown upon potential sodomistic behavior of men who frequented men only establishments (Ibid).

Today, in North America and other societies, a person's sexual orientation is much more than a personal quality. In the case of homosexuality, formal and informal attempts have been made to prevent its practice (see Sandfort, Schuyf, Duyvendak, and Weeks, 2000) even though the well publicized study by Kinsey et al. (1948) found a surprising high level of homosexual activity among the population surveyed. No doubt, this is the major reason that lesbian and gay men remain, to a considerable degree, Canada's "hidden minority" (Fassinger, 1991).

▉ Defining "Lesbians" and "Gay Men"

Like other minorities, homosexual women and men have been subjected to slang and derogatory labels. As well, there has been an evolution in socially acceptable terms that reflect their social identity.

What are the common terms related to homosexuals?

- **Homosexual**
  This term is traditionally used in a more clinical manner to refer to individuals who had sexual relationships with individuals of the same gender. The term was primarily related to describing a type of sexual activity and not the social identity or status of individuals.[31]
- **Lesbians and Gay Men**
  Once generally used within a derogatory context, today these terms are used to represent the social identities that homosexual women and men have in society. As well, these terms acknowledge that gay men and lesbians have separate and distinct social identities.

---

[29] In 1965, a NWT man (George Kippert) was jailed because he was a homosexual ("Gaysbian…", 2006). He was charged with four counts gross indecency, all involving consensus acts. Canada's first gay march was held on August 28, 1971. In 1976, John Damien, a horse race judge in Ontario was fired from his job because of his sexual preferences (Ibid). There are additional stories marking the evolution of gay and lesbian rights at the CBC site: http://archives.cbc.ca/IDD-1-69-599/life_society/gay_lesbian/.

[30] Adams (1987) notes that in earlier times a number of societies such as the Melanesia, Amazonia, and Western Egypt, males were openly involved in homosexual relations.

[31] Germany was the first country to advance the civil rights of homosexual people in 1897. In England, the trial of Oscar Wilde brought to light the "social purity movement" lead by early feminists who tried to curb the sexual lust of men in all its various manners of expressionism. One of the results was the highly publicized and controversial trials of the Irish born playwright, poet, and novelist, Oscar Wilde in 1895. Wilde was found guilty of violating a new amendment to the criminal law and spent two years imprisoned for having sexual intimacy with a girl under the age of sixteen (Adam, 1987).

In 2001, Statistics Canada initiated an inquiry as to how the Canadian Census might go about collecting data on Canadians sexual orientation. Some $55,000 was spent establishing a focus group to figure out how such an inquiry could be phrased—clearly reflecting the degree of sensitivity around the concept! ("Gay market statistics: …", 2002) (see Same-sex partnership below).

Same-sex Partnerships

Changes in the legal status of same-sex common-law partnerships in 2001 were the primary reason for collecting data on same-sex partnership. Although not necessarily meaning that such relationships constitute gay or lesbian relationships, it was a means of trying to obtain estimates of such relationship.

The 2001 Census estimates that approximately 0.5% of the Canadian population live as same-sex partners.[32]

Learning Activity 2 - Reflect

Oftentimes, the slang terms we use for members of a particular minority group are an expression of prejudice, discrimination and segregation. Consider some of the slang terms you have heard referring to lesbians and gay men. Why do people use these terms? Do the terms have any hidden purposes?

The "Hidden Minority"

Canadian social science research exploring the social identities of gay men and lesbian women is very sparse.[33]

Why is there so little research on lesbians and gay men?

1. Unlike most other minorities (e.g., Aboriginals, young persons, older adults and women), lesbians and gay men are "non-visible minorities." Becoming visible is more a matter of choice for gay men and lesbians than most other minorities in Canada.[34]

2. Because of the social consequences of revealing their identity, many gay men and lesbians are disinclined to be open about their sexual preference (generally, see Sandfort et al., 2000). Oftentimes, social scientists cannot gain access to these two groups in order to conduct their research.

---

[32]   According to Statistics Canada, only a few other countries collect data on same-sex partnerships. Data for the United States set same-sex partnerships at around 1% and in New Zealand around 0.6%.

[33]   For a listing of some of the publications relating to gays and lesbians in Canada see: http://www.cha-shc.ca/cchs/resources/bib.htm (retrieved Oct. 01/07).

[34]   Some well known Canadians such as Mark Tewksbury, Rick Mercer, Rufus Wainwright, Emanuel Sandhu, Sven Robinson among others spent some time covering up their sexual preference until finally "risking" their status and/or reputation to disclose their sexual orientation.

3.   In comparison to other diversity issues, the level of academic expertise on gay and lesbian social identities/issues is somewhat limited. This fact results in research generally being conducted by persons of similar sexual persuasion and to a much more limited extent than other diversity issues.

4.   Some suggest that the traditional social sciences are blind to lesbian and gay issues (Adam, 1987, Foster and Murray, 1972). In other words, traditional social scientists exhibit some of the same prejudice and discrimination towards lesbians and gay men that is found in other parts of Canadian society.

It is likely that aspects of all of the above reasons are at work to limit the amount of Canadian research related to lesbian and gay men. Unfortunately, the lack of research has left us with little empirical data.

What don't we know about gay men and lesbians in Canada?

Here are some of the things **we do not know** about gay men and lesbians in Canada:

- the number of individuals who consider themselves lesbian or gay
- the demographic distribution of gay men and lesbians in Canada
- the true degree of prejudice and discrimination these groups experience
- the social profile (e.g., age, financial status, health) of gay men and lesbians
- the true rate of criminal victimization against gays and lesbians
- the rate of criminality among these two groups[35]

Learning Activity 3 - Discuss

Using the course's discussion board or in class, discuss what might be the negative consequences of the fact that gay men and lesbians are a "hidden minority." What does this mean for lesbians and gay men? What does this mean for Canadian justice system? What does this mean for Canadian society in general?

The Legal Status of Gay Men and Lesbians in Canada

Wasn't homosexuality once illegal in Canada?

Throughout all of Canada's history, the Criminal Code has prohibited some sexual activities between individuals, regardless of the consensual nature of the activity (Adam, 1987; Pilon, 2001).

---

[35] A recent report by the British government revealed that England, New Zealand and Canada have been exploring the option of including questions regarding sexual orientation in their Census collections. However, all three countries choose not to do so for social and politically sensitive reasons. Based on a focus group study, the Statistics Canada found that most Canadians were not comfortable with asking such questions in a census but were amenable to such questions in health surveys, surveys of safety, human rights and victimization ("Sexual orientation…", 2007).

This remains true today as legal restrictions are placed on the age of sexual consent; as well as certain types of sexual activity (e.g., anal intercourse or "buggery") before the age of 18 (see Pilon, 2001).

However, homosexual activity between males (but not females) was given particular attention in past criminal laws. For example, according to section 148 of the 1955 Criminal Code of Canada (Criminal Code and Selected Statutes, 1955:47):

> Every male person who assaults another person with intent to commit buggery or who indecently assaults another male person is guilty of an indictable offence and is liable to imprisonment for ten years and to be whipped.

Seeds of Change

When did things start to change?

The concern over the 1965 Supreme Court of Canada decision to deny the appeal of George Klippert is considered by many to be the catalyst for change regarding the legal status of gay men and lesbians. In 1965, Klippert was arrested, charged and convicted for engaging in homosexual activity, even though the activity was consensual. In the process of determining the appropriate sentence, the court concluded that Klippert was not likely to ever stop having sexual relations with other men. Because of this, he was declared the equivalent of today's dangerous offender and received an indeterminate sentence. This meant that he could be kept in prison for the rest of his life.

In 1967, Canada's Minister of Justice, Pierre Trudeau (who became Prime Minister the following year) introduced legislation to "decriminalize" homosexual behaviour between consulting adults. It was within this context that Trudeau made the now famous statement, "There is no place for the state in the bedrooms of the nation."

What are some of the more important ways things have changed for gay men and lesbians?

Here are other important legal changes regarding gay and lesbian rights in Canada (Canadian Broadcasting Corporation, 2007):

- In 1977, Quebec added sexual orientation as a prohibited ground for discrimination.
- In 1978, the *Canada Immigration Act* was changed to remove the ban on immigrants who were known to be gay or lesbian.
- In 1982, the *Canadian Charter of Rights and Freedoms* was approved. It states that all persons are equal before the law.
- During the 1980s, Ontario (1986) and Manitoba (1987) followed Quebec's lead and changed their Human Rights legislation to prohibit discrimination on the basis of sexual orientation:
- In 1995, the Supreme Court of Canada ruled that discrimination on the basis of "sexual orientation" is prohibited under the equality provisions of the Canadian Charter (even though it does not explicitly state "sexual orientation").

- During the 1990s, all governments, except Alberta changed their Human Rights legislation to prohibit discrimination on the basis of sexual orientation.
- In 1999, the Supreme Court of Canada ruled that same-sex partnerships have the same legal rights as "common-law" partnerships.
- In 2005, the Parliament of Canada passed the Civil Marriage Act that recognized the legal basis of same-sex marriage.

Learning Activity 4 - Watch and Listen

The Canadian Broadcasting Corporation has developed a valuable online archive of many contemporary and historical television and radio clips covering a wide range of Canadian topics. You can visit the online archive at **http://archives.cbc.ca/index.asp?IDLan=1**

Two clips are particularly relevant to this topic.

Follow this link to hear a CBC radio clip regarding reaction to the Supreme Court of Canada's decision to reject George Klippert's appeal of his prison sentence for engaging in homosexual activity:

    http://archives.cbc.ca/IDC-1-69-1917-12538-11/life_society/klippert/

Follow this link to watch a CBC television clip in which then-Justice Minister Pierre Trudeau discusses the logic behind the "decriminalization" of homosexual relationships between consulting males:

    http://archives.cbc.ca/IDC-1-73-538- 2671/politics_economy/omnibus/clip1

Violence towards Lesbians and Gay Men

What is a "hate" or "bias crime"?

Hate/bias crime is a loaded term, which does not carry a commonly understood meaning. In a general context, "hate/bias crime" refers to offences against individuals because of their disability, ethnicity, race, religion, or sexual orientation.[36] Perry (2002) observed that such crimes are more likely to involve crimes against a person than crimes against property.

    According to sections 318 and 319 in the Criminal Code, hate crime is committed to intimidate, harm or terrify not only a person, but an entire group of people to which the victim belongs. The victims are targeted for who they are, not because of anything they have done. Typically, hate

---

[36] The Ottawa city police were the first police department in the country to establish a Bias Crime Unit in 1993. It was in large response to the brutal beating of a young gay man in the city. (see: http://ww4.ps-sp.gc.ca/en/library/publications/general/models/ottawa.html).

crimes include crimes of violence (murder, assault, sexual assault, kidnapping) and some property crimes (vandalism, arson).

The collection of statistics on hate crimes in Canada is incomplete.[37] First, police agencies have been slow to collect separate statistics on crimes motivate by hate. Second, it is likely that some victims of hate/bias crimes do not come forward to the police because they do not want to expose themselves to more victimization. For these reasons, the amount of hate/bias crime against gay men and lesbians is probably under-reported. Roberts (1995) and Jeffery (1998) have both noted that it is extremely difficult to conduct any research on the subject as there is no formal collection of such data in Canada.

How much hate/bias crime against lesbians and gay men is there in Canada?

The most current nationwide data on hate crimes in Canada comes from a 2001/2002 Statistics Canada study. This study looked at the amount of hate crimes reported by 12 major Canadian police departments. Key findings of the study include (Statistics Canada, 2004b):

- There was a total of 928 hate crime incidents (as classified by the police departments
- About 90% of the crimes were motivated by race, ethnicity or religion
- 10% were motivated by sexual preference
- In terms of the type of offence:
    - about 50% were threats of violence or actual violence
    - about 33% were property offences such as vandalism or arson
    - about 17% were hate propaganda
- Slightly 50% of the hate crimes resulted in someone being charged:
    - 90% of the accused were male
    - the average age of the accused was 29 years
    - 1 in 10 had been involved in previous criminal activity
    - 3% were connected to a gang or an extremist organization[38]

Learning Activity 5 - Case Study

Matthew Shepard attended Catawba College in Salisbury, N.C, and Casper College. Moving to Denver he worked several jobs. Later he was attending the University of Wyoming in Laramie. There his major was political science/foreign relations and the minors were languages. Matthew was selected as the student representative for the Wyoming Environmental Council, and was very active in politics.

Matthew started acting in community theatre at the age of 5, and was very active in front of and behind the scenes in several Casper College and Stage III Theater plays. Matthew also enjoyed soccer, swimming, running, snow skiing and dancing. He knew he was not the best athlete in the world but he had a very competitive spirit. Matthew loved the nature, enjoying hunting, fishing and camping. Matthew was a member and an acolyte in St. Mark's Episcopal Church in Casper, Wyoming.

Matthew was lured from a campus bar shortly after midnight on October 7 by two men (Aaron McKinney, 22 and Arthur Henderson, 21) who told him they were gay. He was driven to a remote area near the Sherman Hills neighborhood east of Laramie, tied to a split-rail fence, tortured, beaten and pistol-whipped by his attackers, while he begged for his life. He was then left for dead in near freezing temperatures. A cyclist who found him on Snowy Mountain View Road at 6:22 pm, some 18 hours after the attack, at first mistook him for a scarecrow. He was unconscious and suffering from hypothermia. His face was caked with blood, except where it had been partially washed clean by tears.

Matthew died at 12:53 am on Monday 12th October 1998, at Poudre Valley Hospital in Fort Collins, Colorado, with his family at his bedside. Hospital officials said Matthew had a fracture from behind his head to just in front of his right ear and a massive brain stem injury which affected his vital signs, including his heart beat, body temperature and other involuntary functions. There were also approximately a dozen small lacerations around his head, face and neck. He was so badly injured in the attack that doctors were unable to operate. He never regained consciousness after being found.

*Source: Matthew Shepard Foundation, n.d.

In Canada, and many states in the United States, hate crimes are legally considered more serious than other crimes. Why is a "hate crime" assault on a member of a minority considered more serious than a "non-hate crime" assault?

■ A Question of Homophobia and Heterosexism

What does homophobia and heterosexism mean?

First coined in 1972 by the American psychologist George Weinberg, the term "homophobia" is a non-scientific term generally defined as "denoting an aversion to, active hatred of, or even violence towards the fact of same-sex desire and those who experience it" (Angelini, 2007:370). "Hetero-sexism" is the legal, social and cultural advantages that are given to heterosexuals and heterosexual partnerships in laws, policies, procedures, customs and traditions (Ibid.). Mihalik (1991) notes that heterosexism is considered normative and that non-heterosexualism is deviant and less desirable. This has in-part been reflected in the lack of research conducted in the area (see Ryan, Brotman and Rowe, 2001; Goldfreid, 2001).

The incidents of hate/bias crime towards gay men and lesbians is evidence that homophobia exists in some Canadians. The fact that some lesbians and gay men are reluctant to report the violence they experience because of their sexual orientation suggests that the amount of homophobia in Canada is greater than the official statistics indicate (see Banks, 2003). However, one recent attempt to gage the impact that homophobia might have on the health and well-being of gay and lesbian Canadians was the work of Banks (2003) who conducted an extensive study relying on health related data to try and obtain a representative picture of the impact of homophobia. Along with his associates they estimated that pre-mature deaths that could be associated to homophobia included:

- Suicide = 818 to 968 deaths per year
- Smoking = 1,232 to 2,599 deaths per year
- Alcohol abuse = 236 to 1,843 deaths per year
- Illicit drug use = 64 to 74 deaths per year (Banks, 2003:9).[39]

Perhaps a most telling account comes from the Forward to the Banks report. Gens Hellquest writes (p.10): "If there's been one constant in my nearly 40 years of participation in the gay and lesbian community and my over 30 years as a gay activist, it has been death."

Under the legal authority of Canada's Charter of Rights and Freedoms, significant advances have been made in removing formal discrimination against gay men and lesbians in Canada's laws (e.g., Criminal Code of Canada, family law, civil law). However, the question remains—*Does heterosexism remain in our culture?*

Learning Activity 6 - Reflect

Some people believe that homophobia causes heterosexism. Others believe it is the other way around—that heterosexism causes homophobia. Which do you think is true? Why?

In this chapter, we have examined the theme of sexual orientation as a topic of diversity. Borrowing the phrase "hidden minority," we examined some of the issues surrounding gay and lesbian lifestyles and noted the general lack of research in the area, especially in comparison to the other themes of diversity covered in this text.

References

Adam, B.D. (1987). *The rise of a gay and lesbian movement.* Boston, MA: Twayne.

Banks, C. (2003). "The cost of homophobia: Literature review on the impact of homophobia in Canada." *Report submitted to the Gay and Lesbian Health Services.* Saskatoon, SK.

Canadian Broadcasting Corporation. (2007). "The Supreme Court and same-sex marriage." Retrieved April 12, 2007, from http://www.cbc.ca/news/background/samesexrights/.

Canadian Broadcast Corporation, Digital Archives Website. (2003b). "There's no place for the state in the bedrooms of the nation." Retrieved May 8, 2007, from http://archives.cbc.ca/IDC-1-73-538-2671/politics_economy/omnibus/clip1.

Canadian Broadcast Corporation, Digital Archives Website. (2005b). "Jailed for homosexuality."

---

[39] Banks' report notes that there is insufficient data to determine how many incidents of depression, unemployment, murder, and HIV/AIDS may be attributable to homophobia.

Retrieved May 8, 2007, from http://archives.cbc.ca/IDC-1-69-599-3226/life_society/gay_lesbian/.

Criminal Code and Selected Statutes, 1955. (1955), Ottawa, ON: The Queen's Printer.

Fassinger, R. (1991). "The hidden minority: Issues and challenges in working with lesbian women and gay men." *The Counseling Psychologist* 19(2):157-176.

Gabbidon, S. and Greene, H. (2005). *Race and crime.* Thousand Oaks, CA.: Sage.

"Gay market statistics: Facts and misfigures." (2002). Retrieved October 1, 2007, from http://www.wildemarketing.com/facts.html

Goldfried, M. (2001). "Integrating gay, lesbian, and bisexual issues into mainstream psychology." *American Psychologist* 56:975-988.

Jeffery, B. (1998). *Standing Up to Hate: Legal Remedies Available to Victims of Hate-Motivated Activity—A Reference Manual for Advocates.* Ottawa, ON: Canadian Heritage.

Kinsey, A. et al. (1948). *Sexual behaviour in the human male.* Boston, Mass.: Sanders.

Matthew Shepard Foundation, (n.d.). "Matthew's life." Retrieved May 8, 2007 from http://www.matthewsplace.com/mattslife.htm

Mihalik, G. (1991). "Homosexuality, stigma, and biocultural evolution." *Journal of Gay & Lesbian Psychotherapy* 1:15-29.

Perry, B. (2002). "Defending the color line: Racially and ethnically motivated hate crime." *American Behavioral Scientist* 46:72-92.

Pilon, M. (2001). "Canada s Legal Age of Consent to Sexual Activity." Retrieved October 1, 2007, from http://www.parl.gc.ca/information/library/PRBpubs/prb993-e.htm.

Roberts, J. (1995). *Disproportionate Harm: Hate Crime in Canada.* Department of Criminology University of Ottawa, Department of Justice Canada, Working Document 1995-11e.

Ryan, B., Brotman, S., and Rowe, B. (2000). *Access to care: Exploring the health and well-being of gay, lesbian, bisexual and two-spirit people in Canada.* Montreal: McGill Centre for Applied Family Studies.

Sandfort, T., Schuyf, J., Duyvendak, J., and Weeks, J. (eds.). (2000). *Lesbian and gay studies: An introductory, interdisciplinary approach.* Thousand Oaks, CA.: SAGE.

"Sexual orientation and the 2011 census: background information. (2006). Retrieved October 1, 2007, fromhttp://www.statistics.gov.uk/about/consultations/downloads/2011Census_sexual_orientation_background.pdf.

Statistics Canada. (2004). *Pilot survey of hate crime.* Retrieved April 22, 2007, from http://www.statcan.ca/Daily/English/040601/d040601a.htm.

Statistics Canada. (2005). *Criminal victimization in Canada, 2004.* Catalogue no. 85-002-XPE, vol. 25, no. 7. Retrieved April 10, 2007, from http://www.statcan.ca/bsolc/english/bsolc?catno=85-002-X20050078803.

PART TWO

Unit Four: Gender and Sexual Preferences

Chapter 12

Women, Justice and (In)Equality

Wendy Chan and Dorothy E. Chunn

Learning Activity 1 - Fun Quiz

Take this fun quiz before you read the chapter. Answer "True" or "False":

1. Traditionally, gender has been an important research topic in criminology and criminal justice.

2. On average, women commit fewer crime than men in Canada.

3. In comparison to all women in Canada, female offenders then to be, on average, younger, single and of Aboriginal ancestry.

4. The rate of reported female criminality in Canada has been rising significantly since 1990.

5. One of the earliest explanations for female criminality was one that focused on the biological differences between women and men.

6. Feminist explanations of women and crime see gender as a source of social power within society which results in unequal gender participation in crime.

7. One feminist argument is that women are treated more leniently in the criminal justice system.

8. The legal defence of infanticide is being increasingly rejected in Canada's courts.

9. Feminist criminologists are concerned that some women receive more punitive treatment in the justice system because they do not conform to the social ideal of how a female should behave.

10. The criminal justice system is one way that society creates a "culture of control" over women.

ANSWERS: 1F, 2T, 3T, 4F, 5T, 6T, 7F, 8T, 9T, 10T

Introduction

Historically, women were virtually invisible in analyses of crime and criminal justice. Academics, experts, criminal-justice practitioners, and political decision-makers all seemed to be in agreement that there were "too few to count" (Adelberg and Currie, 1987). Since the late 1960s, however, an explosion of research and writing about criminalized women has occurred in Canada and other liberal states. Feminists initiated and carried out much of this work, beginning with detailed critiques of traditional male-dominated criminology for a failure to incorporate women in the analysis of crime and justice, and ultimately establishing the foundation for feminist criminologies (see, e.g., Comack, 1996, 2007; Daly, 1994; Daly and Chesney-Lind, 1988; Gavigan, 1983, 1988; Heidensohn, 1985; Naffine, 1987, 1996; Roberts, 1993; Smart, 1976; Rafter and Heidensohn, 1995; Snider, 1994).

The picture of the criminalized woman that emerges from the spate of feminist and non-feminist literature in recent decades is by no means a uniform or homogeneous one, however. While they have challenged and rejected traditional conceptions of "the female offender," feminists themselves hold divergent views on how to interpret women's lawbreaking and what to do about it. Moreover, feminist perspectives have by no means displaced the conventional perspectives on women, crime, and justice that historically have shaped explanations of and reactions to women in conflict with the law.

The contradictory findings and conclusions that characterize the post-1960s literature on adult women who are criminalized in liberal states have generated intense debates. In this chapter, we examine three questions that have been, and continue to be, central to these debates through a primary focus on adult women in the Canadian context[40]: (1) Who are Canada's criminalized women? (2) Why do women commit crime(s)? (3) How does the Canadian criminal justice system respond to women accused of crime(s)?

Learning Activity 2 - Reflect

Before reading this chapter, stop and consider your own assumptions on why women have a much lower participation rate in most crimes in Canada? Do you have a single explanation for this fact? What evidence do you have to support this explanation?

Who are Canada's Criminalized Women?

The picture of the extent to which women are involved in criminal behaviour is derived from official and unofficial statistics. Official statistics are generated from records of official criminal justice agencies such as the police, courts, prisons whereas unofficial statistics are produced independently

---

[40]   Under Canadian criminal law, adults are women and men who are 18 years of age and older.

of official control agencies. Sources for unofficial statistics can include data collected from social scientists through observations, surveys of victimization as well as surveys of self-reported criminal involvement. Crime statistics about women offer a range of important information about their involvement in crime, the types of crime they tend to commit, the legal outcome of their criminal cases and the differences between men as well as between women who engage in criminal behaviour.

The official picture of women's involvement in criminal activity reinforces a well establish trend in official crime statistics—that women, on average, tend to commit fewer crimes than men. For example, in 2005, women committed only one quarter of the total crimes recorded (1080 versus 4193 per 100,000 population) in Canada (Kong and AuCoin, 2008). The only exception to this is in prostitution related offences where men and women were apprehended at an equal rate. When women do get involved in criminal activity, they are most likely to do so between the ages of 12 and 17. Young women in this age group were accused by police of Criminal Code offences at a rate 3.5 times higher than older, adult women (Kong and AuCoin, 2008:3).

The most common types of crimes women commit are property related crimes such as shoplifting and fraud. These crimes account for almost half (47%) of all crimes committed by Canadian women in 2005. Women are much less likely to engage in white collar crimes or financial crimes. The second most common type of crime women commit is common assault (28% in 2005)—the most minor form of violation against the person. Many scholars point out that the crimes women commit are strategies for survival (Pollack, 2008:6). That is, women's lack of social, economic and political power results in higher levels of poverty, particularly for marginalized women. As well, women are more likely to be victimized in domestic relationships than men, and there is speculation that many women accused of common assault may be acting in self-defence against an abusive partner. This is not unlikely given that over 40,000 incidences of spousal violence were reported to the police in Canada in 2007 (Statistics Canada, 2009).

When the extent and nature of women's crimes are compared to men's, it is clear that women not only commit less crime than men, but their crimes are typically less serious or violent than men's as well. Women are also less likely to have multiple charges laid against them and are less likely to have a history of criminal offending. It has also been noted that repeat offending by women (21% of women offenders in 2005) does not increase the severity of crimes committed. In fact, 29% of women who were charged with further crimes in 2005 were accused of offences involving the administration of justice (e.g. bail violations, failure to appear in court, unlawfully at large, breach of probation) (Kong and AuCoin, 2008:5).

Amongst women involved in criminal activity, differences arise between women's age, maritial status and racial backgrounds. Data from correctional services indicates that federally sentenced women tend to be young, single and Aboriginal (Kong and AuCoin, 2008:12). Compared to the general population, the average age of a woman serving a federal sentence was 37.7 in 2006, whereas the average age of Canadian women that year was 48.1 (Ibid). In terms of marital status, almost half of federally sentenced women were single (47%) compared to 21% of women in the general population (Ibid). Finally, Aboriginal women are over-represented in the federal correctional system (25% of women incarcerated in 2006) compared to their representation in the general population (3% of Canadian adult women in 2006) (Kong and AuCoin, 2008:12).

Longitudinal data of women's involvement in crime indicates that the rate of women's crimes has not changed much over the last several decades. In fact, crime rates for women have been declining since 1991. What has been noted, however, is the statistical increase in serious violent crimes committed by women since the mid-1980s. Official statistics record an increased charge rate of 11% per 100,000 (from 25% to 46%) between 1986 and 2005 for adult women while the rate for young women more than doubled between this period (from 60 per 100,000 to 132 per 100,000).

Despite these numbers representing a substantially lower rate when compared to men charged with serious violent crimes, anxieties heightened across many western liberal democracies (e.g. Canada, USA, UK) over this discovery. Were women and girls *really* becoming much more violent? If so, why was this happening? While the media sensationalized and exploited the rare occurrences of women's use of violence to perpetuate the myth of "the violent woman" in our midst, feminist criminologists argued that any understanding of women's use of violence needs to be properly contextualized (Luke, 2008; Jiwani, 2005; Pollack and Davis, 2005). They argue that concern over women's increase use of violence reflects the increasing criminalization of women's survival skills. As cuts to social welfare continue in Canada, women, particularly women of colour, suffer the most from the lack of support available (Elizabeth Fry Society, 2009). This is reflected in the high rates of property related offences women tend to commit. Furthermore, Luke (2008) contends that the alleged higher rates of young woman using violence can be attributed to a phenomenon of "relabeling" where previous actions deemed minor and non-delinquent by authorities are now labeled violent assault (p.42). The rise of zero-tolerance policies across many jurisdictions is but one example of the increasing reliance on criminal justice interventions to manage social problems. These kinds of administrative policy changes can give the appearance of higher crime rates while masking other factors like the increasing levels of women's poverty that can also influence the collection of crime data.

This debate highlights how official statistics can be interpreted differently and how the issue can be exaggerated by a non-critical reading of the statistics. The problem can look a lot worse depending on how the data is presented (Chesney Lind and Pasko, 2004). For example, small increases in arrest rates can appear much larger when the overall numbers are small to begin with. Thus a change from 1 to 3 arrests is an increase of 200% while an increase of 250 to 300 is only a 20% increase (Luke 2008:41). Hence, without a proper contextualization of these numbers, confusion and misunderstanding can result.

Unofficial statistics on women's involvement in crime have become increasingly sparse as funding for these types of projects becomes more scarce. As a result, in Canada, there are no recent self-report studies on women and crime, nor has there been any recent in-depth victimization studies completed. The few victimization studies available are generated by government agencies and rely on the use of official statistics for their data. Given these challenges, researchers have focused on re-interpreting official statistics to offer critical analysis of current trends. For example, the Elizabeth Fry Society uses official statistics to generate fact sheets on criminalized women, but they contextualize their discussions by focusing on the treatment of vulnerable women, the challenges and hardships women can face as a result of being criminalized, and the impact of criminalization on different groups of women (Elizabeth Fry Society, 2009). This approach cannot challenge the validity of official statistics, but it does offer an important way to think about how to interpret and understand official statistics.

Why do women commit crime(s)?

Women's low rates of criminal behaviour both past and present are a significant factor in understanding the development of theories put forward to explain their criminality. Their relative absence from official crime statistics has resulted initially in a series of explanations which either ignored women or drew on sexist assumptions about their biological inferiority. Recent feminist theories have sought to challenge these ideas as well as offer new approaches to thinking about women's involvement in crime. In this section, we review both the early explanations made about women's offending and offer a discussion of more recent feminist research in this area.

Early biological explanations

In the late 19th and early 20th century, a number of key works defined the approaches developed during this period to explain women's crimes. Cesare Lombroso and William Ferrero's *The Female Offender* (1895), W.I. Thomas' *The Unadjusted Girl* (1923), Sheldon Glueck and Eleanor Glueck's *Five Hundred Delinquent Women* (1934) and Otto Pollak's *The Criminality of Women* (1950) helped to shape a view of women's crimes that would have a lasting influence until the latter part of the 20th century. The main thrust of these writings was premised on a view of women as biologically different from men and that these differences were "natural" and "intractable." Women's differences in behaviour, psychology and sexuality were attributed to their inherent biological difference from men and accounted for the differences in the nature and extent of their criminal involvement. Men were seen as naturally more aggressive, dominant, independent and rational and hence not only were they more likely to engage in criminal behaviour, but it would often be regarded by authorities as a rational response. Women, on the other hand, were viewed as dependent, nurturing, emotional and passive. Their criminality was seen as irrational and pathological because it contradicted this prevailing view of who women were, and therefore, researchers at the time assumed it was women's sexuality and mental instability that resulted in their deviant behaviour.

The work of Lombroso and Ferrero (1895) highlights the way women's crimes were understood as different from men's. The development of their theory involved studying pictures of female offenders, measuring their craniums and counting the moles and tattoos of imprisoned women to search for signs of degeneration and atavism. They found that women were less evolved than men, and this was why they exhibited fewer signs of degeneration. As a result, women would have fewer visible criminal characteristics marking them as "true" criminals. Moreover, Lombroso and Ferrero noted that women's primitive nature and biologically determined role helped to explained why women were more likely to lead less active and more solitary lives, and less likely to engage in criminal behaviour. However, the few women that did engage in crime were regarded as having an excess of masculine traits combined with possessing the worst traits of women. These women were depicted as excessively vile, cruel, cunning, spiteful and deceitful. They were regarded as abnormal for possessing an unnatural combination of both sexes and because they lacked any maternal instinct. Lombroso and Ferrero clearly saw women's crimes as antithetical to women's biologically predisposed nature. If a woman did engage in criminal behaviour, not only was she seen as an abnormal woman, but she was also seen as biologically more like a man.

Other researchers at the time also understood sex differences to be biologically based. The work of W.I. Thomas (1923) viewed women's sexuality to be the basis for their criminality. Thomas claimed that women's greater need for love combined with her inferior sense of morality meant that women and girls were more predisposed to using their sexuality to deceive and manipulate men to achieve their ends. Unlike men and boys, women's active sexuality is not normal, but a reflection of the fact that they are ill and maladjusted, and in need of treatment and protection. Thomas believed that women's criminality could be reigned in by domesticating and socializing women, particularly lower class women, to control their sexual behaviour. He also argued that women's increasing participation in the public sphere was also contributing to their increased promiscuity and immorality, thereby weakening the middle class values and family ties that kept women in check.

Sheldon and Eleanor Glueck's (1934) study of delinquent women drew on similar themes to that of W.I. Thomas when they concluded that women's crimes reflected the inability of certain women, particularly those from disadvantaged backgrounds, to control their sexual impulses. Their view of women reflected a prevailing belief at the time within criminology, that these women were pathetic, a "sorry lot" and that given their "brain disease, illegitimacy and unhappy matrimony," it is surprising that so many of them did not remain delinquent throughout their lives (p.96).

The work of Otto Pollak (1950) is regarded by many scholars as the most important research on women's crimes in this early period of criminological writings about women (Smart, 1976; Leonard, 1982). He challenged the extent and nature of women's involvement in crime and attempted to explain women's crimes through a mix of biological, psychological and sociological factors. According to Pollak, the true rate of women's crimes was hidden or masked, and if properly accounted for, would likely be similar to that of men. The reason why women's crimes did not come to the attention of authorities as often as men is because they were more likely to be the instigators than the perpetrators of crime, many of the crimes women commit took place in the home, and a gender bias at the time blinded men from seeing women's "true" nature. Women's devious acts included prostitution, blackmail, stealing from employers and hurting family members. Pollak observed that social factors such as poverty, crowded living conditions, broken homes, delinquent companions, and the impact of spending time in reform schools or prisons were important in understanding women's criminality (Pollak, 1950:139). However, Pollak, like his predecessors, emphasized women's biological and physiological differences as a fundamental theme in his theory about women. For Pollak, women had an inherently deceitful nature. Their ability to trick and deceive was related to their sexuality and physiology. He believed that since women are born without a penis, they are able to fake orgasms, and this gave them a lot of practice at deception (p.138). As well, Pollak's work also reinforced the belief that a strong link exists between women's reproductive cycle and her criminal offending. He claimed that women's generative phases (i.e., menstruation, pregnancy, and menopause) elicited a negative reaction in a male-dominated society, and this resulted in shame, secrecy and guilt for many women (p.157). Women responded to their perceived inferior status by engaging in revenge and criminal activity. When this is combined with a double standard of treatment whereby women were less likely to be arrested or prosecuted, and male victims are less likely to report women offenders, women will be underrepresented in official crime statistics.

Women, according to these theories, are defined by their domestic and sexual roles. Women are not only shaped by their biology, but women offenders are seen as inherently pathological. As Balfour and Comack (2006) note, many of these earlier criminologists saw women as "monsters, misfits or manipulators" (p.27). Biological determinism dominated these theories and even though they have been largely discredited, their legacy continues into contemporary times. Research in the 1960s continued to rely on stereotypical assumptions about women's biological imperatives to formulate explanations of women's crime and delinquency. For example, women who suffered from premenstrual syndrome (PMS) and engaged in violent behaviour were believed to have been suffering from the effects of PMS (Ibid). By locating women's criminal behaviour in their biology, even when social factors were considered, the effect has been to reinforce traditional stereotypes of women.

These writings exemplified the "legacy of sexism" that sharply influenced societal views of women at the time (Klein, 1973). Frances Heidensohn (1985) points out a curious omission in these theories when she notes how biology is seen as a determining factor in crimes women commit, but not in the crimes men commit. She argues that these theories are over-deterministic since a much higher crime rate would be expected from women due to changes in their physiology yet this has not materialized over time (Heidensohn, 1985:112). Feminists, in general, have been very critical of these explanations because they reduce an understanding of women's crimes to a set of unchanging, biologically determined set of characteristics about women (Carlen, 1985; Gavigan, 1983). The idea that women's crimes may be caused by social, cultural or economic reasons is rarely entertained. So too is the idea that her actions may be regarded as rational and purposeful. Instead, for these theorists, women who commit crimes are seen as flawed, irrational, as going against their true nature, and they are women who have failed to learn their proper role in society.

Learning Activity 3 - Journal Entry

In your course journal, discuss the following questions:

1. How are the biological explanations of female criminality linked to the concept of patriarchy and the traditional notions of sex/gender roles that were found in our society?
2. In your mind, what value do these biological explanations have today?

Sociological accounts of women's lawbreaking

Contemporary studies of women's involvement in crime focused on extricating the study of women's criminality from a biological, medical science approach and locating explanations of female criminality in external factors. The belief was that sociological approaches offered more promise than earlier biological and psychological theories. Sociological themes that traditionally were applied to explain men's criminality were scrutinized to determine their applicability to women. However, feminists examining these criminological theories found that the themes of blocked opportunity, anomie, power-control, and labeling, to name a few, were less than satisfactory in explaining the criminality of women (Leonard, 1995). Anomie theory, for example, offers little value for explaining the crimes that women commit. It cannot explain why women deviate the way they do or what type of strain leads to each outcome (p.57). The theory is more applicable to men and focuses on the goal of financial success. The general conclusion drawn from the evaluation of mainstream theories of crime has led critics to contend that they are, at best, inconsistent in their relevance to women (Naffine, 1987; Jang and Krohn, 1995) and at worst, inapplicable or irrelevant to women (Gelsthorpe and Morris, 1988). Women did not respond in the same way as men and these theories either excluded women entirely or were insufficient in explaining the gender differences in behaviour. This led many feminists to argue that mainstream criminology was really "malestream" criminology due to its failure to adequately consider women's involvement in crime. The response by some feminist criminologists was to try and make these theories "fit" women by reformulating mainstream criminological theories (Leonard, 1982), but other feminists pointed out that this "add women and stir" approach still located women at the margins of theory development (Gelsthorpe and Morris, 1988). That is, women were not integral to the arguments being developed and were merely regarded as an afterthought.

All of this changed with the publication of Freda Adler's *Sisters in Crime* and Rita Simon's *Women and Crime* in 1975. Women were now central to the development of theories seeking to explain their offending and their treatment in the criminal justice system. Adler and Simon's books generated significant interest due mostly in part to their claim that the women's liberation movement is linked to the rate of female crime. Their approach suggests that the women's movement is largely responsible for the changing sex roles taking place since the 1960s. While women have gained greater equality from the women's movement in a variety of legitimate contexts (education, occupations, politics), women now also have greater opportunities in the illegitimate or criminal context. Adler and Simon claim that women are not only committing more crimes as a result of the increased opportunities available, but they are also committing crimes that were once traditionally dominated by men. They argued a "new female criminal" was now emerging. Their theories about women's criminality were very similar, although they did differ about what types of crimes committed by women would increase. While Simon believed that only property crime rates would increase as a result of women's liberation, Adler claimed that women's violent crimes would increase as well.

Critics of Adler and Simon's work have noted several flaws with their assumptions about the link between women's liberation and women's rates of crime. One key criticism concerns the claim that women's criminality would rise substantially—a premise that both Adler and Simon assume to be the case as a result of women's liberation. As Steffensmeier (1978, 1980) highlights, there has been little or no overall change in the gap between men and women's crime rates nor is there any evidence to support the claim that a new "breed" of women criminal has emerged. Any increases in women's crime rates have occurred in traditionally female crimes like shoplifting and fraud. Another criticism leveled against their work is that the increased opportunities they document as the reason for women's greater involvement in crime is highly misleading as they misuse and manipulate statistics to prove that gender equality leads to crime (Naffine, 1987; Smart, 1976). Statistics continue to show a significant gap between men's and women's access to high-paying occupations and professions. Moreover, women in general have not experienced increased equality since the increased presence of women in the workforce has not been accompanied by a decrease in their traditional domestic responsibilities (Smart, 1976). Finally, studies with incarcerated women document how these women were generally "traditional," "feminine" and "conformist" in terms of their sex-role, and not the hardened criminals that Adler and Simon assumed would emerge (Bunch, Foley and Urbina, 1983). As Naffine (1987:32) concludes, the focus on women's liberation as the cause of crime by women has been a "time consuming and fruitless exercise."

Although Adler and Simon's work on women's changing gender roles and its link to crime has been widely discredited, other research examining the impact of sex roles on men and women's differential crime rates has merited attention. Sex role theory is based on the idea that boys and girls are socialized differently and that there is a relationship between being socialized as "masculine" or "feminine" and the nature and extent of the crimes men and women commit. The claim is that different personalities emerge from the differential socialization process, where girls are socialized to be non-violent, to seek protection rather than fight back, and to conform to their gender role expectations (Smart, 1976:66-67). As a result, women are less likely to engage in crime, and where they do, their participation reflects their gender role and expectations. For example, they are more likely to engage in violence within the home, using weapons such as a knife (Wolfgang, 1958). Men, on the other hand, are encouraged to be tough, independent and aggressive; making them more prone to involvement in crime. Although they too may be encouraged to conform, they are also rewarded for flouting conventional standards. Role theorists argue that the process of differential socialization begins at birth and is continually reinforced throughout one's life. Thus, men and women's differential crime rates are a reflection of how the values, expectations and standards of behaviour for men and women have been differently internalized.

A more recent variation of differential socialization and sex roles can be found in the work of Hagan and his colleagues (1979, 1987) where they combined gender roles, differential socialization and control theory to create a power-control theory that explained the sex differences in rates of delinquency. They argued that a relationship exists between levels of parental control and delinquent behaviour, and depending on what type of family form is in place, this would impact delinquency rates. Two types of family forms were identified: patriarchal families where the husband is the breadwinner and the authority figure and the wife stays at home, and the egalitarian family, where both the husband and wife share the authority position. Hagan (1987) predicted that delinquency rates between girls and boys from patriarchal families would likely be wider than girls and boys from egalitarian families because in patriarchal families, girls will be socialized to focus on domestic activities and have less freedom relative to boys in patriarchal families. In egalitarian families, girls and boys will have similar levels of freedom and hence, the differences in delinquency rates will not be as wide (Hagan, 1987:792).

Researchers seeking to replicate this thesis have not been as successful in demonstrating that gender differences in delinquency are related to family type or that levels of parental control are a significant predictor of delinquency rates (Akers, 1994). Several feminists have pointed out the similarities between power-control theory and the women's liberation thesis and take issue with the claim that Hagan's theory effectively makes, which is that "mother's liberation causes daughter's crime" (Chesney-Lind, 1989:20).

Overall, there are several limitations with focusing on sex roles and differential socialization as a way of explaining the different rates of crime between men and women. First, this approach fails to challenge the idea of sex roles as "natural" or biologically determined. These theorists do not historically situate or contextualize women's socially inferior position and leave intact the view that women's subordinate status is naturally given or inevitable (Smart, 1976:69). By substituting "role as destiny" for "biology as destiny," a biologically based determinism continues to dominate our view of women's criminality (Smart, 1976). Second, differential gender role socialization emphasizes why women conform, but completely ignores women's motivations for engaging in crime and therefore, cannot explain why some do get involved in criminal activity. Poor or unsuccessful socialization becomes the default view to explaining women's criminality even though this relationship has not been adequately tested (Morris, 1987:64). Finally, discussions of male and female sex roles make no reference to race and class differences in socialization even though black girls, for example, are encouraged to be assertive, responsible and independent (Sharpe, 1976). For these reasons, the contribution of sex role theory and differential socialization to our understanding of women's involvement in crime is of limited value. As Carol Smart (1976) points out, if this approach is to have an impact, then there is a need to locate sex roles in the context of social, economic and political processes which recognizes the structurally produced position of women (p.70).

Feminist accounts of women's lawbreaking

Given the marginalized, sexist, and often invisible status women occupied within mainstream criminological theories, feminist involvement in criminology began with critiques of past criminological approaches. They demonstrated how explanations of crime reflected a male view of the world and failed to adequately explain the differential crime rates between men and women (Morris, 1987; Naffine, 1987; Daly and Chesney-Lind, 1988). The need for "alternative modes of conceptualizing the social world" (Smart 1977:180) was evident, and many feminist researchers heeded Carol Smart's warning in the late 1970s when she stated that a "critique alone cannot constitute a new theoretical approach … in particular more research is needed in the area of women and crime" (p. 183).

Feminist criminology thus developed with the intent of taking a "woman centered" approach—that is, making women the central figure of criminological analysis. Since the 1970s, feminist approaches to understanding women's involvement in crime take as their starting point that the entirety of women's lives—their life experiences and social context—needs to be considered for developing an effective understanding of women's criminality. Such an approach also involves interrogating the assumptions and beliefs about the origins and consequences of gendered social structures and relations (Simpson, 1989:606). The belief is that gender, power and social relations shape social life along gendered lines through a social process that needs to be understood if it is to be challenged and changed.

The variety of feminist perspectives in criminology that have emerged since the 1970s emphasize several key themes—women's economic marginalization, the social control of women, the role of sexual and physical victimization, and women's pathways into crime. Economic explanations for criminal behaviour are not new, but only recently have researchers sought to understand the link between women's poverty and crime. The rise in property crimes by women is, contrary to the liberation thesis, a result of women's poverty, a problem experienced more harshly by single mothers (Chapman, 1980; Jurik, 1983) and women of colour. Carlen (1988:162) concluded that women in these situations were more likely than not to choose to commit crimes. Another theme examined by feminist criminologists is the influence of control theory on women's behaviour.

Unlike earlier discussions of control theory, feminist approaches to the social control of women emphasize women's agency in determining their own fates within systems which seek their conformity. For example, Worrall's research on women offenders shows how women were able to resist stereotypical constructions of femininity by exploiting the contradictions of official discourses (Worrall, 1990:163). A third theme developed by feminist criminologists is the attempt to draw greater attention to the relationship between women's victimization and criminality. Feminist researchers noted the connection between women's history of abuse and their criminal offending, highlighting the blurred boundaries between victim and offender (Comack, 2006). In particular, women who use violence were understood to be acting in a self-defensive manner (Browne, 1987; Jones, 1994; Dobash and Dobash, 1992) and were women in need of help rather than punishment. This body of work challenged the legal logic of individual culpability and reconstituted women criminals as "women in trouble" (Comack, 1996). In a similar vein, feminist pathways research examines how events in women and girls' "life course" places them at risk of offending. By sequencing the major events in women's lives, researchers were able to link, for example, childhood experiences and traumas to women's "pathways" to offending (Silbert and Pines, 1981; Chesney-Lind and Rodriguez, 1983). They found that by examining women's life histories, women who experienced childhood abuse (physical or sexual) (Widom, 1989; Shaw, 1991; Gilfus, 1992), women who were labeled and process as deviants and delinquents as young girls for refusing to accept their victimization (Arnold, 1990) or women who were in abusive relationships (Daly, 1992) turned to deviant and criminal behaviour as strategies for survival (Richie, 1996). Clearly, these interpretations of women's criminality are markedly different from previous theories and attempt to offer an understanding of women that includes a wide range of social, economic and political influences.

These important contributions were set against cautions as well, in particular, that feminists should not assume that women as a group behave in a similar manner. To that end, feminist researchers have also sought to recognize the heterogeneity of women by carrying out intersectionality research that examines the impact of race and class differences as sources of inequality and identity (Razack, 1998; Austin, 1991). More recently, feminists have eschewed the "add women and stir" approach to theorizing women's criminality drawing their influences from sociological notions of "doing gender" (West and Zimmerman, 1987) and examining the role of "gender regimes" (Williams, 2002) in shaping women's behaviour. Finally, in an effort to avoid deterministic accounts of women and crime, researchers have given greater emphasis to the complexity, tentativeness and variability in which women negotiate and resist their gender identity (Kelly, 1993; Thorne, 1993), thereby highlighting how the "gender order" (Connell, 2002) of social life is "complex and shifting" (Chesney-Lind, 2006:8).

Clearly, overcoming the limitations of previous theorizing about women's crimes involves recognizing that gender is a social process and that gender interacts in complex ways with other social characteristics. Daly and Maher (1998) identify two major roles for the future of feminist criminological research—"to continue building feminist knowledge while also challenging and correcting a non-feminist field for its gender blindnesses, enthocentrisms and theoretical rigidities" (p.12). While feminist theories of crime have yet to be fully integrated within mainstream criminology, continued critiques and development will help to ensure that successive generations will not replicate the existing biases of the past.

Learning Activity 4 - Watch and Listen

The Canadian Broadcasting Corporation (CBC) has developed a valuable online archive of many contemporary and historical television and radio clips covering a wide range of Canadian topics. You can visit the online archive at: **http://archives.cbc.ca/index.asp?IDLan=1**

The "highway of tears" is a stretch of highway in northern British Columbia that has become infamous for the number of women, mostly Aboriginal, who have gone missing along the highway. Watch this CBC television clip about the "highway of tears":

http://archives.cbc.ca/society/crime_justice/clips/17274/

Women, Criminal Law and Criminal Justice

The debates about why relatively few women engage in crime and what motivates them, are linked to a third dispute in the literature about whether criminal law and the administration of criminal justice are gender-based and thus discriminatory. The question, "Are women lawbreakers treated more leniently or more severely than men?", has generated a substantial literature on gender bias and criminal justice, both feminist and non-feminist. While Canada lacks systematic, longitudinal, national data on the various stages of the criminal justice process (for instance, reporting, policing, prosecution, and sentencing) the available information reveals patterns similar to those in other jurisdictions where researchers do have access to such data.[41]

The Chivalry-Paternalism Thesis

The most influential and enduring non-feminist perspective on how women fare in the criminal justice system was articulated in detail by the American sociologist, Otto Pollak (1950; see also Moulds, 1980). He argued that a woman lawbreaker is less likely to be detected and if detected, is treated more leniently than her male equivalent because she benefits from the operation of chivalry-paternalism. According to Pollak, men are naturally inclined to be protective toward women and, therefore, even men who make and enforce law and men who are victimized by women, are supposedly reluctant to invoke the criminal law against women lawbreakers. Consequently, women are much more likely than men to be processed informally, outside the justice system, when they commit crimes.

As evidence of this attitude, proponents of the "chivalry-paternalism thesis" cite criminal justice statistics across time in liberal states which consistently show that overall, women are reported to and charged by police much less often than men, and when brought before the courts

---

[41] Canada is particularly lacking in comprehensive, national court data which include a gender breakdown with respect to convictions and sentencing. In this section, we rely primarily on periodic statistical overviews produced by the Canadian Centre for Justice Statistics (see, e.g., Kong and AuCoin, 2008).

they are convicted less often and receive lighter sentences *vis-à-vis* men, particularly with respect to incarceration (Kong and AuCoin, 2008:10-11). They also point to the emergence and utilization of certain sex-specific offences and criminal defences that have resulted in reduced sentences for women, particularly in cases involving serious violence. For example, the offence of infanticide in the Canadian Criminal Code (SC, c.46, s.233, s.237) stipulates that the maximum sentence for women who kill their infant children by reason of post-partum depression is five years imprisonment, and in practice, women charged with infanticide have often been acquitted and serve no sentence at all. In contrast, a father who kills his infant child will likely be charged with murder or manslaughter and, if convicted, face a much longer prison term.

Since the 1980s, women defendants have also used sex-specific defences such as premenstrual syndrome (PMS) and the battered-woman syndrome (BWS) with some success, usually in cases of serious violence. Canadian law does not recognize PMS as a cause of diminished responsibility, but in a handful of cases, judges have directly considered it as a mitigating factor in sentencing (McArthur, 1989; Osborne, 1989). In 1986, for instance, proof of PMS and the necessity of "proper treatment" mitigated the sentence of a London, Ontario woman who had seriously assaulted her husband (Osborne, 1989).

Unlike PMS, the existence of BWS has been acknowledged in Canadian law through the landmark case of R. *v.* Lavallee (1990) when the Supreme Court of Canada upheld the original trial court acquittal of Angelique Lavallee. She had shot and killed her long-time abuser and common law spouse, Kevin Rust, who was not assaulting her at the time but had threatened to kill her later that evening. Speaking for the Court, Madam Justice Wilson said that to require a battered woman to wait until a physical assault is under way before she can legally defend herself is akin to "sentencing her to murder by installment" (R. *v.* Lavallee, 1990:120). While the SCC wanted to use BWS to counteract what they regarded as the systemic, informal tolerance of violence in Canadian courts and society more generally, many people consider the judgment in Lavallee (and similar cases) to be excessively lenient, essentially giving women a "licence to kill" (Comack, 1993; Grant, Chunn and Boyle, 1994:6.35-6.56).

Assuming that the "chivalry-paternalism thesis" is valid, why does protectiveness towards women translate into lenient treatment *vis-a-vis* men who commit crime(s)? Two factors are often discussed in the literature. First, the widespread assumption that women lawbreakers are "sick" or pathological individuals acting on irrational impulses may actually work to their advantage because being viewed as a "double deviant"—both mad and bad—is an image that resonates strongly with the nature of much of women's lawbreaking. For example, women shoplifters are frequently depicted as PMS-propelled kleptomaniacs. Similarly, women who kill their children are often assumed to be mentally ill because it seems inconceivable that a "normal" mother would commit such an act (Allen, 1987; Hyman, 2004). Thus, such women are legally guilty of a crime but not held morally culpable—they are bad but they cannot help it—and the result is less severe treatment than a comparable male would receive. A second factor that historically may have lead to lenient treatment of women accused of crime is the common perception of them as either helpless victims or unwilling accomplices of men. When men and women commit crimes together, for instance, the men are generally viewed as the planners and implementers and the women as passive, even reluctant, participants who are therefore less accountable for their actions (Pollak, 1950).

The Enforcement of Patriarchy

Not everyone is convinced by the "chivalry-paternalism thesis," however. Many feminists have argued that exactly the opposite is true because historically and in the contemporary context, those who enact and enforce the criminal law are predominantly men. Therefore, (criminal) law and its administration necessarily reflect and support the interests of patriarchy (i.e., male dominance). They constitute a consciously deployed mode of control that contributes directly to the ongoing subordination and inequality of women (Chunn and Lacombe, 2000:5-6). Inevitably, then, women lawbreakers are subjected to sexist and discriminatory treatment relative to the treatment of their male counterparts.

Not surprisingly, Canadian feminists who link patriarchy to harsher treatment for women than men in criminal law and the criminal justice system offer a radically different interpretation of the same statistical data cited by proponents of the "chivalry-paternalism thesis." They agree that aggregate statistics show women are less likely to be convicted of an offence and if convicted, more likely than are convicted men to receive a non-custodial disposition and, if incarcerated, more likely to be released on full parole, and that these trends have not changed fundamentally over time (Johnson, 1993; Kong and AuCoin, 2008:10-13). However, they argue that these patterns do not reflect chivalry-paternalism toward women but, rather legal differences between women and men who are criminally charged. Specifically, women are less likely than men overall to be charged with multiple offences; they generally face less serious charges; and they have shorter criminal histories than do men (Ibid).

Feminists also dispute the leniency argument with respect to sex-specific offences and defences. While infanticide carries a lesser penalty than murder, for instance, the law applies only to mothers who kill babies less than a year old and such cases are not automatically handled under that legislation. On the contrary, the infanticide law has faced increasing challenge in recent decades and since the 1990s, a growing number of women have been convicted of murdering their children, not only in Canada but also in other liberal states (Cunliffe, 2009; Kramar, 2005). Indeed, the recent Alberta decision in *R. v. Effert* (2008) in which the jury rejected expert testimony that Katrina Effert suffered an "imbalance of mind" when she killed her newborn baby and found her guilty of second degree murder rather than infanticide, may mark a tipping point for the Canadian infanticide law. She is currently appealing her life sentence and if the appeal fails, the offence of infanticide could well be repealed. Yet it has become increasingly clear that some women convicted of murdering their children in the past fifteen years were wrongfully convicted and given lengthy prison sentences on the basis of flawed evidence provided by coroners and other experts (Cunliffe, 2009; Kramar, 2005).

Similarly, many feminists maintain that the Lavallee decision has not made it easier overall for a woman who kills an abusive spouse when he is not assaulting her at the time, to plead self-defence (Sheehy, 2000; see also Chan, 2001). While the Supreme Court of Canada acknowledged BWS and broadened the interpretation of "reasonable" use of force to include prevention of an anticipated, imminent assault, they also made it clear that not every battered woman would be able to rely automatically on the defence of self-defence in such cases. This turned out to be an accurate assessment of how the Lavallee decision would play out in similar cases. In 1995, the then federal Minister of Justice and the Solicitor General of Canada jointly appointed Judge Lynn Ratushny to review the cases of 98 women who were imprisoned in relation to the deaths of abusive men prior to the Lavallee decision to determine whether they might have been able to use the broader defence of self-defence if it had been available. After a rigorous legal review of the cases, Judge Ratushny recommended that seven women be granted relief, but ultimately no women were released from prison as a result of the Self-Defence Review (Sheehy, 2000). In other words, the recognition of BWS in Canadian law has not "licensed" women to kill their spouses with impunity (Ibid; see also Stubbs and Tolmie, 2005).

How does patriarchy lead to more severe treatment of women lawbreakers than of men who are criminally charged? Many feminists argue that a major source of gender bias in the administration of criminal justice is the historical tendency of lawmakers and enforcers to sexualize women's lawbreaking. Sex outside a marriage relationship has always been considered more unacceptable for (young) women than (young) men and the former have consistently been penalized more heavily than the latter for "promiscuity" and prostitution-related offences (Boyle et al., 1985; Brock, 2009; Sangster, 2001). Moreover, if a woman commits a property offence and a sexual offence, it is more likely that she will be prosecuted for the sexual offence whereas the reverse is true of a man (Ibid).

This double standard of justice also exists because criminal law and its administration reflect man-centered perspectives on reality that are presented as universal and gender neutral. But women experience the world differently from men and therefore the implementation of gender-neutrality in criminal law and its administration still leaves women in a disadvantaged position. Although the police are charging more male clients under the current gender neutral prostitution laws in Canada, for example, it is clear that women sex workers are more likely to be charged and convicted of prostitution-related offences than are men (Lowman, 1998). Thus, the (criminal) law may now be based on the "rational person," but for those who make and enforce law, the legal subject is still the rational man.

Leniency and Severity for Which Women?

Despite compelling arguments on both sides, the existing literature does not provide conclusive evidence on the issue of gender bias and criminal justice. American researchers have produced a spate of quantitative studies in recent decades that do not demonstrate either across-the-board chivalry toward or discrimination against women lawbreakers (see, e.g., Datesman and Scarpitti, 1980; Crew, 1991; Daly, 1994; Grabe et al., 2006; Franklin and Fearn, 2008). Sometimes criminal law and the criminal justice system favour women over men and vice versa.

For some feminists, the conflicting results of research on the chivalry-severity debate suggest that researchers have been asking the wrong question (Edwards, 1989; Daly, 1997). Since no blanket legal privileging or repression of women *vis-à-vis* men has been demonstrated, it is impossible to say that women are always treated either more leniently or more severely than men. The huge and historically consistent gender gap between the numbers of women and men who are criminally charged (Kong and AuCoin, 2008; see also Rennison, 2009) seems to be generally regarded as evidence that women do commit less crime than men rather than conclusive evidence of leniency toward women. Likewise, the gender gap challenges the argument that (criminal) law is an instrument of patriarchy because if men use law to maintain their power over women, why are so many more men than women criminalized (Daly and Chesney-Lind, 1988:116)?

At the same time, it is clear that while criminal law and criminal justice may not always operate directly in the interests of men, they do work as mechanisms for regulating marginalized populations in Canada and other liberal states, thereby reproducing and maintaining structured inequalities based on social relations of gender, race, class, and sexual orientation, among others. Therefore, researchers need to think about how gender intersects with other social relations to create differences *among* women and *among* men which privilege some and disadvantage others in criminal law and the administration of criminal justice. In short, the questions researchers should be addressing are: Which women and which men are treated more leniently or severely than others in the criminal justice system and why?

It is generally agreed that the administration of criminal justice is based on both legal factors, including number of charges, seriousness of the offence(s), prior criminal record, and extra-legal factors, such as the family and employment status of the accused. More controversially, many feminists and other critical scholars argue that the administration of criminal justice is a human process and therefore the ways in which legal and extra-legal factors are assessed and influence the processing of women and men lawbreakers will reflect prevailing ideas about gender and gender relations and about crime, law and justice at particular moments in time.

With regard to ideas about gender and gender relations, many feminists have conducted studies that point to what Kathleen Daly has called "familial-based justice" (1989; see also Eaton, 1986; Okin, 1989). What their cross-jurisdictional research demonstrates is how the decision-making of legal and non-legal agents alike historically has reflected and reinforced, to a greater or lesser extent, a belief that the nuclear family unit organized around a heterosexual, monogamous marriage relationship and a sexual division of labour is the only appropriate form of family (Gavigan, 1988:293). This conception of family incorporates two assumptions about the acceptable relations between women and men, adults and children. First, "normal" women and men marry, have children, and carry out sex-specific duties and responsibilities that are related to their "natural" roles within the nuclear family—the husband as the primary breadwinner/provider and protector of his dependents, the wife/mother as the primary caregiver/homemaker and socializing agent. Second, "normal" parents prevent their children from behaving like adults, and they are particularly careful to guard the sexual purity of daughters (Sangster, 2001).

What this means is that ideas and discourses about normality are inextricably tied to assumptions about gender roles within a traditional nuclear family unit. Thus, women (and men) who conform to heteronormative, white, middle class behavioural norms are more likely to encounter the criminal justice system as agents (e.g., police, prosecutors, and judges) than as criminally charged persons; and, if they are charged, such women are more likely to receive "lenient" treatment, other things being equal, than women who cannot or refuse to conform. Only "bad" mothers, wives/spouses and daughters go to prison (Daly, 1989; Roberts, 1993; Swift and Callahan, 2009).

Women's differential ability to meet the normative standards that underpin familial-based justice is also intertwined with and influenced by shifting ideas about crime and justice. It is clear that criminal law and policy in liberal states such as Canada have been framed within the parameters of ideas and discourses about sameness and difference from the 19th century to the present (Deutschmann, 2007). Initially, an emphasis on (gender) sameness was the dominant influence on criminal law and justice which were based on the ideas that: (1) crime is a rational choice, albeit a bad one, by both women and men; (2) lawbreakers are responsible for their bad choices; and (3) they should be punished in proportion to the seriousness of their crimes. From the late 19th century to the 1960s, an emphasis on (gender and age) difference increasingly became the primary influence on criminal law and justice which were now based on the ideas that: (1) crime is an irrational act by women and men who are afflicted by sex-specific pathologies; (2) lawbreakers cannot, therefore, be held fully accountable for their actions; and (3) the appropriate response is individualized diagnosis and treatment of the crime-causing pathologies by non-legal experts (e.g., social workers, psychiatrists) rather than punishment (Ibid).

From the 1960s to the present, most liberal states have witnessed the emergence of a criminal justice system based on a hybrid of assumptions about sameness and difference that has created what David Garland (2001) calls "the culture of control." Specifically, ideas about rational choice, accountability, and punishment are intertwined with ideas about identifying "risky" women and men before they can cause harm, or to prevent future harm, working with the ones who can be "responsibilized" and containing the ones who cannot. In most contemporary liberal states, criminal justice rests on a conception of sameness as identical treatment and differences among women (and among men) are acknowledged only to pinpoint and control risk, not to develop individualized responses to criminalized women which address their needs (Hannah-Moffat, 2005; Swift and Callahan, 2009). Moreover, the conception of equal treatment as identical treatment when there are such obvious differences (i.e., inequalities related to race/class/gender/sexual orientation) among criminalized women, works to reproduce and exacerbate those differences, thereby increasing the severity of the criminal justice process for many women (Daly, 1989; Roberts, 1993; Chigwada-Bailey, 2003).

Racialized women (and men), for example, are vastly over-represented in the criminal justice systems of all contemporary liberal states (see, e.g., Chan and Mirchandani, 2002; Chigwada-Bailey, 2003). Canadian reforms implemented in recent decades that are aimed at improving police-community relations and reducing imprisonment rates, particularly with respect to Aboriginal people, clearly have been ineffectual (Williams, 2009). In 2006, a decade after the implementation of a sentencing reform that instructed judges to consider all reasonable alternatives to prison for Aboriginal people (SC, c.46, s. 718.2(e)), the incarceration rates for both women and men had increased while the rates for non-Aboriginal prisoners actually declined (pp. 80-81). Aboriginal women, who are dramatically over-incarcerated even relative to their male counterparts, are among the most marginalized women in Canada and therefore among the least able to meet familial-based norms and to achieve self-sufficiency and independence in their lives. Yet in passing sentence, judges have tended to focus on the individual circumstances and "risky" characteristics of Aboriginal women without considering the broader social context, including the legacy of colonialism, in which they live. As a result, sentencing decisions about Aboriginal women over the post-1996 decade were dominated by a judicial desire to control for risk with little attention to the ways in which criminalized Aboriginal women are also at risk (Williams, 2009:81; see also Comack, 1996; Swift and Callahan, 2009).

Research reveals similar patterns with criminalized women who openly flout heterosexual norms and are often marginalized in other ways as well. Studies of women on death row in the United States, for example, show an over-representation of lesbians, or prisoners perceived to be lesbians, who do not project the "hetero-feminine" persona that is critical "in engendering chivalry and leniency" toward criminalized women (Farr, 2000:49; see also Robson, 2004). Rather, they are depicted as "manly and man-hating women" who kill out of rage and an "irrational desire for revenge"; a portrait of "homosexualized … female evil" that may be an additional aggravating circumstance in the sentencing of women for offences that carry the ultimate penalty of death (Ibid). Finally, it is important to note that even middle class, white, heterosexual women can find themselves in the "undeserving" category of offender if they seriously breach the norms of femininity and propriety. In the Canadian context, for instance, Karla Homolka has achieved iconic status as the epitome of the "monstrous feminine" for her participation in the killings of several women, including her younger sister (Kilty and Frigon, 2006).[42]

Initially, she was constructed in law and in the media as a fairy tale princess who thought she had married a prince, but he turned into an abusive husband and coerced her into committing acts of sexual sadism and murder. Ultimately, this construction of Homolka as a victim was erased and replaced by the enduring image of Homolka as an evil witch who manipulated criminal justice officials into granting her an undeserved plea agreement (Ibid.). In exchange for testifying against her former husband, she was allowed to enter a guilty plea to manslaughter charges and was released from prison after serving a twelve year sentence whereas Paul Bernardo was convicted of first degree murder, declared a dangerous offender and sentenced to life imprisonment. Many Canadians were outraged at what they perceived as the appalling leniency that criminal justice authorities extended to Karla Homolka (Pearson, 1997). Arguably, however, if she is viewed as *both* endangered and dangerous, she should receive a lesser sentence than Paul Bernardo; to give her an identical sentence would be to punish her more severely than him (Kilty and Frigon, 2006).

Learning Activity 5 - Summarize

In your own words, summarize the key provisions of the application of feminist approaches to the topic of female criminality. In particular, pay particular attention to the following:

- "under-representation" of women as perpetrators of crime
- the "chivalry-paternalism" thesis
- the "culture of control"

Conclusion

Our point of departure for this overview of women, crime and criminal justice was the historical silence with respect to criminalized women. Since the late 1960s, feminists have attempted to fill the silence, first with critiques of the few writers who did talk about criminalized women during the first half of the twentieth century, and second, with their own attempts to analyze and theorize how gender influences explanations of and responses to criminalized women. While it is obvious that feminists hold diverse perspectives, their collective work highlights several things that are key

---

[42]   The young women were Leslie Mahaffy, Kristen French, and Tammy Homolka.

to conducting research on and theorizing about women's lawbreaking. One is the need to conduct both inter-gender and intra-gender comparisons; that is, to examine similarities and differences *between* women and men and also *among* women and *among* men. Men commit much more crime than do women, and most of the serious violent crime, but it is also the case that the majority of women and men who enter the criminal justice process are charged with relatively minor property and/or other non-violent offences. Likewise, the intersection of gender with other social relations of race/class/sexual orientation generates differences among criminally charged women (and men) which translate into differential treatment in the criminal justice system.

A second issue that emerges from feminist criminology is the need to locate criminalized women (and men) within the wider structural context(s) in which they are expected to be responsible and accountable. To that end, researchers should also focus attention on the intersecting institutional regulation of marginalized women and the extent to which they are caught up in social welfare, child welfare, and (mental) health systems as well as the criminal justice system. The current one-sided emphasis on disciplining and controlling "risky" women ignores the unmet needs of women that put them at risk in the first place and which often create pathways into lawbreaking (Daly, 1992).

Perhaps the most important issue that feminist criminology has highlighted, however, is feminists' over-emphasis, even reliance, on legal reform strategies as a means of bringing about change (Snider, 1994). In liberal states such as Canada, criminal law is among the most repressive mechanisms of state control that are deployed against some of the least powerful women and men in those societies and should be used as a last, not a first, resort. The spectacular failure of criminal justice reforms, such as the 1996 sentencing provision aimed at reducing the incarceration rate of Aboriginal peoples, clearly demonstrates that criminal law is simply not an appropriate vehicle for resolving social problems. Feminists and their allies will need to develop non-legal strategies for change in other arenas (e.g., politics) if criminalized women are ever to achieve social justice.

References

Adelberg, E. and C. Currie (eds.). (1987). *Too few to count: Canadian women in conflict with the law.* Vancouver: Press Gang Publishers.

Adler, F. (1975). *Sisters in crime.* New York: McGraw-Hill.

Akers, R. (1994). *Criminological theories: Introduction and evaluation.* Los Angeles: Roxbury Publishing Company.

Arnold R. (1990). "Women of color: Processes of victimization and criminalization of black women." *Social Justice* 17(3):153-166.

Austin, R. (1991). "The black community: Its lawbreakers and a politics of identification." *Southern California Law Review* 65:1769-1818.

Balfour, G. and E. Comack (eds.). (2006). *Criminalizing women.* Halifax: Fernwood Press.

Boyle, C., Bertrand, M.-A., Lacerte-Lamontagne, C., and R. Shamai. (1985). *A feminist review of criminal law.* Ottawa: Minister of Supply and Services Canada.

Brock, D. (2009). *Making work, making trouble: The social regulation of sexual labour.* 2nd ed. Toronto: University of Toronto Press.

Browne, A. (1987). *When battered women kill.* London: Collier Macmillan.

Bunch, B. L. Foley and Urbina, S. (1983). "The psychology of violent female offenders: A sex-role perspective." *The Prison Journal* 63:66-79.

Carlen, P. (1985). *Criminal women: Autobiographical accounts.* Cambridge, UK: Polity Press.

Carlen, P. (1988). *Women, crime and poverty.* Buckingham: Open University Press.

Chan, W. (2001). *Women, murder and justice.* New York: Palgrave.

Chan, W. and K. Mirchandani (eds.). (2002). *Crimes of colour: Racialization and the justice system in Canada.* Peterborough, ON: Broadview Press.

Chapman, J.R. (1980). *Economic realities and the female offender.* Lexington: Lexington Books.

Chesney-Lind, M. (1989). "Girls' crime and women's place: Towards a feminist model of female delinquency." *Crime and Delinquency* 35:5-29.

Chesney-Lind, M. (2006). *Patriarchy, crime and justice.* Feminist Criminology 1(1):6-26.

Chesney-Lind, M. and Pasko, L. (2004). *The female offender: Girls, women, and crime.* 2nd ed. Thousand Oaks, CA: Sage Publications.

Chesney-Lind, M. and Rodriguez, N. (1983). "Women under Lock and Key." *Prison Journal* 63:47-65.

Chigwada-Bailey, R. (2003). *Black women's experiences of criminal justice.* 2nd ed. Winchester: Waterside Press.

Chunn, D.E. and D. Lacombe, (eds.). (2000). *Law as a gendering practice.* Toronto: Oxford University Press.

Comack, E. (1993). *Feminist engagement with the law: The legal recognition of the battered woman syndrome.* Ottawa: CRIAW/ICREF.

Comack, E. and S. Brickey. (2007). "Constituting the violence of criminalized women." *Canadian Journal of Criminology and Criminal Justice* 49:1-36.

Comack, E. (1996). *Women in trouble.* Halifax: Fernwood Press.

Connell, R. (2002). *Gender.* Cambridge: Polity Press.

Crew, B.K. (1991). "Sex differences in criminal sentencing: Chivalry or patriarchy?" *Justice Quarterly* 8(1):59-84.

Cunliffe, E. (2009). *Getting away with murder? Law, science and motherhood in R. v. Kathleen Folbigg.* Unpublished doctoral thesis, University of British Columbia, Vancouver, BC.

Daly, K. (1989). "Rethinking judicial paternalism: Gender, work-family relations, and sentencing." *Gender and Society* 3(1):9-36.

Daly, K. (1992). "Women's pathways to felony court: Feminist theories of lawbreaking and problems of representation." *Review of Law and Women's Studies* 2:11-52.

Daly, K. (1994). *Gender, crime and punishment.* New Haven, CT: Yale University Press.

Daly, K. (1997). "Different ways of conceptualizing sex/gender in feminist theory and their implications for criminology." *Theoretical Criminology* 1(1):25-51.

Daly, K. and L. Maher (eds.). (1998*). Criminology at the crossroads.* New York: Oxford University Press.

Daly, K. and Chesney-Lind. M. (1988). "Feminism and criminology." *Justice Quarterly* 5(4):497-538.

Datesman, S.K. and F.R. Scarpitti (eds.). (1980). *Women, crime and justice.* New York: Oxford University Press.

Deutschmann, L. (2007). *Deviance and social control.* 4th ed. Toronto: Nelson Thomson Learning.

Dobash, R. and Dobash, R. (1992). *Women, violence and social change.* London: Routledge.

Eaton, M. (1986). *Justice for women? Family court and social control.* MiltonKeynes, UK: Open University Press.

Edwards, A.R. (1989). "Sex/gender, sexism and criminal justice: Some theoretical considerations."

International Journal of the Sociology of Law 17(2):165-184.

Elizabeth Fry Society. (2009). *Fact sheet: Issues associated with increased criminalization of women.* Accessed online at: http://www.elizabethfry.ca/eweek09/factsht.htm.

Farr, K.A. (2000). "Defeminizing and dehumanizing female murderers: Depictions of lesbians." *Women and Criminal Justice* 11(1):49-66.

Franklin, C.A. and Fearn, N.E. (2008). "Gender, race, and formal court decision-making outcomes: Chivalry/paternalism, conflict theory or gender conflict?" *Journal of Criminal Justice* 36(3):279-290.

Garland, D. (2004). *The culture of control: Crime and social order in contemporary society.* Chicago: The University of Chicago Press.

Gavigan, S.A.M. (1983). "Women's crime and feminist critiques." *Canadian Criminology Forum* 6(1):75-90.

Gavigan, S.A.M. (1988). "Law, gender and ideology." In A. Bayefsky (ed.), *Legal theory meets legal practice.* Edmonton: Academic Press.

Gelsthorpe, L. and A. Morris (eds.). (1988). *Feminist perspectives in criminology.* Milton Keynes: Open University Press.

Gilfus, M. (1992). "From victims to survivors to offenders: Women's route of entry and immersion into street crime." *Women and Criminal Justice* 4:63-90.

Glueck, S. and E. Glueck. (1934). *Five hundred delinquent women.* New York: Knopf.

Grabe, J.E., Trager, K.D., Lear, M. and J. Rauch. (2006). "Gender in crime news: A case study test of the chivalry hypothesis." *Mass Communication and Society* 9(2):137-163.

Grant, I., Chunn, D.E. and C. Boyle. (1994). *The Law of homicide.* Scarborough, ON: Carswell/Thomson.

Hagan, J., J. Simpson, and A. Gillis. (1979). "The sexual stratification of social control: A gender-based perspective on crime and delinquency." *British Journal of Sociology* 30(1):25-38.

Hagan, J., J. Simpson, and A. Gillis. (1987). "Class in the household: A power-control theory of gender and delinquency." *American Journal of Sociology* 92:788-816.

Hannah-Moffat, K. (2005). "Criminogenic need and the transformative risk subject: Hybridizations of risk/need in penality." *Punishment and Society* 7:29-51.

Heidensohn, F. (1985). *Women and crime.* Basingstoke, UK: MacMillan.

Hyman, R. (2004). "Media of suburbia: Andrea Yates, maternal infanticide, and the insanity defense." *Women's Studies Quarterly* 32(3/4):192-210.

Jang, S. and M. Krohn. (1995). "Developmental patterns of sex differences in delinquency among African American adolescents: A test of the sex-invariance hypothesis." *Journal of Quantitative Criminology* 11(2):195-222.

Jiwani, Y. (2005). "Walking a tightrope: The many faces of violence in the lives of racialized immigrant girls and young women." *Violence Against Women* 11(7):846-875.

Johnson, H. (1993). "A statistical overview of women and crime in Canada: Women and the Canadian justice system." In E. Adelberg and C. Currie (eds.), *In conflict with the law.* Vancouver: Press Gang Publishers.

Jones, A. (1994). *Next time she'll be dead.* Boston: Beacon Press.

Jurik, N. (1983). "The Economics of Female Recidivism." *Criminology* 21(4):3-12.

Kelly, D. (1993). *Last chance high: How girls and boys drop in and out of alternative schools.* New Haven, CT: Yale University Press.

Kilty, J.M. and S. Frigon. (2006). "Karla Homolka-From a woman *in danger* to a *dangerous* woman: Chronicling the shifts." *Women and Criminal Justice* 17(4):37-61.

Klein, D. (1973). "The Etiology of female crime: A review of the literature." *Issues in Criminology* 8(2):3-30.

Kong, R. and K. AuCoin. (2008). *Female offenders in Canada.* Juristat 28(1). Statistics Canada Catalogue no. 85-002-XIE. Ottawa.

Kramar, K. (2005). *Unwilling mothers, unwanted babies: Infanticide in Canada.* Vancouver: UBC Press.

Leonard, E. (1982). *Women, crime and society.* New York: Longman.

Leonard, E. (1995) ."Theoretical criminology and gender." In B. Price and N. Sokoloff (eds.), *The criminal justice system and women.* 2nd ed. New York: McGraw Hill.

Lombroso, C. and W. Ferrero. (1895). *The female offender.* London: Fisher Unwin.

Lowman, J. (1998). "Prostitution law reform in Canada." *In Toward comparative law in the 21ˢᵗ century: The 50ᵗʰ anniversary of the Institute of Contemporary Law in Japan* . Tokyo: Chuo University Press.

Luke, K. (2008). "Are girls really becoming more violent? A critical analysis." *Affilia* 23(1):38-50.

McArthur, K. (1989). "Through her looking glass: PMS on trial." *University of Toronto Faculty of Law Review* 47(Autumn):826-873.

Messing, J.T. and J.W. Heeren. (2009). "Gendered justice: Domestic homicide and the death penalty." *Feminist Criminology* 4(2):170-188.

Morris, Alison. (1987). *Women, crime and criminal justice.* Oxford: Basil Blackwell.

Moulds, E. (1980). "Chivalry and paternalism: Disparities of treatment in the criminal justice system." In S.K. Datesman and F.R. Scarpitti (eds.), *Women, crime and justice.* New York: Oxford University Press.

Naffine, N. (1996). *Feminism and criminology.* Philadelphia: Temple University Press.

Naffine, N. (1987). *Female crime: The construction of women in criminology.* Sydney: Allen and Unwin.

Okin, S.M. (1989). *Justice, gender, and the family.* New York: Basic Books.

Osborne, J. (1989). "Perspectives on premenstrual syndrome: Women, law and medicine." *Canadian Journal of Family Law* 8(Fall):165-184.

Pearson, P. (1997). *When she was bad: Violent women and the myth of innocence.* Toronto: Random House.

Pollack, O. (1950). *The criminality of women.* Philadelphia: University of Pennsylvania Press.

Pollack, S. (2008). "Labeling clients 'risky': Social work and the neo-liberal welfare state." *British Journal of Social Work* 38:1-16.

Pollock, J. and S. Davis. (2005). "The continuing myth of the violent female offender." *Criminal Justice Review* 30(1):5-29.

Rafter, N. and F. Heidensohn, (eds.). (1995). *International feminist perspectives in criminology: Engendering a discipline.* Philadelphia: Open University Press.

Razack, S. (1998). *Looking white people in the eye: Gender, Race and culture in courtroom and classrooms.* Toronto: University of Toronto Press.

Rennison, C.M. (2009). "A new look at the gender gap in offending." *Women and Criminal Justice* 19(3):171-190.

Richie, B. (1996). *Compelled to crime: The gender entrapment of battered black women.* New York:

Routledge.

Roberts, D. (1993). "Motherhood and crime." *Iowa Law Review* 79:95-141.

Robson, R. (2004). "Lesbianism and the death penalty: A 'hard core' case." *Women's Studies Quarterly* 32(3/4):181-191.

Sangster, J. (2001). *Regulating girls and women: Sexuality, family, and the law in Ontario, 1920-1960.* Toronto: Oxford University Press.

Sharpe, S. (1976). *Just like a girl—how girls learn to be women.* Harmondsworth: Penguin.

Shaw, M. (1991). *Survey of federally sentenced women.* Ottawa: Ministry of the Solicitor General.

Sheehy, E.A. (2000). "Review of the self-defence." *Canadian Journal of Women and the Law* 12(1):197-134.

Silbert, M and A. Pines. (1981). "Sexual abuse as an antecedent to prostitution." *Child Abuse and Neglect* 5:407-411.

Simon, R. (1975). *Women and crime.* Lexington, Mass.: Lexington Books.

Simpson, S. (1989). "Feminist theory, crime and justice." *Criminology* 27(4):605-31.

Smart, C. (1976). *Women, crime and criminology: A feminist critique.* London: Routledge and Kegan Paul.

Snider, L. (1994). "Feminism, punishment and the potential of empowerment." *Canadian Journal of Law and Society* 9(1):75-104.

Statistics Canada. (2009). *Family violence in Canada: A statistical profile.* Catalogue no. 85-224-X. Ottawa.

Steffensmeier, D. (1978). "Crime and the contemporary woman: An analysis of changing levels of female property crime, 1960-1975." In Lee H. Bowker (ed.), *Women and crime.* New York: MacMillan.

Steffensmeier, D. (1980). "Assessing the impact of the women's movement on sex-based differences in the handling of adult criminal defendants." *Crime and Delinquency* 76:344-357.

Steffensmeier, D. and S. Demuth. (2006). "Does gender modify the effects of race-ethnicity on criminal sanctioning?" *Journal of Quantitative Criminology* 22(3):241-261.

Stubbs, J. and J. Tolmie. (2005). "Defending battered women on charges of homicide: The structural and systemic versus the personal and particular." In W. Chan, D.E. Chunn and R. Menzies (eds.), *Women, madness and the law: A feminist reader.* London: The GlassHouse Press.

Swift, K. and M. Callahan. (2009). *At risk: Social justice in child welfare and other human services.* Toronto: University of Toronto Press.

Thomas, W. (1923). *The unadjusted girl.* Boston: Little, Brown.

Thorne, B. (1993). *Gender play.* New Brunswick, NJ: Rutgers University Press.

West, C. and D.H. Zimmerman. (1987). "Doing gender." *Gender and Society* 1:125-151.

Widom, C. (1989). "The cycle of violence." *Science* 244:160-166.

Williams, L. (2002). "Trying on gender, gender regimes, and the process of becoming women." *Gender and Society* 16:29-52.

Williams, T. (2009). "Intersectionality analysis in the sentencing of aboriginal Women in Canada." In E. Grabham, D. Cooper, J. Krishnadas, and D. Herman (eds.), *Intersectionality and beyond: Law, power, and the politics of location.* Abingdon, Oxon: Routledge-Cavendish.

Wolfgang, M. (1958). *Patterns in criminal homicide.* Philadelphia: University of Pennsylvania Press.

Worrall, A. (1990). *Offending woman.* London: Routledge.

POSTSCRIPT

System Responses to Justice-Related Diversity Issues in Canada

Take this fun quiz before you read the chapter. Answer "True" or "False":

1. "Affirmative action" programs are illegal because they discriminate against non-minorities.

2. The rights of First Nations Peoples were established when Canada was founded in 1867.

3. In Canada, it was once impossible for a husband to be charged with raping his wife.

4. Quota hiring of minority individuals is a common practice in most Canadian police departments.

5. Most First Nations communities have their own police.

6. Community policing originated in the United States during the 1970s and 1980s.

7. Under the Youth Criminal Justice Act, a young person must be found guilty before extrajudicial sanctions can be applied.

8. Early intervention by domestic violence courts is a way to ensure that the offender gets the stiffest sentence possible.

9. Probation is a form of suspended sentence.

10. Female inmates are housed in an isolated part of prisons that also house male inmates.

ANSWERS: 1F, 2F, 3T, 4F, 5T, 6T, 7F, 8F, 9F, 10F

Introduction

Diversity-related issues gained greater recognition in much of Canadian society starting sometime after World War II. However, the justice system was somewhat slower to recognize and attempt to address these concerns. It was not until the 1970s, with the introduction of community policing initiatives in some Canadian cities, that we see the first significant changes within the justice system (Seagrave, 1997).

Each part of the Canadian justice system has responded to diversity-related concerns in somewhat different ways. Within policing, there has been little in the way of a coordinated system-wide approach. It has been left up to individual police agencies to address diversity-related issues. Within federal correction, there has been as system-wide and coordinated response to many diversity-related concerns.

The purpose of this chapter is to introduce readers to some of the different approaches used within the Canadian justice system to deal with diversity issues. Specifically, the chapter will review:

- Federal Government initiatives such as changes to the Criminal Code of Canada, same-sex marriage provisions and residential school reconciliation,
- police initiatives such as diversity hiring, officer training and specialized diversity units,
- changes within the operation of criminal court system in response to the over-representation of youths and aboriginals, and
- approaches within federal corrections related to aboriginal offenders, female offenders and young offenders.

Federal Government Initiatives

When the Canadian Constitution, including the *Charter of Rights and Freedoms*, became law in 1982, it rapidly formed the foundation for a series of Federal Government initiatives to attempt to remedy justice-related diversity concerns. The new Charter lead to a massive revision of the Criminal Code of Canada, the ultimate recognition of gay and lesbian legal equality and the push towards formal resolution of the damages done by residential schools.

Charter Rights of Equality

How does the Canadian Constitution and Charter of Rights and Freedoms relate to diversity issues?

There are two very important parts of the Canadian Constitution that provide the legal basis for diversity rights in Canada. These are:

1. The establishment of equality rights in section 15 of the *Canadian Charter of Rights and Freedoms*, and
2. The separate recognition of Aboriginal rights in Part 2 of the Canadian Constitution.

Part 1 of the Canada's Constitution is the *Canadian Charter of Rights and Freedoms*. The Charter articulates the rights of individuals such as democratic rights, mobility rights, legal rights, language rights and equality rights. Section 15 of the Charter reads as follows (*Constitution Act 1982*, 2004):

Equality Rights

15. (1) Every individual is equal before the and under the law and has the right to the equal protection and equal benefit of the law without discrimination and, in particular, without discrimination based on race, national or ethnic origin, colour, religion, sex, age, or mental or physical disability.

(2) Subsection (1) does not preclude any law, program or activity that has as its object the amelioration of conditions of disadvantaged individuals or groups including those that are disadvantaged because of race, national or ethnic origin, colour, religion, sex, age, or mental or physical disability.

Don't affirmative action programs discriminate against non-minorities?

Subsection (2) of the equality rights section of the Charter is worth noting. It allows governments to establish laws, policies and programs that are designed to address the negative social consequences of discrimination and prejudice in Canada. The Court was concerned that claims of "**reverse discrimination**" over some government diversity programs could prevent attempts to "right past wrongs."[43] Subsection (2) allows governments to continue with "affirmative action" programs. This usually involves the process of creating and/or allowing marginalized groups and individuals access to education and/or employment otherwise not availed in the past. Such actions are considered essential to people human rights.

The Special Constitutional Rights of Aboriginals in Canada

Are Aboriginal people viewed the same as other minorities in Canada?

The unique historical position of Canada's First Nations people is given special attention in Canada's Constitution.

■ **Section 25 of the Charter**
This section is important because it affirms the legal recognition that Aboriginal peoples have a historical claim to land ownership. The Royal Proclamation of 1763 established legal precedence to their claim and all subsequent treaties remain enforce.

---

[43] Social theories such as **egalitarianism** claim that social equality should exist for all regardless of any social, cultural, ethnic, or other differences upon which diversity and discrimination or prejudice could be founded. An example of reverse discrimination might be the granting of rights to Aboriginals, gays and lesbians, the elderly, etc. at the expense of a historically socio-politically dominant group (e.g., whites, heterosexuals, middle-age, etc.).

Section 25 of the Canadian Constitution Act 1982 (2004)

25. The guarantee in this Charter of certain rights and freedoms shall not be construed so as to abrogate or derogate from any aboriginal, treaty or other rights or freedoms that pertain to the aboriginal peoples of Canada including

(a) any rights or freedoms that have been recognized by the Royal Proclamation of October 7, 1763; and

(b) any rights or freedoms that may be acquired by the aboriginal peoples of Canada by way of land claims settlement.

Learning Activity 2 - Research

Section 25 of the Canadian Charter guarantees that it "shall not be construed so as to abrogate or derogate from any aboriginal treaty or other rights and freedoms that pertain to the aboriginal peoples of Canada." What do the terms "abrogate" and "derogate" mean?

Re-read section 25 to make sure you fully understand what it means.

Part 2 of the Canadian Constitution

Aboriginal rights are given additional protection. Part 2 of the Canadian Constitution is entitled "Rights of Aboriginal Peoples of Canada." In this part of the Constitution, the following provisions to the rights of Aboriginal people are made (*Constitution Act 1982*, 2004):

- The Constitution recognizes the definition of "Aboriginal people" in the Indian Act (e.g., Indian, Inuit, and Métis);
- The legal recognition is given to all existing aboriginal and Treaty rights;
- The legal right for Aboriginal people to negotiate future Treaty rights;
- The equal gender rights among Aboriginal people; and
- The Federal Government's commitment to consult with Aboriginal peoples before changing the Canadian Constitution.

The Recognition of the Rights of Lesbians and Gay Men

In comparison to Aboriginal rights, the recognition of the Charter rights of lesbians and gay men has been slow.[44] One reason is the omission of "sexual orientation" as one of the stated illegal grounds for discrimination the Section 15 of the Charter (see above).[45]

Has the Supreme Court ruled on the rights of lesbians and gay men?

The rights of gay men and lesbians were advanced by two critical legal challenges:

- **Egan v. Canada**
  In 1995, the Supreme Court of Canada ruled that Section 15 of the Charter also provided protection from discrimination on the basis of sexual orientation (Eagle Canada, 2007a). The Court ruled that it was covered under the Charter's prohibition of sex discrimination. However, the Court did not accept the claim that a same-sex partnership was the same as a marriage.
- **Same-sex Marriages**
  After several years of controversy, the Government of Canada recognized that same-sex partners could be legally married within Canada in 2005 (Egale Canada, 2007b). The federal legislation was following the lead of 8 out of 10 provinces and 1 territory. Under federal law, religious organizations can decline to perform same-sex marriages on the basis of their freedom of religious belief.[46]

Hate Propaganda Laws

In response to concerns about the growing incidents of hate literature and speeches, the Federal Government amended the Criminal Code of Canada in 1970 to include new "hate propaganda" laws (Sections 318-320) (Rosen, 2000:2-3).

What is "hate propaganda"?

Specifically, Canada's hate propaganda laws prohibit (Department of Justice Canada, 2007):

- The advocacy and promotion of genocide (killing or deliberately promoting the killing of the members of a minority group);
- The willful promotion of hatred against and identifiable group;
- Communicating, other than in private, willful hatred against an identifiable group.

---

[44]   It wasn't until 2003 that under then Prime Minister Jean Chretien efforts were made to change the definition of marriage to include same-sex marriage. Finally, in July 2005, Canada became only the fourth country in the world to recognize same sex marriage through the Civil Marriage Act (see below).

[45]   In 2006 at the world's first Outgames held in Montreal, the city also hosted the International Conference on LGBT Human Rights out of which emerged the Declaration of Montreal Declaration which outlines the rights to lesbians, gays, bisexuals, and transgender people.

[46]   For more information on legal and related issues pertaining to same-sex marriage, visit: http://www.samesex-marriage.ca/.

During the 1970s and 80s, these laws were primarily used to prosecute individuals and groups that promoted anti-Semitic views. Most notably, individuals such as Ernst Zundel and James Keegstra[47]were charged under the hate propaganda legislation for denying the attempted genocide of Jews in World War II. Keegstra expressed his views in high-school classrooms as a social studies teacher. Zundel published and distributed his views in books, brochures and public speeches.

How many hate propaganda crimes are there in Canada each year?

According to Statistics Canada (2004:16), 124 hate propaganda incidents were reported to the police in 12 major Canadian municipalities during 2001/2002. This was just over 13% of all "hate crimes" reported in Canada.

Sentencing Guidelines for Hate-Motivated Crimes

In 1995, the Federal Government included in the Criminal Code of Canada a new section entitled "Purpose and Principles of Sentencing." The rationale for Section 718 is to provide direction to the courts on those factors that must be considered as a judge is determining the appropriate sentence.

How are hate crimes handled in Canada?

Section 718.2 (a) reads as follows (Department of Justice Canada, 2007):

Section 718.2 of the Criminal Code

718.2. A court that imposes a sentence shall also take into consideration the following principles:

(a) a sentence should be increased or reduced to account for any relevant aggravating or mitigating circumstances relating to the offence or the offender, and, without limiting the generality of the foregoing,(i) evidence that the offence was motivated by bias, prejudice or hate based on race, national or ethnic origin, language, colour, religion, sex, age, mental or physical disability, sexual orientation, or any other similar factor.

Source: Department of Justice Canada, 2007

---

[47]   Ernest Zundal, German born, moved to Canada in 1958 and began to advocate anti-Semitic literature and denied the Holocaust (a crime in Germany). Over the years various efforts to constrain him failed. In 2001 he moved to Knoxville, Tenn. In 2005, Canada was able to lay charge against him under the new hate laws and had Zundal returned to Canada where was later extradited back to Mannheim, Germany where was found guilty in Feb. 2007 of inciting racial hatred and denying the Holocaust. He received a 5 year sentence ("Nazi policies…", 2007). James Keegstra was a high-school teacher as well as a former mayor in a small town in Alberta who pushed the boundaries of "freedom of speech" by declaring that the Holocaust never happened and promoting anti-Semitic statements with his students. In 1984 he was charged with unlawfully promoting hatred against an identifiable group under s. 319(2) of the Criminal Code. (For a more detailed account see: http://www.chrc-ccdp.ca/en/timePortals/milestones/128mile.asp).

Doesn't Canada have any specific criminal laws regarding hate crime?

Outside of the hate propaganda laws, Canada does not have separate laws to address crimes of violence (i.e., assaults, homicides, and robberies) or crimes against property (i.e., vandalism and arson) that are motivated by prejudice or hate. The Canadian approach is to direct judges to consider more severe sentences for hate motivated crimes. Nevertheless, judges must keep punishment within the prescribed range that is outlined in the Criminal Code for each offence.

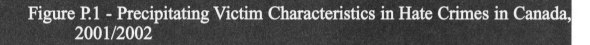

Learning Activity 3 - Discuss

Share your thoughts on why you think Canadian law allows for stiffer sentences for hate-motivated crimes? Why should we consider these crimes more serious? If they are so serious, why don't we have separate criminal code charges for hate crimes like they do in some jurisdictions in the United States?

How many hate motivated crimes are there in Canada?[48]

According to a Statistics Canada survey (Statistics Canada, 2004a:1), there were 928 reported incidents of hate crime in 12 major Canadian cities in 2001/2002. Figure P.1 below illustrates which specific minority groups were targeted.

Figure P.1 - Precipitating Victim Characteristics in Hate Crimes in Canada, 2001/2002

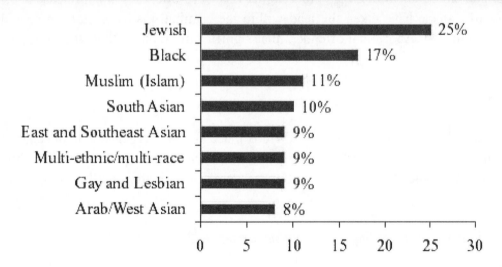

Source: Statistics Canada (2004b).

---

[48]   For an interesting comparative look at hate crime and how it is dealt with internationally consider accessing: Under the Shadow of Weimar Democracy, Law, and Racial Incitement in Six Countries by L. Greenspan and C. Levitt (1993).

The same survey indicates that nearly 50% of the reported hate crimes involved threats and 34% involved physical violence (Statistics Canada, 2004a:12). In 17% of the reported hate crimes, a weapon of some variety was used. However, in many instances, hate-motivated crimes go unreported to the police. Fear of future victimization and a belief that the police will not take the crime seriously are two common reasons why some people do not report crimes (Statistics Canada, 2005a:19).

Sentencing Guidelines for Aboriginal Offenders

Are sentences given to Aboriginal offenders different than non-Aboriginals?

Within the Criminal Code of Canada's "Purpose and Principles of Sentencing," judges are given directions to consider when sentencing an Aboriginal offender. As Section 718.2(e) states:

Section 718.2e of the Criminal Code

(e) all available sanctions other than imprisonment that are reasonable in the circumstances should be considered for all offenders, with particular attention to the circumstances of aboriginal offenders.

Source: Department of Justice Canada, 2007

As we shall see in the upcoming unit of corrections, incarcerating Aboriginal offenders in a traditional prison environment often lead to a higher risk of re-offending upon release. Correctional Services of Canada have taken the lead within the criminal justice system in providing effective programming for Aboriginal offenders that significantly reduces their likelihood of re-offending.[49]

Sexual Violence

Massive revisions to the Criminal Code of Canada took place in 1983, largely due to the enactment of the Canadian Charter of Rights and Freedoms one year earlier. The equality rights within the Charter illustrated that some of criminal code offences were discriminatory on the basis of gender and/or sexual orientation.

How have the criminal laws regarding sexual violence changed?

Perhaps the most obvious example of the need to revise the Criminal Code of Canada was found in pre-1983 Criminal Code offence of rape. According to criminal law, rape was an act that could

---

[49]   For more details see: http://198.103.98.138/text/prgrm/correctional/ab_e.shtml.

only be committed by a "male person" (Criminal Code and Selected Statutes, 1955:45). Further, the rape victim had to be a "female person who is not his wife."

The 1983 revisions to the Criminal Code removed rape as an offence and added the current 3-tiered sexual assault law. Equally important, the new law removed any presumptions about the gender of both the victim and offender. As well, the family relationship between the victim and the offender became irrelevant (Goff, 2003).

Criminal Harassment

Canada's Criminal Code was amended in 1993 to include criminal harassment as a criminal law. Often referred to as the "stalking law," the new law was enacted in response to growing concerns about violence in intimate relationships.

What is criminal harassment?

Section 264 of the Criminal Code of Canada defines the offence of criminal harassment:

Section 264 of the *Criminal Code*

Criminal Harassment
264. (1) No person shall, without lawful authority and knowing that another person is harassed or recklessly as to whether the other person is harassed, engage in conduct referred to in subsection (2) that causes that other person reasonably, in all the circumstances, to fear for their safety or the safety of anyone known to them.

Prohibited conduct
(2) The conduct mentioned in subsection (1) consists of
    (a) repeatedly following from place to place the other person or anyone known to them;
    (b) repeatedly communicating with, either directly or indirectly, the other person or any-one known to them;
    (c) besetting or watching the dwelling-house, or place where the other person, or anyone known to them, resides, works, carries on business or happens to be; or
    (d)engaging in threatening conduct directed at the other person or any member of their family.

Source: Criminal Code of Canada, 2007

Why is criminal harassment a diversity issue?

The link between diversity issues and the crime of criminal harassment is two-fold.

1.   According to a Statistics Canada study, 66% of the victims of criminal harassment are women (Statistics Canada, 2006:44).

2.   About 81% of the perpetrators of criminal harassment are men (53% in a male—female relationship and 28% in a male—male relationship) (p.36).

Learning Activity 4 - Summarize and List

In your own words, list the 4 types of prohibited conduct outlined in the criminal harassment law. Why is the criminal harassment law related to diversity issues?

Diversity-Related Responses among Canada's Police

Police departments were among the first justice agencies to respond to diversity-related concerns (Seagrave, 1997). While other parts of the justice system used a system-wide approach, it has largely been left up to individual police departments to address diversity concerns. Many police departments adopted community-based policing initiatives, such as decentralized personnel deployment and diversity hiring, as their core approach. As well, officer training in diversity issues is a common strategies used in Canadian policing.

Personnel Deployment in Community Policing

Where did community policing originate?

Community policing has its origins in the civil rights movement in the United States during the 1960s. Distress over perceived racism within the justice system were fuelled by the over-representation of Black Americans in prisons, instances of police brutality and the under-policing in Black communities.[50] In response to these growing concerns, public officials required police departments to "do things differently." Community policing was soon being adopted by many police agencies (Gabbidon and Greene, 2005).

One of the primary goals of community policing is to encourage public confidence with the police, increase community involvement in preventing crime and to reduce the fear of crime.[51] Decentralized police deployment is an important tactic to meet this goal.

---

[50]   While the use of criminal profiles by the police has been effective for identifying prospective offenders, they have also been accused of *racial profiling*–using race or ethnic origin to assume responsibility for a particular type of crime. Various research reports in the United States have reported that one of the most blatant examples or racial profiling in the 1990s was DWB (driving while Black). Research showed that Blacks stood a greater likelihood of being scrutinized than non-Blacks while driving (Gabbidon and Greene, 2005).

[51]   For further details on community policing in Canada see: http://www.mts.net/~dcaskey/CP.HTM.

How is personnel deployment different in community policing?

The core features of decentralized police deployment involve (Seagraves, 1997:214-220), (Griffith, Whitelaw and Parent, 1999:239-253):

- Dividing the city into small geographic areas and building a district office within each geographic area to house policing services (patrol, investigation, crime prevention);
- Assigning police officers to one of the city's districts for several years to encourage them to become familiar with the district, its people and businesses;
- Adding foot and bike patrols in key areas of the district; and
- Establishing community or neighbourhood "mini-stations" or storefront operations to reinforce police visibility.

These initiatives are particularly relevant in ethnically and culturally diverse neighbourhoods. They work to breakdown the traditional barriers between the police and minority groups (Gabbidon and Greene, 2005).

Diversity Hiring in Community Policing

Diversity hiring by police agencies is among the more controversial community policing initiatives. Unfortunately, much of the controversy is based on a poor understanding of how diversity hiring in most Canadian police departments works. The Ottawa Police Service has produced a useful document which reflects the rationale and criteria for hiring with diversity in mind (see, Police Sector Council, 2007).

Why is diversity hiring important in community policing?

There are two chief reasons why diversity hiring is central to community policing (Seagraves, 1997:92-97):

1. Traditionally, police recruits were over-represented by Caucasian, relatively young, male, heterosexual individuals with limited education and life experience. Because of this profile, the vast majority of police officers did not "mirror" the communities in which they worked. By increasing the number of minorities hired by police departments, police departments would be seen as more open and accessible to minority groups.
2. Because of the traditional profile of police officers (e.g., white, relatively young, male, etc.), many police departments fostered an internal culture of insensitivity towards cultural diversity (Gabbidon and Greene, 2005). In some instances, policing practices were prejudiced and discriminatory against members of minority groups. Diversity hiring help police agencies to change this internal culture.

Learning Activity 5 - Online Research

Review the Calgary Police Service website information on requirements and standards to become a Calgary police officer. What, if anything, does it say about different standards for women or minorities?

http://www.calgarypolice.ca/recruiting/html/requirements.htm

Now follow the link below to the RCMP website information on recruiting. What does it say about diversity hiring?

http://www.rcmp-grc.gc.ca/recruiting/application_process_e.htm

What is "quota hiring"?

In many cities in the United States, diversity hiring was imposed upon police departments by law. In cities such as Milwaukie, St. Louis, Cleveland and Miami, "quota hiring" by police departments was legislated (Seagraves, 1997:228). This meant that each round of hiring of new police officers had to meet an established quota for minority hires. In some instances, more qualified non-minority individuals were denied employment in favour of a less qualified minority.

Do Canadian police departments use quota-hiring?

In Canada, diversity hiring by police departments has been very different. Most Canadian police departments follow these practices (Griffith, Whitelaw and Parent, 1999:77-82):

- Police departments in Canada adopted diversity hiring practices without having to be legislated to do so;
- "Quota hiring" was not the tactic most Canadian police departments adopted;
- To increase the number of applicants from minority groups, Canadian police departments engage in "active recruitment" among minority groups;
- With the exception of the RCMP, police agencies in Canada use the same standards in hiring a minority applicant as they do a non-minority applicant.

How is the RCMP different?

The RCMP is somewhat different in terms of the final point above. In order to increase the number of minority applicants who become RCMP officers, the minimum passing grade of the written examination stage of the recruit selection process is different for white males, females and non-white males (Griffith, Whitelaw and Parent, 1999:83). The passing grade is somewhat higher for white males. However, as noted recently by the organization Immigration Watch Canada, the series of negative incidents that have befallen the RCMP in recent years has not only dramatically limited the number of white applicants but undermined their "equity employment for visible minorities" ("RCMP Pursuit...", 2005).

Diversity Training in Community Policing

How are police officers trained in diversity-related issues?

As part of community policing, police recruits in Canadian police training academies must pass a diversity training module before they become officers. While these modules may vary in length and contact between police agencies, they share common objectives (Seagraves, 1997:80-83):

- Educate police recruits on the social reality of prejudice and discrimination in Canadian society;
- Assist individual police recruits to assess their own personal beliefs and opinions about different minority groups;
- Provide recruits with basic information about the history, culture and customs of various minority groups;
- Increase the awareness of the possible barriers between the police and minority groups;
- Educate recruits in interpersonal techniques to demonstrate respect and build trust with various minority group.

Learning Activity 6 - Journal Entry

In your course journal or notes, address the following questions. In your own words how importance is diversity training for police officers? Why or Why not? How often should police officers go through this training? Why?

Aboriginal Policing

The RCMP began withdrawing from policing First Nations communities in Ontario and Quebec in the 1960s. By 1971, when the Indian Act came into effect, there were some 121 Band constables across Canada. But a series of inquiries between 1989-92, across the country, revealed that there was a lack of "sensitivity to cultural considerations, lack of community input, biased investigations, minimal crime prevention programming, and fostering alienation from the justice system by Native people" (Clairmont, 2006). Finally in 1991, the Federal Government established the First Nations Policing Policy with the goal of improving the administration of justice on Aboriginal reserves (Ibid). The policy provided Aboriginal reserves with two options regarding policing services:

- *Community Tripartite Agreement*
  Aboriginal reserves could contract with the RCMP, their provincial police or a nearby municipality to provide policing services on the reserve (Royal Canadian Mounted

Police, 2007). The Canadian Government agreed to cover the policing costs as outlined in the Indian Act.

■   *First Nations Police*
     Aboriginal reserves can establish a separate police agency that is under the administration and supervision of the reserve's Band Council (Royal Canadian Mounted Police, 2007). These First Nations police departments are legislated under the respective provinces Police Act and Police Regulations. Police training is provided by the RCMP, their provincial police or a nearby municipal police department. The Canadian Government agreed to cover the policing costs as outlined in the Indian Act.

Is Aboriginal policing common in Canada?

According to Goff (2004:145), 319 Aboriginal communities with a total population of nearly 250,000 have signed policing agreements by 2005. Approximately 1,000 police officers, mostly of Aboriginal ancestry, are working on reserves. Nearly 70% the reserves in the program have taken the First Nations Police option.

Diversity-related Responses by Canada's Criminal Courts

In Canada, the court system is responsible for the determination of guilt or innocence of accused persons. Also, it is at the sentencing phase in criminal that the judge sentences guilty individuals to an appropriate punishment. In response to many of the diversity-related issues confronting the justice system, Canada's courts have developed several key innovations. In particular, Canada's Aboriginal court initiatives, youth courts and domestic/family violence courts have gained worldwide recognition.

Aboriginal Justice Strategy

The Federal Government's Aboriginal Justice Strategy (AJS) was established in 1996 following the publication of the final report from the Royal Commission on Aboriginal Peoples.

Why was the AJS established?

The five-year mandate for the AJS was to (Department of Justice Canada, 2006:1):

■   Help Aboriginal people assume greater responsibility for the administration of justice in their communities;
■   Promote the inclusion of Aboriginal values within the Canadian justice system;
■   Contribute to a reduction in rates of crime, victimization and incarceration among Aboriginal people.

The mandate of the AJS has been renewed several times since 1996 as it has been successful in 3 specific areas (p.3):

■ **Policy Development and Support**
Because several different levels of government are involved in Aboriginal justice initiatives, the AJS serves to coordinate and oversee most new initiatives. It ensures that program policies are in place and management of the new initiatives is accountable.

■ **Aboriginal Justice Learning Network**[52]
The AJS provides a forum for Aboriginal communities to exchange "best practices and creative solutions." It also supports training and educational support to help establish and run new Aboriginal justice initiatives.

■ **Community-Based Justice Program Funding**
Through the AJS, the Federal Government establishes cost-Sharing agreements with provincial and territorial governments to develop and launch new Aboriginal justice initiatives.

In partnership with Aboriginal communities and provincial/territorial governments, the AJS has supported such Aboriginal justice programs as diversion/alternative measures, community sentencing and mediation in non-criminal matters.

Aboriginal Sentencing Circles[53]

Sentencing circles (also known as circle sentencing or healing circles) were first developed in the Yukon Territorial Court in the early 1990s but are now widely used throughout Canada (Department of Justice Canada, 2005a).

How do sentencing circles operate?

The key features of a sentencing circle are:

■ Offenders are not eligible for circle sentencing until they are found guilty.
■ The court invites interested members of the community to join the circle including
  ▪ the judge, prosecutor, defense counsel,
  ▪ police, social service personnel,
  ▪ offender and his/her family and supporters,
  ▪ victim and his/her family and supporters,
  ▪ community elders.
■ The participants gather to discuss, in turn, the offence, damage that has been done to victims, their family and the community.
■ All participants discuss what factors contributed to the offence (e.g., history of substance abuse, dysfunctional upbringing, disrespect).
■ The circle agrees on an appropriate punishment for offenders that can include restorative community service, restitution and treatment/counselling.

---

[52]   For further information visit: http://www.usask.ca/nativelaw/publications/jah/ajln.html.
[53]   For a list of material related to sentencing circles in Canada visit the website listed in footnote 10.

■   The circle participants volunteer to make sure offenders live up to their obligations.

■   If the offender "fails" the circle, they are returned to the court for traditional sentencing.

As Goff (2004:227) points out, circle sentencing only works if the offender has deep roots within the community and is not coerced into participating. In addition, the other circle participants must be willing to follow the circle's direction, as well as maintain contact with the offender after deciding on the appropriate sentence.

Learning Activity 7 - Journal Entry

In your course journal or notes, address the following questions. Be sure to give your rationale:

1. What are the possible strengths and weaknesses of circle sentencing?
2. Is it possible that this approach to sentencing could work outside of Aboriginal communities?
3. How do sentencing circles relate to the concept of restorative justice?
4. Is there any particular non-aboriginal offenders that might be better dealt with using circle sentencing?

Aboriginal Peacemaker Courts

A Peacemaker court is a concept borrowed from the Navajo tradition of justice. In their traditional ways and language, the Navajo have no word for "guilt." Guilt implies a moral wrong while in Navajo tradition justice comes through healing within the community by driving away that which caused the problem. It is not about laying blame and accepting or administering punishment for wrongdoing (Yazzie, 1994; Tso, 1996). In the Aboriginal context, Aboriginal courts share some similarities to sentencing circles. Both ensure that victims, offenders, families and the community are involved in resolving conflicts, addressing underlying causes of offending behaviour, and promoting a more peaceful community.

How do peacemaker courts operate?

Peacemaker courts more closely mirror the appearance and operation of a non-aboriginal Canadian court of law. However, there are some key differences (Indian and Northern Affairs Canada, 2006):

■   Peacemaker courts are mostly found on Aboriginal reserves.

■   The judge, Crown prosecutor and court clerks are Aboriginal.

■   The court deals with criminal matters, provincial statutes First Nations' bylaws.

■   The court has more latitude to use alternative conflict resolution mechanism and culturally appropriate mediation than non-aboriginal courts.

The Youth Criminal Justice Act's Extrajudicial Measures

The Federal Government's decision to replace the Young Offender Act (YOA) with the Youth Criminal Justice Act (YCJA) was informed by research into the effectiveness of formal youth court proceedings. It was found that youth who were 1st time offenders of less serious crimes were much less likely to re-offend if *they were not sentenced to incarceration*. In other words, sentences that included such things as restitution, counselling and community service were more effective for first-time offenders of less serious crime (Statistics Canada, 2005b).

In response to the above finding, the YCJA introduced "extrajudicial measures." Extrajudicial measures give police officers an option between charging a youth and doing nothing. If an officer has "reasonable grounds" to believe that a young person has committed an offence, the officer can consider using an extrajudicial measure.

What are extrajudicial measures?

These include such things as:

- Warn the young person;
- Issue a formal (written) caution; and
- Refer the young person to a community program.

The purpose of extrajudicial measures is to give police officers more latitude in dealing with a likely first-time offender of a less serious crime. These measures rely on a police officer's judgment that some young persons are more effectively dealt with outside the formal criminal justice system.

The Youth Criminal Justice Act's Extrajudicial Sanctions

Extrajudicial *sanctions* are different than extrajudicial *measures*. Sanctions are used in instances where the offence committed by a young person is somewhat more serious or the young person is a repeat offender. In keeping with the more serious circumstances, extrajudicial sanctions are stern and are applied through a more formal process. Police officers and Crown prosecutors can apply an extrajudicial sanction.

How is an extrajudicial sanction different from an extrajudicial measure?

Here are some of the important aspects of the process (Department of Justice Canada, 2005b):

- There must be sufficient evidence to proceed with a charge against the young person.
- The young person must accept responsibility for the "offence."
- Before extrajudicial sanctions are applied, the young person must be allowed to consult with a lawyer and parents or guardians.
- The young person must accept the extrajudicial sanction as an alternative to a formal criminal charge.

■   The victim must be informed of the name of the young person and the extrajudicial sanction that is being applied.

Each province has established a list of possible sanctions that could be applied to a young person. For example, Alberta refers young persons to local Youth Justice Committees (YJC) that are established throughout the province.[54] The YJC operates in much the same was as Aboriginal sentencing circle in that the committee decides on appropriate conditions that the youth must satisfy. These conditions range from a personal apology to the victim, personal services to the victim, community service, financial restitution to the victim and participation in counselling and/or treatment programs (Alberta Solicitor General and Public Security, 2007).

Learning Activity 8 - Online Research

Youth Justice Committee's are found across Ontario. Follow the link below to provincial website and read how youth justice committees work. As you are reading this information, consider how similar they are to our earlier discussion of Aboriginal sentencing circles.

http://www.yjcontario.ca/overview.php

Domestic or Family Violence Courts

Women make up the majority of victims of domestic violence (sometimes called "spousal abuse" or "family violence") ("Family violence in Canada...", 2006:6). The growing concern about the amount and seriousness of domestic violence have resulted in both police and court programs.

How are family violence courts different?

The first FVC was established Winnipeg in September 1990. Today, many jurisdictions have established family violence courts (FVC) or domestic violence courts (DVC). The mandate of these specialized courts is to (Statistics Canada, 2003:52):

■   Provide early intervention for first-time offenders to prevent future incidents of domestic violence.

■   Provide "coordinated prosecution" to ensure that domestic violence cases result in a conviction.

---

[54]   In 2005 Alberta became the first province to establish a youth justice committee made up of youth volunteers and the same year the 100th YJC was established on the Siksika Nation (Youth and the justice system, 2003).

What do family violence/domestic violence courts operate?

Early Intervention

The Ontario Domestic Violence Court Program provides an example of early intervention. It has several key components (Statistics Canada, 2003:52-53):

- The accused must have no prior domestic violence conviction, used no weapon in the offence and cause no significant harm to the victim.
- The accused must plead guilty to the current offence.
- Prior to sentencing, the offender attends the provincial Partner Assault Response (PAR) program which is a 16-week treatment/counselling program.
- When the program has been completed, the offender returns to court for sentencing. The court hears about the offenders progress (or lack thereof) in PAR. The judge determines the appropriate sentence.

Coordinated Prosecutions

Because victims of domestic violence are often hesitant to provide testimony or evidence against the accused, Ontario's Domestic Violence Courts have implemented measures to enhance prosecutions. These include the following (Statistics Canada, 2003:53-54):

1. Specialized training for police officers to recognize the dynamics involved in domestic violence and the collection of evidence in these calls for service;
2. Designated Crown prosecutors who handle most domestic violence court cases;
3. Specialized training for domestic violence Crown prosecutors to assist with interviewing accused and victims; and
4. Specialized training to assist local experts in giving testimony regarding the causes and consequences of domestic violence and effective sentencing for offenders.

Learning Activity 9 - Summarize

In your own words, summarize the advantages of separate domestic or family violence courts. Why is early intervention valuable? Why are coordinated prosecutions considered valuable to the process?

Diversity-Related Responses by Canada's Correctional System

The corrections system in Canada has implemented a wide range of programs in response to diversity-related issues. Specific attention has been given to Aboriginal, youth and female offenders to address the different circumstances associated with their criminal behaviour. The ultimate purpose is to reduce the likelihood of recidivism among these offenders (Goff, 2004). In addition, Canada s correctional system has a Correctional Advisory Committee (CAC) that is made-up of community volunteers ad membership attempts, as much as is possible, to ensure the ethnic, gender, socio-economic and cultural diversity of the community and endeavour to be the "public presence" in Corrections (Correctional Service Canada, nd.).

Overview of Canada's Corrections System

The personnel, facilities, programs and administration of criminal sentences make up Canada's corrections system.

What are the common types of criminal sentences in Canada?

Once an offender is convicted, the criminal court next determines the appropriate sentence. Judges have only a limited amount of latitude in applying a sentence because the Criminal Code of Canada outlines the maximum possible sentence for each criminal offence. In Canada, there are basically three types of sentences:

- **Incarceration**
  An offender can be sent to prison under one of the following conditions:
    - If the prison sentence is 2 years or more, the inmate serves the time in the federal prison system operated by the Correctional Services of Canada.
    - If the sentence is "2 years less a day," the inmate goes into provincial/territorial custody.
    - Lastly, remand facilities (sometimes referred to as "jails") hold those individuals who are have been detained before or during their trial.
- **Probation**
  If the Criminal Code of Canada does not outline a **minimum** sentence for an offence, a judge can consider a sentence of probation. After sentencing an offender, a judge can suspend the sentence and place the offender on probation. An offender must meet all of the conditions in the probation order (such as meeting regularly with a probation officer, and attending treatment/counselling). Violating the probation order can result in the offender serving the original sentence. Probation is administered by provincial/territorial authorities.
- **Conditional Sentences**
  Unlike probation which is part of a suspended sentence, conditional sentences are intended to be more punitive than probation but less punitive than incarceration. Typically, conditional sentences will restrict the movement of an offender through such things as house arrest, curfews, mandatory residence in a treatment facility, and so forth.

Recidivism and Criminogenic Needs

Section 718 of the Criminal Code outlines the objectives of criminal sentencing in Canada (Department of Justice Canada, 2007). They include such objectives as:

- Denouncing criminal behaviour;
- Deterring future behaviour by the offender and others; and
- Rehabilitating offenders.

The correction system in Canada is organized to implement these objectives.

What is recidivism?

Besides fulfilling the Criminal Code's objective of rendering a "fair and just" punishment, preventing the offender from future criminal behaviour is central to Canada's correctional system. The technical term for re-offending is "recidivism."

What are criminogenic needs?

A significant body of research indicates that the likelihood of an inmate recidivating is linked to their "criminogenic needs." This term refers to those psychological, emotional, and behavioural factors that can increase an individual's risk of breaking the law. Substance abuse problems, a history of unemployment, a lack of education, poor job skills, an anti-social personality disorder and a peer group of criminals are examples of criminogenic factors (Hannah-Moffat, 2005).

Criminogenic factors link to our earlier discussions of Aboriginals, young persons and women in Canadian society (see Module 2). Many of the factors that define these groups as minorities are mirrored in each group's different criminogenic factors. In simpler terms, the criminogenic factors for Aboriginal offenders, for female offenders, for young offenders and for male offenders vary somewhat from group to group.[55]

In response to these diversity-related criminogenic needs, Canada's corrections system provides targeted programming for Aboriginal offenders, young offenders and female offenders.

---

[55] Drawing on data over a 10-year period the Bureau of Justice in the United States found that nearly two-thirds of released offenders were rearrested within three years ("In a 15 State study…", 2002). Based on additional investigation and a pilot project to test their observation, Gilbert (2006) reports that the most important criminogenic factor was employment upon release. Hence, in Lancaster County, Pennsylvania they introduced a Job Court in which judges helped to assign jobs based on skill levels. They found a notable drop in recidivism when compared to those not provided employment opportunity (Ibid).

■ **Learning Activity 10 - Reflect**

The concept of "criminogenic needs" is very closely related to many of the diversity-related themes that have been presented in Unit 2 of this text. Review the social conditions that confront First Nations peoples, women, young persons and the elder. Consider how the information on the social conditions facing these minority groups informs the criminogenic needs of offenders from these groups.

Programming for Aboriginals in Custody

Because of the over-representation of Aboriginal people in the Canada's corrections system, specialized Aboriginal programming is a top priority at both the federal and provincial/territorial level.

Are there separate Aboriginal prisons?

Separate Aboriginal Facilities

While most incarcerated Aboriginal offenders are housed in penitentiaries and prisons with non-Aboriginal inmates, the Correctional Services of Canada operates or funds nine "healing lodges" across Canada (Correctional Services Canada, 2003). The concept of healing lodges was first proposed by the Native Women s Association of Canada. The basic philosophy behind healing lodges is that Aboriginal criminality is largely rooted in their socially disadvantaged position in society. By reintroducing a new generation of Aboriginal people to their cultural roots, these lodges can being the healing process for Aboriginal offenders.

How are healing lodges different?

The basic features of a healing lodge are as follows:

■   Exclusively for Aboriginal inmates who are supervised by mostly Aboriginal personnel;
■   Focused on spiritual/cultural reintegration; specialized treatment for such things as substance abuse problems, low self-esteem, anger management, poor cognitive skills; educational upgrading; and job skills upgrading;
■   Located in both rural and urban settings; and
■   Range in size from about 20 beds to 120 beds.[56]

---

[56]   For additional information visit: http://www.csc-scc.gc.ca/text/prgrm/correctional/abissues/challenge/11_e.shtml.

Institutional Programs

Aboriginal programs exist in the vast majority of federal, provincial and territorial prisons that house a large number of Aboriginal inmates.

How are Aboriginal programs different?

Besides accessing the range of programming available to all inmates (in areas such as anger management, substance abuse, cognitive skills and self esteem), these institutions provide specialized programming for Aboriginal offenders such as the following:

■ **Native Liaison Services**
   Bicultural Aboriginal workers work with Aboriginal offenders throughout their sentence (Correctional Services Canada, 2002). These workers act as a guide or counsellor to inmates on the criminal justice process and day-to-day prison life. This service facilitates and encourages the involvement of Aboriginal inmates in prison programs.

■ **Spiritual Services**
   By law, all institutions are required to make available to Aboriginal inmates the services of an Aboriginal Elder. Elders are the "spiritual leaders, general counsellors and teachers within Aboriginal societies" (Correctional Services Canada, 2002).[57] They organize spiritual and cultural ceremonies for Aboriginal inmates.

Programming for Women in Custody

Correctional services in Canada have a long tradition of separating programs for female offenders from those offered to male offenders. This is, in part, due to the fact that women commit far few crimes than men. Also, women tend to commit less serious crimes and are therefore not incarcerated at the same rate as men.

Do female offenders stay in the same prisons as male offenders?

Separate Facilities for Women

Women make up about 10% of the adult offenders in provincial/territorial custody (or about 2,000 inmates) and 5% of the offenders in federal custody (or about 500 inmates) (Statistics Canada, 2006:15). Each province and territory operates separate correctional facilities for female offenders.

---

[57]   "There is no clear definition of an Elder as it varies from nation to nation. For example, the Six Nations' definition of their Elders include: Faith Keepers, Clan Mothers, Hereditary Chiefs and Spiritual Leaders. The Algonquin Nation in their teachings an Elder is defined as someone who possesses spiritual leadership which is given by one's cultural and traditional knowledge. This knowledge is found in the teachings and responsibilities associated with sacred entities such as the Pipe, Wampum belt, Drum and Medicine people" (Kumik – Council of Elders, 2005).

The Correctional Services of Canada houses federal inmates in seven separate facilities for women that are situated across Canada.

What are the different types of programs for female offenders?

Institutional Programs

The range of specialized correctional program varies from institution to institution. The more common programs include (Correctional Services Canada, 2006):

- **Programs for Survivors of Abuse and Trauma**
  Recent research has shown that the majority of incarcerated women have experienced some form of abuse or trauma. These programs help female offenders understand the causes and effects of abuse.
- **Parenting Programs**
  Two thirds of incarcerated women have a child under the age of 5 years. These programs are designed to enhance the parenting skills of female inmates who have children. Research demonstrates that increasing the bond between a mother and child helps female inmates acquire more "pro-social" attitudes.
- **Women Offender Substance Abuse Programs**
  These programs focus on the underlining cause of substance abuse such as low self-esteem and low self-efficacy.
- **Educational and Employment Skills Upgrading**
  These programs are designed to upgrade the social functioning of female offenders once they are released. Successful employment following release is directly related to the reduced risk of re-offending.

Learning Activity 11 - Online Research

Follow the link below to the Correctional Services Canada website list of federal institutions and facilities. Scan through the list and click on the following institutional links:

- Nova Institution for Women
- Jolliette Institution
- Grand Valley Institution for Women
- Edmonton Institution for Women
- Fraser Valley Institution for Women

http://www.csc-scc.gc.ca/text/region/institutional_profiles_e.shtml

Programming for Young Offenders in Custody

In the second year of the Youth Criminal Justice Act (YCJA), the number of young offenders sentenced to custody (open and secure) was about 4,400 (Statistics Canada, 2007:4). This represented a decrease of about 7% from the previous year.

Are young offenders in the same facilities as adult offenders?

Separate Facilities for Young Offenders

Young offender facilities are administered at the provincial and territorial level. In those instances when an incarcerated young offender turns 18 years of age and still has time left to be served on the sentence, he/she is transferred to an adult facility.

What types of programs do young offenders take?

Institutional Programs

The range of specialized correctional program varies from province to province. The more common programs include programs such as the following (Bell, 2003:295-303):

- **Educational Programs**
  Many young offenders have a history of failed academic performance and truancy. One key to reduce the risk of re-offending is to encourage educational success. Besides basic elementary and high school academic subjects, vocational training is often provided.
- **Life Skills and Cognitive Skills Program**
  These programs focus on necessary life skills such as self-control, critical thinking, anger management and problem solving.
- **Substance Abuse Treatment**
  Young offenders are educated in terms of the appropriate and inappropriate use of alcohol, prescription medication and illegal drugs. The key to these programs is to involve community support groups such as Narcotics Anonymous, Alcoholics Anonymous and Al-Anon and Alateen. These groups provide support to the young offender after release.
- **Recreation Programs**
  These programs help young offenders improve their self-esteem and sense of teamwork and belonging. Programs can include such things as arts and crafts, team sports, wilderness camping and so forth.
- **Work Activities and Incentives**
  Daily work activities within youth facilities are common. Young offenders take an active role in the day-to-day operation of the facility by completing jobs such as cleaning and cooking. Many facilities offer an allowance to those who perform well in order to reinforce positive behaviour.

In this final section we have provided an overview of how diversity issues are being dealt with within the criminal justice system and beyond. Ever since the issue of diversity became recognized as an issue within Canada, we noted that efforts have been made, and continue to be made to address them. Respecting diversity and accommodating it has been the cornerstone of Canada in many ways. And, while some areas of diversity still require considerable attention and work, it is evident that concerted efforts are being made.

■ References

Alberta Solicitor General and Public Safety. (2007). *Youth justice committees.* Retrieved May 2, 2007, from http://www.solgen.gov.ab.ca/yjc/default.aspx?id=2513.

Bell, S. (2003). *Young offenders and juvenile justice: A century after the fact.* Scarborough, ON: Thomson Nelson.

Clairmont, D. (2006). "Aboriginal policing in Canada: An overview of developments in First Nations." Atlantic Institute of Criminology, Dalhousie University, Halifax.

Constitution Act, 1982. (1984). Retrieved April 27, 2007, from http://www.solon.org/Constitutions/Canada/English/ca_1982.html.

Correctional Services Canada. (2002). *Aboriginal programs and issues.* Retrieved May 12, 2007, from http://www.csc-scc.gc.ca/text/prgrm/correctional/ab4_e.shtml.

Correctional Services Canada. (2003). *Aboriginal healing lodges.* Retrieved May 12, 2007, from http://www.csc-scc.gc.ca/text/prgrm/correctional/abissues/know/6_e.shtml

Correctional Services Canada. (nd). Retrieved Oct. 11, 2007, from www.abcgta.ca/docs/csc-citizens.doc.

Correctional Services Canada. (2006). *Women offender programs and issues.* Retrieved May 4, 2007, from http://www.csc-scc.gc.ca/text/prgrm/fsw/fsw_e.shtml.

Criminal Code and Selected Statutes, 1955. (1955), Ottawa, ON: The Queen's Printer.

Department of Justice Canada. (2005a). *How the courts are organized.* Retrieved April 23, 2007, from http://www.justice.gc.ca/en/dept/pub/trib/page3.html.

Department of Justice Canada. (2005b). *Types of extrajudicial sanctions.* Retrieved April 12, 2007, from http://www.justice.gc.ca/en/ps/yj/repository/3modules/01extjud/3010301d.html.

Department of Justice Canada. (2006). *Annual activities report 2002-2003, 2003-004, 2004-2005: Aboriginal justice strategies.* Retrieved Mat 12, 2007, from http://www.justice.gc.ca/en/ps/ajs/report/1-1.html.

Department of Justice Canada. (2007). *Criminal Code (R.S., 1985, c. C-46).* Retrieved April 12, 2007, http://laws.justice.gc.ca/en/C-46/.

Egale Canada. (2007a). *Egan case in Supreme Court.* Retrieved May 4, 2007, from http://www.egale.ca/index.asp?lang=E&menu=1990&item=731

Egale Canada. (2007b). *Equal marriage bill passes final hurtle.* Retrieved May 4, 2007, from http://www.egale.ca/index.asp?lang=E&menu=20&item=1161.

Family violence in Canada: A statistical profile 2006. (2006). Catalogue no. 85-224-XIE. Ottawa, Statistics Canada.

Gabbidon, S.L. and Greene, H.T. (2005). *Race and crime.* Thousand Oaks, CA.: SAGE.

Gilbert, S. (Sept. 28, 2006). Job Court: Sentencing convicts to work. Retrieved Oct. 11, 2007, from http://www.npr.org/templates/story/story.php?storyId=6161848.

Goff, C. (2004). *Criminal justice in Canada.* 3rd ed. Toronto, ON: Nelson.

Griffiths, C., Whitelaw, B., and Parent, R. (1999). *Canadian police work.* Scarborough, ON: ITP Nelson.

Hannah-Moffat, K. (2005). "Criminogenic needs and the transformative risk subject." *Punishment and Society* 7(1): 29-51.

Indian and Northern Affairs Canada. (2006). *Observations.* Retrieved May 12, 2007, from http://www.ainc-inac.gc.ca/wige/usm/obser_e.html.

"Nazi policies toward Jews and minorities." (2007). Retrieved October 10, 2007, from http://topics.nytimes.com/top/reference/timestopics/subjects/n/nazi_policies_toward_jews_and_minorities/index.html?query=ZUNDEL,%20ERNST&field=per&match=exact.

Police Sector Council. (2007). Retrieved October 10, 2007, from http://www.policecouncil.ca/pages/research_ppm.html.

RCMP Pursuit of "Equity Employment for Visible Minorities' " Policies Has Become a Truly Public National Embarrassment. (July 6, 2005). Retrieved October 10, 2007, from http://www.immigrationwatchcanada.org/index.php?module=pagemaster&PAGEuser_op=view_page&PAGE_id=198.

Rosen, P. (2000). *Hate propaganda.* Ottawa, ON: Library of Parliament, Parliamentary Information and Research Services.

Royal Canadian Mounted Police. (2007). *Community, contract and aboriginal policing.* Retrieved May 12, 2007, from http://www.rcmp-grc.gc.ca/ccaps/fncps_e.htm.

Seagraves, J. (1997). *Introduction to policing in Canada.* Scarborough, ON: Prentice Hall Canada.

Statistics Canada. (2003). *Family violence in Canada: A statistical profile.* Catalogue no. 85-224-XIE. Retrieved April 23, 2007, from http://www.statcan.ca/english/freepub/85-224-XIE/85-224-XIE03000.pdf.

Statistics Canada. (2004a). *Hate crime in Canada.* Catalogue no. 85-002-XPE, vol. 24, no. 4. Retrieved April 23, 2007, from http://dsp-psd.tpsgc.gc.ca/Collection-R/Statcan/85-551-XIE/0009985-551-XIE.pdf.

Statistics Canada. (2004b). *Pilot survey of hate crime.* Retrieved April 22, 2007, from http://www.statcan.ca/Daily/English/040601/d040601a.htm.

Statistics Canada. (2005a). *Criminal victimization in Canada, 2004.* Catalogue no. 85-002-XPE, vol. 25, no. 7. Retrieved April 10, 2007, from http://www.statcan.ca/bsolc/english/bsolc?catno=85-002-X20050078803.

Statistics Canada. (2005b). *Youth court statistics, 2003/2004.* Catalogue no. 85-002-XPE, vol. 25, no. 4. Retrieved April 12, 2007, from http://www.statcan.ca/bsolc/english/bsolc?catno=85-002-X20050047948.

Statistics Canada. (2006). *Women in Canada: A gender-based statistical report.* Catalogue no. 89-503-XPE. Retrieved April 28, 2007, from http://www.statcan.ca/Daily/English/060606/d060606b.htm.

Statistics Canada. (2007). *Youth custody and community services in Canada, 2004/2005.* Catalogue no. 85-002-XPE, vol. 27, no. 2. Retrieved May 2, 2007, from http://www.statcan.ca/english/freepub/85-002-XIE/85-002-XIE2007002.htm.

Tso, T. (1996). "The process of decision making in tribal courts." In M.O. Nielson and R.A. Sil-verman (eds.), *Native Americans, crime, and justice.* Boulder, CO: Westview Press.

Yazzie, J.R. (1994). "Life comes from it." Retrieved Oct 10, 2007, from http://www.context.org/ICLIB/IC38/Yazzie.htm.

"Youth and the Justice System." (2003). Retrieved October 10, 2007, from http://www.justice.gov.ab.ca/JustIN/spring2003/page4.htm.

EPILOGUE

A Comparative Approach to Equality and Diversity: Lessons from the United Kingdom Justice System

Theo Gavrielides

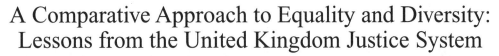

Learning Activity 1 - Fun Quiz

Take this fun quiz before you read the chapter. Answer "True" or "False":

1. Ethnic minorities, juveniles and men are over-represented in both the Canadian and the UK criminal justice systems.

2. The 2001 census showed that Canada has more people from visible ethnic minority groups than the UK.

3. Both in the UK and Canada, youths have the highest criminal victimization rates.

4. Discrimination in the criminal justice system is a reality for both Canada and the UK.

5. The UK does not have a written Bill of Rights but Canada does.

6. At the current rate of change, it will take until 2105 to close the ethnic employment gap in the UK.

7. In both Canada and the UK, ethnic minority groups that have a high crime and/or imprisonment rate typically belong to socially and economically disadvantaged social classes.

8. In the UK, girls now have better educational outcomes than boys at 16 and more women now have higher education qualifications than men in every age group up to age 44. However, women are paid 21 percent less than men.

9. In the UK, nearly all minority ethnic groups are less likely to be in paid employment than White British and women.

10. The impact of social background and class on someone's future and chances in life is more significant in the UK than in Canada.

ANSWERS: 1T, 2T, 3T, 4T, 5T, 6T, 7T, 8T, 9T, 10T

▇ Introduction and Learning Outcomes

As noted in the Introduction, diversity within the justice system can involve a broad range of issues ranging from the elderly to the young, ethnic minorities, class and socio-economic disadvantage, gender and people who are disabled or with mental health problems. In broad terms, equality matters for:

- *individuals* claiming their inherent rights of respect, fairness and dignity and the opportunity to fulfil their potential;
- *societies* aiming to promote and protect feelings of cohesion, belonging, integration and progression;
- *the economy* because without it many talents, skills and creative minds and ideas will be neglected due to prejudice and discrimination.

Inequality is not a challenge attached to a particular country or nation. It is a reality faced by justice systems worldwide. For instance, a quick look at the case law of the European Court of Human Rights (EcrtHR) is enough to paint a picture of persistent inequalities faced by all 47 members of the Council of Europe. Gavrielides (2005) argued that the inequality and diversity issues faced within the entire Council are so similar and consistent in their manifestation that through the case law of the EcrtHR European justice systems are converging.

Every justice system has its own characteristics, and this applies even to systems that developed from former colonial models. For instance, the Canadian, American and Australian justice systems were based on the British common law model (Nelken, 1997a). Nevertheless, despite their similarities, there are stark differences both in their philosophy and implementation. Identical justice models would mean identical societies, and this is impossible. This does not mean that justice systems cannot learn from each other particularly in relation to issues of diversity and equality. Learning and comparing were the key reasons that led to the development of comparative legal research (Nelken, 1997a), and of this chapter.

This chapter has been designed around three outcomes, which collectively should enable you to develop a more critical and comparative view of diversity and inequality issues as they contrast with the UK justice system. In particular, by the end of this section you will be able to:

- compare and contrast issues of diversity and inequality in the UK and Canada,
- understand why a comparative approach to diversity issues matter, and
- compare and contrast some justice responses that were introduced to protect, respect and promote equality and diversity in the UK.

It is not the intention of this chapter to repeat the information that has already been developed in detail in the book's previous sections. Therefore, to achieve the aforementioned three goals, this section will need to be read in conjunction with other sections of the book, as it aims to complement and not repeat the information that was included there. The focus here will be the UK justice system and how it compares on diversity and inequality issues in Canada as these have already been raised in the book.

Why Compare the Canadian with the UK Justice System?

In 1905, George Santayana said: "A man's feet must be planted in his country, but his eyes should survey the world" (Santayana, 1905). As noted in Chapter 1, diversity is a social fact and hence measures that are introduced to address inequality that relates to issues of diversity should be tailored to each country's realities. However, policy and practice also need to be informed by the latest developments taking place in other countries, particularly if their legal systems have strong historical, sociological, economical, political and cultural ties. Canada and the UK is one example. By looking at the legislative, institutional and policy changes introduced into similar legal systems, the comparative researcher may be able to identify "legal transplants" for addressing inequality and discrimination.

Comparative legal research in not new. The earliest comparative research can be traced back in Ancient Greece at around fifth century BC, in Plato's work "Laws" (Zweirt and Kotz 1998:48). The most obvious reason for comparing justice systems, particularly when it comes to diversity issues, is to attain a deeper understanding of foreign legal systems and through this knowledge improve domestic law and practice.

Zedner also argued that comparative law is now a "policy-oriented imperative" (Zedner 1995:8), due to a pragmatic concern towards legal reforms imposed by international organizations such as the United Nations. Cherif Bassiouni also argued that "traditional sovereignty-based arguments against the recognition of application of internationally protected human rights are no longer valid" (Bassiouni, 1993:225). Human rights and equality law as enforced in the global by treaties, customs and *jus cogens*, has penetrated into areas that in the past were only "a realm of domestic law," and as Nelken pointed out criminal justice is no exception (Nelken, 1997b, and p.251).

It has been a long-standing tradition to think in terms of "systems" when talking about criminal procedures. When we use this word in everyday communication we have in mind something complex with interconnected parts and subsystems with inputs and outputs. The same word is used when referring to the formation of criminal justice agents and organizations. Almost all criminal justice systems are divided into four key subsystems (Davies and Croall, 1998:2): (1) law enforcement officers (police and prosecuting agencies), (2) the machinery of the courts (pre-trial detention, adjudication, and sentencing), (3) the penal sub-system (probation and the prisons), and (4) crime prevention machinery, comprising both private and governmental agencies. Winterdyk (2001) has argued that there an additional sub-system – the public. This plays a key role in the support and demand for change of laws.

Issues of discrimination and inequality are experienced throughout these stages. For instance, in the UK it is well documented that young Black people are over-represented in the criminal justice system both at the prosecution, conviction and prison stages (Home Affairs Committee, 2007). At the same time, statistics indicate that the agents staffing and serving all four stages of the criminal justice system (e.g., police officers, probation officers, prison staff, magistrates and judges) are not representative of the UK's population (CLG, 2007).

The truth is that the structure of a justice system is a reflection of society's attitudes and preferred response to crime. As a former British colony, Canada's justice system was based on the English common law model. As Zweigert and Kotz (1998) said, we only need to look at a country's history and socio-economic development to understand its legal model. If we want to know what led to the adoption of a given legal model, they claimed, then "we only need to look at the nationality of the last soldier who departed the country's shores" (p.48). With the passing of the British North America Act in 1867, Canada entered into a long process of transformation from being a British colony to becoming a Dominion in the British Commonwealth.

History, international policy and politics, the globalization of human rights and equality law and the formation of international organizations are not the only reasons for comparing issues of diversity in the Canadian and the UK legal systems. Just like Canada, the UK has a very diverse population with a strong representation from "Black, Asian and minority ethnic" (BAME) groups. According to the latest census in 2001, 9% of the UKs population is from BAME groups and this is expected to rise to 11-12% by the next census in 2011. The latest Canadian census in 2006 showed that 16.2% of the population comes from a BAME community. To ensure equality of opportunity in the delivery of justice, measures have been taken in legislation, policy and practice. Examples of issues of diversity in the justice system and the responses that were generated as a result will be the focus of the following two sections.

Before moving onto the next section, there is a caveat that needs to be addressed. Although comparison between legal systems may help to put national issues of diversity in context and provide a framework for learning and experimentation, it should not create the assumption that "legal transplants" are always successful. In fact, many have argued that comparative law itself encounters many difficulties, difficulties that are inherent in the process of comparison. According to Zweigert and Kotz (1998:157) "[e]ven today it is extremely doubtful whether one could draw up a logical and self-contained methodology of comparative law which has any claim to work perfectly." Similarly, both Leavitt (1996) and Nelken (1996) argued that there is a great level of relativism in cross-cultural criminological studies and comparative legal research.

Therefore, when entering the area of comparative legal studies we need to be aware not only of the difficulties and limitations that we are bound to envisage, but also of the comparative pitfalls that are certain to block the way to reaching reliable and authentic results. For instance, some of the constraints that this paper had to overcome was the successful use of reliable data, descriptions/ definitions of equality and diversity, cultural variation, the abstention from reliance on law as described "in books," and the support of the claim through reference to "law in action."

Learning Activity 2 - Summarize

1. In your own words, summarize the main reasons for doing comparative legal research. In addition, summarize four reasons for comparing issues of diversity between the Canadian and the UK justice systems.

2. What do you understand by the term "legal transplants"?

The Modern Welfare State and Persistent Inequalities in the UK

As discussed in Chapter 1 of this book, diversity is not a "black or white" quality, but of all individuals and the different levels of groups to which they belong. In the UK, legislation and policy has "grouped" inequalities faced by different people in eight different "equality strands": age, disability, gender, sexual orientation, race and ethnicity, religion or belief, human rights and careers. The cross cutting topic of human rights was introduced through the Human Rights Act 1998 to address multi-strand issues such as multiple identities (e.g., discrimination faced by a Black woman who might also be lesbian or disabled).

Just like in Canada (see previous chapters), several historical events left modern Britain with a number of challenges in the fight for social justice and equality of opportunity. For example, the Beveridge Report of 1942 and the subsequent flurry of legislation in the wake of the World War II put in place a new social security system, the National Health System (NHS) and the Education Act which laid the basis for the modern British welfare state (CLG, 2007). Post World War II legislative reforms aimed to provide to everyone residing in the UK, whether British or not, free access to health, to education, and to social security benefits to cover sickness, disability and unemployment as well as a basic pension and family allowances. Massive investment in social housing also took place throughout the 1950s and 1960s. The principal aim of these initial reforms was to ensure that no one would be deprived of basic provisions such as a good health, a home, income and a basic education. It was hoped that these reforms would also provide a platform for those who were less fortunate to take advantage of their individual talents.

Despite these reforms, evidence suggests that many groups in the UK do not enjoy equality of opportunity (CLG, 2007). In 2007, the Communities and Local Government (CLG) department conducted one of the most thorough Equalities Review. This identified serious inequalities faced by different groups in modern British society extending from the criminal justice system to every public service.

To conduct the Review, the government commissioned the Equalities Review independent panel which looked at existing evidence of inequalities (e.g., statistics, policy documents and demographics) and new data (e.g., through fieldwork with individuals, practitioners, policy makers and service providers). The Panel also reviewed all key legislative initiatives aiming to tackle inequality and discrimination and evaluated their effectiveness.

According to this Equalities Review "the highest concentration of disadvantage in England persists in the North East and North West of the country, and the lowest is to be found in the East and the South East. Disadvantage in Scotland and Wales is also highly persistent and may even be increasing" (CLG, 2007:38). Figure E.1 is indicative of the equality gaps that exist and will remain to exist in Britain.

The findings of the 2007 government's Equalities Review were confirmed and strengthened by the 2010 report, *An Anatomy of Economic Inequality in the UK* (Government Equalities Office 2010). The report, which was commissioned by the Government Equalities Office and carried out by the independent National Equality Panel, is considered the most thorough, evidence based study on the relationships between inequalities in people's economic outcomes and their characteristics and circumstances. Among other things, the report showed that compared with other industrialized countries, including Canada, inequalities in earning and incomes are high in Britain, especially

Figure E.1 - Persistent inequalities in the UK as recorded by the Government's 2007 Equalities Review (CLG 2007)

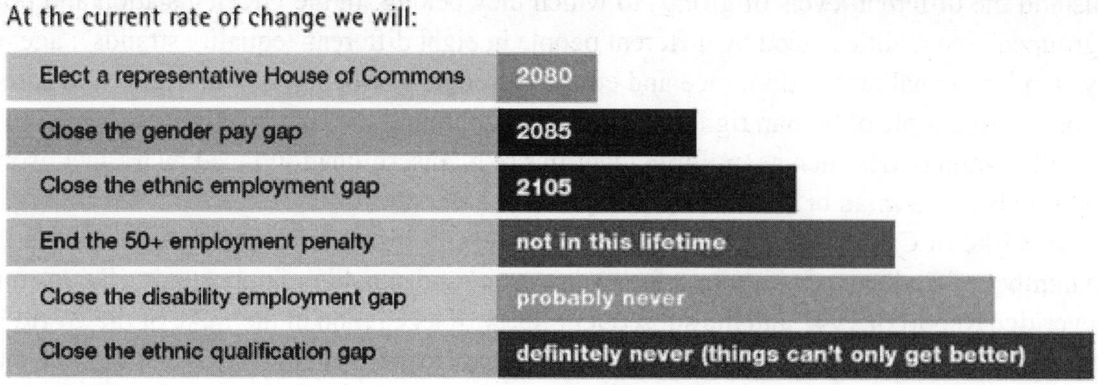

At the current rate of change we will:

Elect a representative House of Commons	2080
Close the gender pay gap	2085
Close the ethnic employment gap	2105
End the 50+ employment penalty	not in this lifetime
Close the disability employment gap	probably never
Close the ethnic qualification gap	definitely never (things can't only get better)

when compared with thirty years ago. For instance, Chapter 8 of this book illustrates how economics and wealth distribution in Canada impact on the choices and quality of life of older people. Chapter 5 also makes this argument for Aboriginal Canadians.

Arguably, one of the most revealing findings of the 2010 UK report is that the top 10 percent of the country's population has wealth 100 times the value of that of the poorest 10 percent. Black, Asian and minority ethnic (BAME) groups are highly represented in that poorest 10 percent, with Pakistani and Bangladeshi Muslim men and Black African Christian men having an income that is 13-21 percent lower than that of White British Christian men. It also became apparent that the poverty of Britain's BAME children shapes their lives and aspirations and leads them to hopelessness and disengagement with society. The report concludes "(t)here remain deep-seated and systematic differences in economic outcomes between social groups across all of the dimensions we have examined—including between men and women, between different ethnic groups, between social class groups, between those living in disadvantaged and other areas, and between London and other parts of the country (Government Equalities Office, 2010:1).

Case Study - Diversity in England's Largest City, London

London presents a unique picture of diversity in the UK, with extreme affluence existing side-by-side with extreme disadvantage. London is one of the largest cities in the developed world in terms of its total land area of 1,584 square kilometres, and is by a considerable margin the most populous city in the European Union, with 7.39 million residents at mid-2003. It is also one of the European Union's most densely settled areas at 4,664 persons per square kilometre.

According to the 2003 Mid Year Estimates, out of the 7,387,900 people living in London, at least 3 million belong to BAME groups. This represents over 40% of the capital's population when nationally BAME groups are 9% of the total population. London is also different from the United Kingdom with regard to its age structure, the population tending to be younger on average than in the country as a whole. The mean age of Londoners is 36.5 compared to 38.9 for the UK population. In 2003, London had proportionally more children at each age under 7 and more adults aged between 22 and 43 than the United Kingdom.

The recent economic downturn highlighted the capital's extreme economic inequalities even further putting an additional burden on those communities that tend to be marginalized.

The latest census in 2001 showed that the unemployment rate for inner London is 8.9% and for Greater London 6.7%; 6.2% and 5.0% respectively are White British and 15.1% and 11.3% are BAME people. The latest census also showed higher proportions of limiting long-term illness and poor health within most BAME groups.

London's population also encompasses at least 14 faiths as well as atheists and agnostics. Fifty-eight percent of all Jews living in England and Wales live in London; 53% for Hindus; 39% for Muslims; 39% for Buddhists and 32% for Sikhs. Following the events of September 11, 2001 and the London bombings in 2006, hate crime statistics have risen particularly in relation to Muslims living in London.

Generally, young people of all ethnic groups in London are better qualified than their elders, but young people of Black African, Caribbean, or Bangladeshi origin are particularly at risk of poor educational outcomes (GLA, 2007a). Over 15% of London's population—nearly 1.2 million people—are aged 60 or over. Older people particularly those belonging to minority groups often suffer double disadvantage. At the opposite end of the age scale, London also has the highest level of child poverty in the country (52%) (GLA, 2007b).

London's BAME communities continue to face persistent inequalities. In particular:

- BAME young people are more likely to suffer from mental health problems and are disproportionately more likely to be found within the social care system (CRE, 2007).
- Young black or mixed race men are more likely than others to be prosecuted and convicted.
- BAME people are over represented in the criminal justice system making up 25% of the male prison population.
- BAME people represent 2.4% of all directors in FTSE 100 companies.
- Anecdotal evidence suggests that ethnic minority businesses find it more difficult to gain opportunities to tender for contracts and are under-represented in both public and private sector supply chains.
- Of the 214 people currently elected to the London Assembly, Welsh Assembly and the Scottish Parliament, only two belong to an ethnic minority and only 4.1% of local councillors come from an ethnic minority background.
- In the 2005 general election, voter turnout was 47% for ethnic minority voters compared with 61% among the population as a whole.
- 67% of BAME people live in the 88 most deprived wards in England.
- London children with a very high risk of living in poverty include those from Pakistani and Bangladeshi groups (69%) those from Black ethnic groups (51?) (GLA, 2006).
- In London, pupils of Chinese and Indian origin perform well above average at school with over 70% of Chinese and 65% of Indian 15+ year olds achieving five or more A – C grade GCSEs, compared with 48% of white children.
- In London in 2007/08 Black people were over 4 times more likely to be stopped and searched than White people under Section 1 of the Police and Criminal Evidence Act (Ministry of Justice, 2009).
- Black people are over three times more likely to be arrested than white people. In 2007/08 Black Londoners experienced proportionally 3 times more arrests than White Londoners.

Although 52% of London's population are female, fewer women are in employment, and those who are tend to be confined to less senior and lower paid jobs (GLA, 2007b). Furthermore, according to the 2001 census, there are more than 8.7 million people in the UK with a disability. Of this number, more than 1.4 million disabled people are in London. Of the working age population, 6.9 million have a disability in the UK and about 810,000 of these people are in London. Disabled workers earn considerably less than non-disabled workers, with a gross average hourly wage for disabled Londoners a fifth lower than for non-disabled Londoners. The LGBT community is also representative of the broader London demographic. Access to services, employment and opportunities are still limited in London, and the face of homophobic discrimination and hate crime is still highly prevalent.

Faces of Diversity and Justice in the United Kingdom

Black, Asian and Minority Ethnic (BAME) Groups

According to the latest census in 2001, 9% of Britain's population are from BAME groups. According to the Equalities Review, Britain's BAME population is forecast to grow to about 11% by the end of the next decade (see Figure E.2).

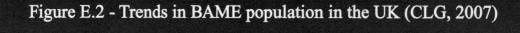

Figure E.2 - Trends in BAME population in the UK (CLG, 2007)

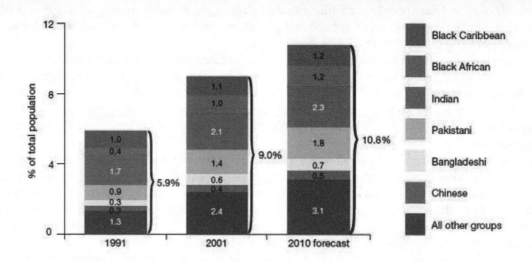

The trends in Canada's Black population are not that different. According to Canada's quarterly magazine *Canadian Social Trends*, Canada's Black population is growing faster than the general population, and it is considerably younger.

According to a 2007 publication by the UK's Commission for Racial Equality (CRE), despite major legislative and policy efforts to achieve racial equality, BAME groups face a number of inequalities and continue to be over-represented in the criminal justice system (CRE, 2007). For example, the CRE reported that Black people are six times more likely, and Asian people twice as likely, to be stopped and searched by the police, and Black people are over three times more likely to be arrested than White British (CRE, 2007:31). There were 955,000 stop and searches recorded by the police for 2006. Of these, 15% were Black, 8.1% were Asian and 1.5% were of Other origin. The number of stop and searches on Black people rose by 12.5% and number of stop and searches on Asian people rose by 11.8%, compared to the overall rise of 9%.

In June 2005, BAME groups accounted for about 25% of the male prison population, and 61% of adult Black offenders were serving a custodial sentence of four years or more, compared with 47% of White prisoners (Home Office, 2006) (see Figure E.3).

In relation to health inequalities, in comparison to the general population BAME people have considerably lower health outcomes, though there is significant variation between different groups in terms of health status and disease patterns. For instance, BAME people are up to six

Figure E.3 - Prisoners per 1000 members of the population in England and Wales by ethnicity in 2004/5 (CLG, 2007:94)

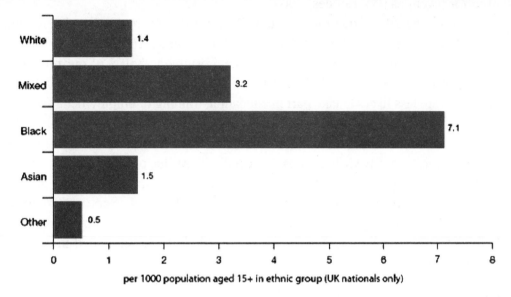

per 1000 population aged 15+ in ethnic group (UK nationals only)

times more likely to suffer from diabetes (Commission for Healthcare Audit and Inspection, 2007). Smoking rates were 40% for Bangladeshi men and 29% for Pakistani men compared to 24% for the general population. South Asians suffer higher rates of heart disease than the general population, in particular Pakistani men, who are twice as likely as men in the general population to suffer from this condition (DCLG, 2007:42).

There is evidence of Gypsy/Roma and Traveller communities having poor access to health-care and dental service. These communities also suffer more from respiratory problems compared with the general population. In this community the asthma prevalence rate is at 65% compared to the 40% national average, and bronchitis at 41% compares to the 10% national average (DCLG, 2007:44)

The finding of the 2007 mental health patients' census shows that rates of admission were proportionately lower for white British, Chinese and Indian groups. Black Caribbean, Black African and mixed groups were up to three times more likely to be admitted to a mental health institution. Moreover, the groups that are more likely to be admitted are generally referred from the criminal justice system rather than from the healthcare services.

Young Offenders

Since 1996, there has been a growing concern of the increased criminality among juveniles (Audit Commission, 1996). The 1996 Audit Commission report pointed out the increased levels of serious youth violence and criticised the juvenile justice system for its failings. The result was the introduction of the Crime and Disorder Act 1998, which according to some represents one of the most serious attempts to reform the English juvenile justice system (Gavrielides, 2003). One of the key reforms introduced through this Act was the use of restorative justice and mediation for crimes committed by young offenders. Previous chapters of this book talked about the application of restorative justice in Canada and therefore repetition will be avoided here. What is worth noticing is that the English legal system and the Crime and Disorder Act 1998 in particular looked at the Canadian experience and application of restorative justice to identify models of mediation that could be used for juveniles (Gavrielides, 2007).

According to the 2007 Equalities Review, Britain's BAME population is predominantly a young one. "While 20% of the White British population is under 16, the figure rises to 38% for those of Bangladeshi origin, 35% for those of Pakistani origin, and 50% of our mixed race population" (CRE, 2007:4). According to the CRE, of all groups, young people of Pakistani and Bangladeshi origin are less likely to take part in education, training or employment. Excluded young people are more than twice as likely to report having committed a crime as young people in mainstream school (Youth Justice Board, 2004). In England, the risk of permanent exclusion is much higher for pupils from some BAME groups, especially Traveller of Irish Heritage pupils (CLG, 2007:65). Not being in employment, education and training for six months or more between 16 and 18 is the single most powerful predictor of unemployment at age 21 (Scottish Executive, 2006). The CRE also noted that young Black or mixed race men are more likely than others to be prosecuted and convicted. BAME young men are also more likely to be remanded in custody prior to sentencing (CRE, 2007).

Older Adults

The latest available UK census showed that the older people's group is a fast growing one (see Figure E.4). BAME older people are an even faster growing group. For instance, in the London

Figure E.4 - UK population by Age (Census 2001)

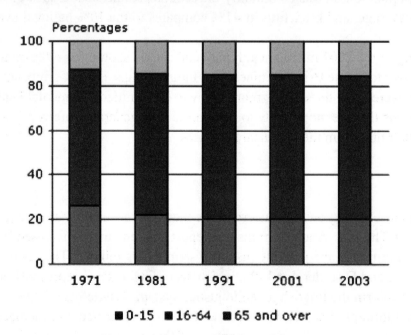

area only, population projections suggest that the number of BAME Londoners aged 65 or over will increase by 50% between 2001 and 2021 (GLA, 2006). The proportion of the total 65 or over population who are from BAME groups will increase from 12% to 23% (GLA, 2006).

According to Race On The Agenda (ROTA), factors such as language barriers, strong religious beliefs, strong cultural awareness, education and employment history, time of immigration, health status, family or lack of family and friends, isolation and depression leave BAME elders more easily exposed to discrimination by providers of public services (ROTA, 2007). Moreover, many BAME older people live in areas of high deprivation, and have poor knowledge and understanding of available services. Older people themselves quote prejudice or discrimination, and the lack of services which are able to meet their special needs, as playing a part in their decision whether to use services or not (CLG, 2007).

Lesbians and Gay Men

Unlike Canada where the latest census includes same sex partners, in the UK there is no definitive figure available that would indicate the population of lesbians and gay men. Government agencies often use the figure of 5-7% of the population, a conservative estimate which many organizations accept (Keogh et al., 2006). It was not until 2003 that the government withdrew legislation that made the protection and promotion of the rights of lesbian and gay men illegal.

Nevertheless, inequalities for this group still persist. For instance, research suggests that lesbians and gay men experience higher rates of mental health problems than the general population (Warner et al., 2004). Moreover, according to a 2008 youth-led survey carried out by Independent Academic Research Studies, young people who are lesbian or gay are one group who don't receive the same levels of fairness, respect, equality and dignity as other young people (IARS, 2008:3). In addition, a survey of adult lesbians and gay men found that over half had considered self-harm as a result of being bullied at school (Rivers, 2001).

▌ Responses to Diversity-Related Issues in the United Kingdom

Over the past 100 years, the UK has seen an immense volume of anti-discrimination laws dealing with racism, sexism, ageism, homophobia, religious intolerance and disablism. For instance, women became part of the political process only after the passing of the Emancipation Act 1918, while institutional racism was publicly recognized for the first time after the murder of Stephen Lawrence in 1993. The first race relations legislation was passed in 1964, but there is still a debate about the need for a consensual definition of equality (CLG, 2007). Section 28 of the Local Government Act 1988, which forbids the promotion of homosexuality by local authorities was repealed only two years ago (Local Government Act, 2003), while the Disability Discrimination Act 1995/2005 was implemented after 20 years of struggle.

Some shifts in policy were driven by high-profile political or social events that illuminated underlying inequalities. Equalities legislation is based on the principle that citizens should not experience abusive and unfair behaviour. This includes a person being deprived, excluded or limited from achieving the opportunities in life by how those characteristics are viewed. That is the characteristics that are not determined by a person's unfettered choice should not determine the opportunities available to a person. In the proposed Single Equality Act this is referred to as "protected characteristics."

Equality legislation was created in response to societal pressure and political movements. Civil unrest and successful challenges to the law have over history disputed what a protected characteristic was; what was discriminatory; what is equality of opportunity; and many other questions in the field. As a result, for race, gender, disability, age, religion, sexual orientation, gender reassignment, marital status and pregnancy the legislation has developed in a patchy way over the past 40 years.

The Scarman Inquiry is one example that followed serious inner city disturbances in 1981, which in turn placed a spotlight on the disadvantage and division in urban areas. Consequently, greater investment in those areas was made while steps were taken to reduce the disadvantage faced by BAME groups in the criminal justice system and in employment (CLG, 2007:35).

Domestic forces were not the only reason that led to the adoption of measures towards equality in the justice system. As a member of the European Union and also of the Council of Europe, the UK had to conform with legislation and case law applicable to all signatory countries. For instance, the Council of Europe's European Convention on Human Rights led to the passing of the Human Rights Act 1998, the UK first Bill of Rights, while the Treaty of the European Union introduced anti-discrimination protections for the first time.

The Government's Equalities Review summarizes the modern changes that have been made in Britain towards greater fairness and increased equality in three domestic drivers: broad social change leading to shifts in public attitudes, action by communities to address their own disadvantage, and some combination of legislative and policy development (CLG, 2007). The same document defined equality as:

"An equal society protects and promotes equal, real freedom and substantive opportunity to live in the ways people value and would choose, so that everyone can flourish. An equal society recognises people's different needs, situations and goals and removes the barriers that limit what people can do and can be" (CLG, 2007:123).

The criminal process and the administration of justice by state agents are the battle fields where human rights and equality are tested. The following Acts and policy initiatives in Table E.2 are indicative of the efforts that have been made over the last years to achieve a more tolerant and equal justice system in the UK.

In an attempt to tackle persistent inequalities in the UK, British Parliament is in the process of passing the Single Equality Bill. This aims to unify the different laws and regulations described in Table E.1 and the legislation that exists for different protected characteristics into one overarching equality law. It also seeks to strengthen the laws to address the persistent inequalities prevalent in society, and uses the same principles and methods established in the past legislation.

Therefore, there is structure of types of discrimination in equalities legislation that is understood and can be applied in many different situations. This structure forms the basis of the Single

Table E.2 - Equalities Law Timeline in the United Kingdom

Key Legislative/Policy Steps	Targeted are of Inequality in the Justice Stytem
Emancipation Act 1918	Gender equality
Equal Pay Act (1975)	Gender equality
Race Relations Act 1964/ 1976 and Race Relations Amendment Act 2000	Race equality
Sex Discrimination Act 1975	Gender equality
Stephen Lawrence Inquiry (1993)	Institutional Racism and discrimination
Crime and Disorder Act 1998, Youth Justice and Criminal Evidence Act 1999	Criminal justice inequalities
Human Rights Act 1998	Human Rights – cross strand discrimination
Disability Discrimination Act 1995/ 2005	Disablism
Local Government Act 2003	Repealing Section 28 of the Local Government Act 1988 which forbade the promotion of homosexuality by local authorities
Equality Act 2006	Cross-strand equality and established Equality and Human Rights Commission
Single Equality Bill (not passed yet)	Will simplify and strengthen existing anti-discrimination and equality legislation

Equality Bill protections. The structure of Single Equality Bill is described below. The same protections will apply to all the protected characteristics:

- *Direct discrimination* based on a protected characteristic is illegal in employment and providing goods and services.
- *Harassment* based on a protected characteristic is illegal.
- *Indirect discrimination* based on a protected characteristic is illegal in employment and providing goods and services.

- Recognizes *dual discrimination*, i.e., the discrimination that arises specifically from the interaction of two protected characteristics such as both someone's race and sex.
- Provide a *public sector equality duty* which will put a duty on public authorities to: eliminate unlawful discrimination; promote equality of opportunity for all people with protected characteristics, and promote good relations between people with protected characteristics and people who don't share the protected characteristics.
- Allows for *positive action* to address underrepresentation of minorities and those sharing protected characteristics in employment.

To champion the Act and to regulate and inspect public authorities, in 2006 the UK government established a single equality body called Equality and Human Rights Commission. This independent body is different from the Canadian Human Rights Commission as it has a much wider remit covering all equality strands, human rights and good relations. It also has regulatory and semi-judicial powers.

Whether the Single Equality Act and the single equality body (EHRC) will prove to be successful reforms is yet to be seen. Comparison and analysis can prove to be beneficial for the Canadian legal system, which faces similar equality and diversity challenges.

Learning Activity 3 - Summarize and Compare

1. In your own words and by using this chapter, summarize the key legislative and policy steps that were taken in the UK to tackle inequality and issues of diversity.

2. In your own words, and by using this book, summarize the key legislative and policy steps that were taken in Canada to tackle inequality and issues of diversity.

3. Compare the two summaries.

Indeed, while much has changed in the UK, as the article argued there is still a long way to go until we can claim that equality and human rights are values that define the way all individuals are treated. The justice system is no exception and as illustrated by the previous chapters of this book, Canada also shares this challenge. From this chapter, it becomes apparent that the UK and Canada share some of the same concerns about diversity in the justice system. There are also similarities in some solutions, proactive measures and policy steps that have been taken to address these concerns. Through comparative legal research, these two systems could benefit from each other by looking at the mistakes and successes of measures that have been long tested and are similar to untested initiatives in the two countries.

Through comparative analysis and legislation these initiatives could provide lessons for others, while at the same time the UK has and should continue to learn from abroad. This means that the UK Equality and Human Rights Commission could learn from Canada's Human Rights Commission that has been in existence since 1977 to implement the Canadian Human Rights Act. The same goes for the UK's Human Rights Act implemented in 2000 to serve as the country's Bill of Rights. Lessons could be drawn from Canada's Constitution and Bill of Rights introduced in 1960.

On the other hand, diversity and inequality issues relating to Aboriginals in Canada could be informed by the well tested policy and legislative measures that have been taken to achieve equality of opportunity for BAME groups residing in the UK. In particular, the continuous challenges surrounding the implementation of the Race Relations Act could serve as a guide in the development of new measures and the revision of existing provisions for ethnic minority groups in Canada. Measures that have been taken to address the over-representation of young people in the criminal justice system constitute another interesting area for comparative legal research. For instance, work that has been carried out by the UK's voluntary and community sector and youth-led non-governmental organizations could be investigated by the relevant Canadian authorities (for links with further information see below).

To conclude, although comparative legal research is not a panacea it can provide useful insights into the historical, economical, societal and cultural reasons that gradually lead to issues of diversity and inequality faced by justice systems. The comparison of the UK's and Canada's justice system is no exception and this chapter has provided examples of similarity and difference in relation to challenges faced by the two systems. Justice responses to these challenges were also looked at and some lessons were drawn as well as words of caution.

Terms used in the field of equality and diversity in the UK

Equality: This term refers to the provision of equality of opportunity and equal access to services and employment. To provide equality in law is to ensure that no person is disadvantaged by sharing a particular protected characteristic, such as being black, or a woman, or gay for example.

Discrimination: This term refers to an act that specifically disadvantages a certain group on the basis of the protected characteristic. It is the specific act that can affect equality. There are two types of discrimination direct and indirect discrimination.

Direct Discrimination: A type of discrimination illegal under the Race Relations Act 1976. *A person 'A' discriminates against another person 'B' if on grounds of gender, race, color, nationality, ethnic or national origins, disability, religion or belief, sexual orientation, 'A' treats 'B' less favorably than s/he treats or would treat other persons."*

Indirect Discrimination: A type of discrimination illegal under the Race Relations Act 1976. *A person 'A' discriminates against another person 'B', if 'A' applies to 'B' a provision, criterion or practice which s/he applies or would apply equally to persons not of the same (group) as' B', but which puts or would put persons of the same (group) as 'B' at a particular disadvantage when compared with other persons, which puts 'B' at that disadvantage and which 'A' cannot show to be a proportionate means of achieving a legitimate aim.*

Multiple Discrimination: This is where discrimination is based on the interaction of 2 or more protected characteristics. This can either be on different occasions, consecutively, or as a combination. Multiple discrimination through the combination of two protected characteristics is not grounds for a case of discrimination in the UK.

Harassment: A type of direct discrimination. *A person subjects another to harassment where s/he engages in unwanted conduct which has the purpose or effect of: (a) violating that other person's dignity, or (b) creating an intimidating, hostile, degrading, humiliating or offensive environment for her/him,* and in the perception of that other person, it should reasonably be considered as having that effect.

Genuine Occupational Requirement: Exceptions to the law covering employment. Employers will be able to recruit staff on the basis of a genuine occupational requirement. That it is a genuine requirement of the job to be of a particular, race or of particular ethnic or national origin.

Victimization: A type of discrimination where a person is treated less favourably because they have brought, or given evidence in a case of discrimination. This is unlawful (under certain circumstances it could amount to a criminal offence).

Positive Action: A term for lawful measures designed to redress imbalances to ensure that people from previously excluded ethnic minority or gender groups can compete on equal terms with other applicants in employment.

Affirmative Action: The action of selecting a person on the basis of the protected characteristic rather than employment based criteria to change the makeup of the workforce to better represent those with protected characteristics. This is unlawful in the UK.

Positive Duty: The general term to describe the statutory duties of race, disability and sex placed on public authorities to take proactive steps to eliminate discrimination and promote equality of opportunity. It is placed in law through specific duties such as the general race duty.

General Race Duty: The duty placed on all public sector authorities by the Race Relations Amendment Act 2000. It obliges public authorities to have *"due regard to the need to eliminate unlawful discrimination, promote equality opportunity, promote good relations between persons of different racial groups."*

Public Sector Equality Duty: The positive duty placed on Public authorities by the Single Equality Bill of 2010. It places a duty on public bodies to show due regard to the need to *eliminate discrimination, harassment, victimization and any other conduct that is prohibited by or under this Act; advance equality of opportunity between persons who share a relevant protected characteristic and persons who do not share it; foster good relations between persons who share a relevant protected characteristic and persons who do not share it.*

Protected Characteristic: A term used in the Single Equality Bill. On the basis of these a person could be discriminated against. These are stated as race (including color and ethnic or national origin), gender, disability, religion or belief, sexual orientation, age, gender reassignment, marriage or civil partnership, and pregnancy and maternity.

Equality Strands: This is reference to bodies of legislation and sectors of activity to eliminate discrimination and promote equality for certain characteristics. As protections for different protected characteristics developed separately so did the activity.

Burden of Proof: A legal term meaning that once the person making the complaint has made out a case that discrimination or harassment has taken place, the onus shifts to the employer to prove on the balance of probabilities, that it did not commit such an act.

Vicarious Liability: Refers to the responsibility carried by an employer for the behavior of his/her employees. Anything done by an individual employee in the course of his/her employment is treated under the Acts as also being done by the employer. This also applies to the public duty.

Useful links

Race equality in the UK: Race on the Agenda www.rota.org.uk
Gender Equality in the UK: Fawcett Society http://www.fawcettsociety.org.uk/
Sexual Orientation Equality in the UK: Stonewall www.stonewall.org.uk
Disability Equality in the UK: RADAR http://www.radar.org.uk
Equality and human rights in the UK: Equality and Human Rights Commission http://www.equalityhumanrights.com/
Youth and justice: Independent Academic Research Studies www.iars.org.uk
Youth justice: Youth Justice Board http://www.yjb.gov.uk/en-gb/
Older people and age equality: Age Concern http://www.ageconcern.org.uk/

References

Audit Commission. (1996). *Misspent youth.* London: HMSO.

Bassiouni, C. (1993). "Human rights in the context of criminal justice: Identifying international procedural protections and equivalent protections in national constitutions." *Duke Journal of Comparative and International Law* 3:235.

Davies, M. and H. Croall. (1998). *Criminal justice: An introduction to the criminal system in England and Wales.* London: Longman.

GLA. (2006). *Child poverty in London: Income and labour market indicators: Summary of findings.* London: Data Management and Analysis Group.

Commission for Healthcare Audit and Inspection. (2007). *Managing diabetes: Improving services for people with diabetes.* London: Commission for Healthcare Audit and Inspection.

Commission for Racial Equality. (2007). *A lot done, a lot to do: Our vision for an integrated Britain.* London: CRE.

Communities and Local Government. (2007). *Fairness and freedom: The final Report of the equalities review.* London: CLG.

Department for Communities and Local Government. (2007). *Improving opportunity, strengthening society: 2 Years On.* London: Crown Copyright.

Gavrielides, T. (2003). "Restorative justice: Are we there yet?" *Criminal Law Forum* 14(4):385-419.

Gavrielides, T. (2005). "Human rights vs. political reality: The case of Europe's harmonising criminal justice systems." *International Journal of Comparative Criminology* 5(2):60-84.

Gavrielides, T. (2007). *Restorative justice theory and practice: Addressing the discrepancy.* Helsinki: HEUNI.

Government Equalities Office. (2010). *An anatomy of economic inequality in the UK.* London: GEO and LSE.

Greater London Authority. (2007a). Equality in our lifetime? *The Discrimination Law Review Green Paper,* London: GLA.

Greater London Authority. (2007b). *The state of equality in London,* London: GLA.

Home Affairs Committee. (2007). *Young black people and the criminal justice system. vol. 1.* London: The Stationery Office Limited.

Home Office. (2006). *Race and the criminal justice system: An overview to the complete statistics 2004-5.* London: Home Office.

Independent Academic Research Studies. (2008). *Homophobic bullying and human rights: Shared values for a shared future*, London: IARS Retrieved September, 08, 2008 from www.iars.org.uk.

Keogh, P., Reid, D. and Weatherburn, P. (2006). *Lambeth LGBT Matters: The needs and experiences of lesbians, gay men, bisexual and trans men and women in Lambeth.* London: Sigma Research for Lambeth Council.

Leavitt, G. (1996). "Relativism and cross-cultural criminology: A critical analysis." In D. Nelken (ed.), *The futures of Criminology.* London: Sage.

Nelken. D. (1996). *The futures of Criminology.* London: Sage.

Nelken. D. (1997a). *Comparing legal cultures.* Dartmouth. Sage.

Nelken, D. (1997b). "The globalisation of crime and criminal justice." *Current Legal Problems* 50:251-295.

Rivers, I. (2001). "The bullying of sexual minorities at school: its nature and long-term correlates." *Educational and Child Psychology* 18(1):32-46.

Race on the Agenda. (2007). "The human rights of older people in healthcare." *Evidence to the Parliamentary Joint Committee on Human Rights*, London: ROTA. Retrieved September, 08, 2008 from www.rota.org.uk.

Santayana, G. (1905-1906) *"Reason in Society," ch. 7, The Life of Reason.*

Scottish Executive. (2006). *Exclusions from schools, 2005/06.* The Scottish Government: Edinburgh.

Tran. K. (2004). "Blacks in Canada: A long history." *Canadian Social Trends* 72(Spring):2-7.

Youth Justice Board. (2004). *Mori Youth Survey 2004.* Accessed September 1, 2008 from http://www.youth-justice-board.gov.uk/Publications/Downloads/YouthSurvey2004.pdf.

Warner, J., McKeown, E., Griffin, M., Johnson, K., Ramsey, A., Cort, C. and King, M. (2004). "Rates and predictors of mental illness in gay men, lesbians and bisexual men and women." *British Journal of Psychiatry* 185:479-485.

Watson A. (1974). *Legal transplants.* Edinburgh: University of Edinburgh Press.

Winterdyk, J. (ed.).(2001). *Corrections in Canada.* Toronto, ON: Pearson Education.

Zedner, L. (1995). "Comparative research in criminal justice." In N. Lesley, L. Michael and M. Maguire (eds.), *Contemporary Issues in Criminology.* Cardiff: University of Wales Press.

Zweigert, K. and Kotz, H. (1998). *An introduction to comparative law.* 3d ed. Oxford: Oxford University Press.

INDEX